Criminology in Brief sets itself apart from the established criminology textbooks by seeking to serve as a foundation for a criminology course rather than trying to serve as a criminology course itself. Heiner discusses key criminological concepts and theories in a way that provides the reader with a foundation upon which they can engage with up-to-date criminological research in class settings and while reviewing empirical articles. This book is highly recommended for instructors who teach introduction to criminology courses.

Michael S. Barton, *Associate Professor of Sociology,*
Louisiana State University

Robert Heiner's *Criminology in Brief* is a unique textbook that bridges the gap between sociology and criminal justice, and is written in a style that is perfect for undergraduates who take courses in either discipline. Heiner's critical approach provides students, practitioners, and indeed informed citizens, with a better understanding of crime and the criminal justice system.

Todd M. Krohn, *Instructor of Sociology, University of Georgia*

Criminology in Brief

This book offers a short and accessible introduction to criminology. Written in a clear and direct style, criminological theories are made more accessible for undergraduates, and the workings of the criminal justice system are explained. Students will learn not only how the criminal justice system works, but also how it does not work. Beyond introducing students to the basics, the book provides a persuasive argument that the criminal justice system we have in the United States comes nowhere close to our ideals for justice, doing little good in terms of crime control, while doing great harm to minorities and the poor.

Engaging and far-ranging, this text offers a condensed approach to the key themes and debates surrounding crime and justice, and covers definitions and measurements of crime, criminological theories, crime typologies, and contemporary issues in the criminal justice system. It includes chapters on:

- Criminological methods and data
- Biological, psychological, and classical theories of crime
- Sociological theories of crime
- Patterns of crime
- The police
- The courts
- Corrections and the American prison system

Written by an experienced textbook author, this book offers a critical approach to the subjects discussed and draws on topical examples such as Black Lives Matter, the militarization of the police, plea bargaining, and the War on Drugs. It is essential reading for Criminology courses within a Sociology Major and will also be of interest to Criminal Justice majors, law students, policymakers, and informed citizens.

Robert Heiner received his PhD in Sociology at the University of Virginia. He is on the faculty at Plymouth State University; and he has authored or edited numerous textbooks, including a Social Problems textbook now in its fifth edition.

Criminology in Brief

Understanding Crime and Criminal Justice

Robert Heiner

R Routledge
Taylor & Francis Group

LONDON AND NEW YORK

First published 2021
by Routledge
2 Park Square, Milton Park, Abingdon, Oxon OX14 4RN

and by Routledge
52 Vanderbilt Avenue, New York, NY 10017

Routledge is an imprint of the Taylor & Francis Group, an informa business

British Library Cataloguing-in-Publication Data
A catalogue record for this book is available from the British Library

Library of Congress Cataloging-in-Publication Data
A catalog record has been requested for this book

ISBN: 978-0-367-32162-8 (hbk)
ISBN: 978-0-367-32163-5 (pbk)
ISBN: 978-0-429-31707-1 (ebk)

Typeset in Giovanni, Stone Sans, and Helvetica
by Wearset Ltd, Boldon, Tyne and Wear

For those who want more justice from our justice system.

Contents

Illustrations

BOX

Acknowledgments

There are a number of people whose help made this book possible. Many thanks go especially to Kristine Levan and Mark Fischler for their expertise and advice. I want also to thank Robin Dorff and Ann McClellan for their support. A shout out to Joyce Bruce, Kathryn Melanson, Alice Staples, and David Mackey for being there when I needed them.

The people who worked with me at Routledge made this project a delight. Tom Sutton and Jessica Phillips were both so professional, encouraging, and responsive that they gave me no reason to complain, not even behind their backs. Once they became involved, everything sailed smoothly and this project was quite a pleasure to work on.

Lastly, I want to thank my partner, Sheryl, who encouraged me and put up with me spending mornings in the office on weekends and breaks for years.

Portions of Chapter 3 were previously published in *Criminological Theory: Just the Basics*, Robert Heiner, College Publications, 2015.

CHAPTER 1

Criminological methods and data

Criminology is the scientific study of crime. There are two fundamental components of the scientific enterprise; these are methods and theory. Methods are the techniques we use to uncover and gather facts. A theory is an attempt to explain the relationship between facts. Thus, criminologists employ methods to gather facts about crime and criminals, develop theories to explain those facts, and then gather more facts to test their theories.

Today, most criminologists in academic settings have been trained to use the methods developed by the social sciences. Very often they employ statistical analyses of data collected by government agencies (in particular, law enforcement agencies); sometimes they may use data generated by surveys (for example, of victims, or of the general public); and sometimes they may interview key players in the criminal justice process (for examples, police officers, convicted criminals, and victims).

People who study crime outside of academia often employ methods developed in the natural sciences. DNA research was developed in the biological sciences; and the study of bomb fragments and shrapnel trajectories may employ methods developed in chemistry and physics. We use the term "criminalistics" or "forensics," rather than "criminology," to refer to the application of methods developed in the natural sciences to the investigation of individual crimes.

WHAT IS CRIME?

In order to collect and measure facts about crime, we must first define it. Our definition will determine what it is that we are measuring. Criminologists are not all agreed on how to define crime, but most employ, either explicitly or implicitly, a legalistic definition of crime. Such a definition allows the law to define crime. According to the legalistic definition, a crime is an act prohibited by law. When we use the law to define crime, we are relying on a *mala prohibita* definition of crime. *Mala prohibita* is Latin for "wrong because it is prohibited."

A number of legal provisions are built into the legalistic definition. By law, for an act to be criminal it must the accompanied by the intent to do something wrong, or *mens rea* (Latin for a "guilty mind"). The law does not require that the actor have the intent to achieve a particular result to be guilty of a particular crime; it only requires that the actor have criminal intent. To be guilty of murder, for example, one does not have to have the intent to kill the victim; one only has to have the intent to do something wrong at the time of the act. One also has to have the *capacity* to form criminal intent. The law, for example, makes exceptions for the "insanity defense," as well as for cases when the act was committed by a minor under a certain age. Lastly, there are acts that would otherwise be criminal, but that are justified by law, such as killing someone in self-defense.

Some criminologists take exception to the legalistic definition of crime, arguing that the law is a political artifact. Scientific findings, they argue, should be applicable over time and throughout the world; but legal definitions of crime vary from time to time and place to place. Politicians make the law and no other sciences would willingly allow politicians to define their subject matter. Acceptance of a legalistic definition of crime, critics argue, aligns the work of criminologists with the interests of those who have the power to make the law and directs our attention to crimes committed by the poor and powerless. (The relevance of this position will come into more focus when we discuss conflict theory in Chapter 3.)

Critics of the legalistic definition of crime suggest criminologists employ a *mala in se* definition. *Mala in se* is Latin for "wrong in and of itself," and such a definition would include acts that are universally wrong; that is, acts that are wrong in all cultures throughout time, regardless of who is writing the law. The problem with *male in se* definitions is that it is difficult or impossible to provide examples of so-called "universal crimes." For example, the act of killing someone is murder in the context of a robbery, and heroism in the context of battle. Incest is often given as an example of a universal crime because it is often held that "the incest taboo is universal." This assertion is misleading, though, because, indeed, all societies do have *an* incest taboo, but different societies define incest differently. Thus, a sexual act between certain relatives may be considered taboo in one society, but not in another. In any case, if criminologists were to confine their research to universal crimes, they would be restricting themselves to a very limited field of subject matter that would be of little interest or practical utility to people outside of the discipline.

To summarize the debate on how best to define crime, the *mala prohibita* definition is far more practical and concrete than the *mala in se* definition, which is more abstract and may belong as much or more within the realm of philosophy than in the science of crime. However, *mala in se* proponents have made a valuable contribution to criminology when they point out that the criminologist should be mindful of the moral and political implications of how we define crime.

IMAGINE IF

Imagine if you were a Martian sent to Earth to study earthling society. Early in your observations, you see a vehicle with flashing blue lights pull up beside a man. Two people wearing uniforms rush out of the vehicle, grab the man, force him against the vehicle, pull his arms behind his back, chain his wrists together, and recite some incantation, "You have the right to remain silent. Anything you say can and will be used against you in a court of law. You have the right to an attorney …" Given your assignment, you wonder if these observations could be a clue to understanding something fundamental about earthling society. You follow the vehicle with the lights on top and you witness the same rituals being performed several times over the week, with the exact same incantation. After a while, you start to follow the men with their wrists chained together. You see them hold numbers above their chest and then a flash of light; you see them forced to roll their fingers in ink, and then make marks on a piece of paper. Later you see them paraded before a very officious looking person wearing black robes, whom you come to realize has a great deal of power over these men's fate. Everything you observe happening to these men is highly ritualized and you become convinced that a great deal of history and meaning is embedded in these rituals.

All societies have constructed very elaborate rituals around their reactions to wrongdoers in their midst, and anthropologists inform us that rituals tell us much about a culture. In fact, the kinds of crimes that are prevalent in a society, and the way a society defines and reacts to crime do, indeed, tell us much about a society. *Crime is a representative characteristic of a society.* If we think about particular examples, this assertion becomes self-evident.

Consider the kind of crime and societal reactions that typified Salem, Massachusetts at the end of the seventeenth century. "Witchcraft" and the ensuing trials tell us much about Salem society then. Consider the kinds of crime that typified the city of Chicago in the 1920s. Bootlegging, gangland violence, and police corruption tell us much about Chicago society during Prohibition. Consider the kinds of crimes and reactions that typified Mao's China and Stalin's Russia. Political dissent and harsh repression of real and imagined enemies of the state tell us much about those societies. Consider the kinds of crimes and reactions that typified the American South in the late 1950s and early 1960s. Peaceful protests on behalf of civil rights met with police brutality and a court system that would look the other way on white-on-black violence—these tell us much about society in the American South during that era. We can also looks at acts that are or were *not* defined as crime. Consider that slavery was not defined as crime for much of American history. This speaks volumes about American society for much of its past. The fact that wholesale genocide of Native Americans and the expropriation of their land were not considered crimes also speaks volumes.

It is easy to see the truth to the assertion that crime is a representative characteristic of a society when we have the advantage of hindsight, and also when we are looking through American lenses at what goes on in other countries. We are appalled and our biases are confirmed when we hear about thieves' hands being amputated in one country, or an adulterer being stoned to death in another country. But crime and reactions to it in the United States today also represent American society to people in other parts of the world, and they too are sometimes appalled. They take note that the United States has the highest incarceration rate in the world, that poor people and minorities are vastly over-represented in our prison population, that guns are easily accessible, that the United States has very high rates of gun fatalities, and that the United States is among a very few industrialized countries that still uses the death penalty. These facts represent the United States to people throughout the world.

There are the obvious reasons for the scientific study of crime: crime costs thousands of lives and causes billions of dollars in financial losses every year in the United States. An understanding of crime that comes from scientific research can be used to better inform policy-making decisions, which will reduce the enormous losses caused by crime. But, as we have seen in this discussion, the study of crime can also open a window into an understanding of our own society.

MEASURING CRIME

First, we should note that among all human behaviors, criminal behavior is likely the most difficult to study. Since crime is most often met with shame, ostracism and punishment, its perpetrators want to keep it a secret. To the extent that they are successful in keeping their secret, perpetrators and their behaviors may never come to the attention of criminologists. Those that do come to the attention of criminologists may be different from those who do not and, therefore, those who are "caught" may not *represent* those who are not caught. Coming up with random samples is often difficult in the social sciences, but even more so in criminology.

How do criminologists gauge the effectiveness of a given policy? How do we know if crime rates are going up or down? How do we know that certain groups are more likely to be perpetrators or victims of crime? How do we know that some cities or countries are more dangerous than others when it comes to crime? The answers to these questions require that we compare numbers: the number of crimes occurring before policy implementation compared with the number afterward, the number of crimes today compared with the number from 20 years ago, the number of black victims compared with the number of white victims, the number of crimes in Detroit compared with the number in Miami. Thus, *in order for crime statistics to be meaningful to criminologists, they must be comparable.*

Comparability is difficult to achieve because of the secretive nature of criminal behavior discussed above. There are vast numbers of crimes that never come to the attention of the authorities. Criminologists call these the "dark figure" of crime. The dark figure makes the comparability of crime statistics problematic. For example, if Miami's crime statistics include one-half of all crimes committed during a given year, while Detroit's statistics include only one-third, then a comparison of the two cities' crime statistics would likely yield erroneous conclusions. However, as we will see below, there are different sources of crime data, and some of them take into account the dark figure.

The *Uniform Crime Report*

The Federal Bureau of Investigation compiles crime statistics voluntarily submitted to them by some 18,000 state, local, county, federal and tribal jurisdictions and then publishes its data annually. (These data are now published online in a variety of formats that anyone can use for quantitative analyses.) The publication's title is *Crime in the United States*, but it is better known as the *Uniform Crime Report* (UCR) as it is produced by the FBI's Uniform Crime Reporting Program, which has been collecting such data since 1930. The UCR's more detailed analyses are applied to the so-called "index crimes" or "Part I" offenses. These include those offenses

TABLE 1.1 Index crimes Included in the *Uniform Crime Report*	
Violent crimes	**Property crimes**
Homicide	Burglary
Rape	Larceny/Theft ($50 or more)
Robbery	Motor Vehicle Theft
Aggravated Assault	Arson

listed in Table 1.1. Note that these offenses are broken down into violent crimes and property crimes. When the FBI is reporting trends in "violent crime" and/or "property crime," it uses this breakdown.[1]

The UCR consists of three types of crime data: (1) crimes known to the police; (2) crimes cleared by arrest; and (3) crime rates. *Crimes known to the police* are crimes reported to the police and that subsequent investigation has determined that these crimes did actually occur. If an investigation determines that the crime did not occur, that report is considered "unfounded" and is not included in the data; *crimes cleared by arrest* include those crimes that result in an arrest (whether or not the person arrested is prosecuted or convicted); and *crime rates* consist of the number of reported crimes adjusted for the size of the population. That is, to obtain a homicide rate, the UCR will take the number of homicides known to the police and divide it by 100,000 population. Thus, the murder rate of 5.0 reported in 2018 indicates that five people were killed for every 100,000 people in the United States' population. Crime rates are better indicators of crime trends than the other data described above because they take into account changes in the population size.

The UCR numbers are often referred to as the "official" crime statistics, most likely because they have been reported by an official government agency for 90 years, and because they are the crime data most often cited by the media. However, since these data are generated by voluntary reporting from thousands of agencies, the FBI has limited opportunity to exercise quality control. Crime data have political ramifications and law enforcement agencies are sometimes motivated to either inflate or deflate their crime statistics. If an agency or an official wants to show the efficacy of recent crime control initiatives, decreasing crime rates will help make their case. If they want to demonstrate a need for more budgetary resources, then increasing crime rates will benefit their argument. Cities worried about how crime will affect tourism and universities concerned about how it will affect student enrollments may both be motivated to "fudge" their data.

There are myriad opportunities—up and down a jurisdictional hierarchy—to manipulate crime data. For example, one retired police officer reports,

> Burglaries would be reclassified to trespasses. Even attempted burglaries with smashed windows and damaged doors would be charged to criminal mischief. This prevented corresponding stats for the Uniform Crime Reports and gave wiggle-room for the chief to tell the public that property crime was down across the city.[2]

The problem of data manipulation is so significant that even New York City's Patrolmen's Benevolent Association addressed the issue,

So how do you fake a crime decrease? It's pretty simple. Don't file reports, misclassify crimes from felonies to misdemeanors, under-value the property lost to crime so it's not a felony, and report a series of crimes as a single event.[3]

Making the interpretation of UCR data more problematic is the fact that they are confined to crimes that are known to the police; as such, they are substantially hindered by the dark figure of crime. In examining the data, we should be mindful of the *reportability of crime*, or the likelihood that a given crime will be reported; that is, some crimes are more likely to be reported after they occur than others. For example, homicides are extremely likely to be reported because a person has gone missing or a body is found. Therefore, homicide rates are very reliable and can be reasonably compared over time. Since the vast majority of automobiles are insured, victims of motor vehicle theft almost always report the crime to the police so that they may collect on their auto insurance. Therefore, motor vehicle theft is highly reportable and the interpretation of the relevant UCR data is relatively straightforward. However, rape, for example, suffers a relatively low degree of reportability, and so does larceny; therefore, interpreting the corresponding data is less than straightforward.

Further confounding our interpretation of crime rates is the fact that reportability may change over time. Decades ago, for example, when rape victims were more likely to be blamed for their own victimization, they were less likely to report the crime than they are today. Reportability may also vary from place to place. Rape victims may be more likely to report the crime in urban areas than in rural areas where their victimization will be known to the vast majority of residents, where many residents know the perpetrator and may take his side, and where the victim's interactions with others may be affected for years to come. Thus, depending on the circumstances, rising crime rates may be as much or more a reflection of increased reporting rather than increasing incidence of crime.

As this book goes to press, the Uniform Crime Reposting program is scheduled to transition from the UCR's Summary Reporting System (SRS) to the National Incident-Based Reporting System (NIBRS) in 2021. NIBRS has been providing more details than provided by the SRS, including "circumstances and context for crimes like location, time of day, and whether the incident was cleared."[4] As such, it allows for more detailed analyses by law enforcement, policymakers, and criminologists; but it will still suffer many of the problems endemic to voluntary reporting from thousands of law enforcement agencies as well as from the dark figure of crime. While plans to phase out the SRS have been in the works for decades, NIBRS may be off to a rocky start because (as of April 2020) eight states have not switched to the NIBRS format for reporting; and the participation rate in other states ranges from 1 percent to 100 percent of law enforcement agencies.[5]

Victimization surveys

In the 1960s, President Lyndon Johnson appointed the Commission on Law Enforcement and the Administration of Justice to examine the nature and extent of crime in the United States. Aware of the dark figure of crime, the Commission directed that victimization surveys be conducted in several major American metropolitan areas, and the National Opinion Research Center (NORC) surveyed some 10,000 randomly selected households nationwide about whether household members had been victims of crime in the past year. The NORC survey proved to be a milestone in the history of criminology as it demonstrated that there were far more crimes being committed than were being reported to the police. The survey suggested, for example, that roughly two-thirds of all rapes and burglaries were *not* being reported. The survey also asked respondents why they had not reported their victimization to the police. The most common answer was that victims felt the police could do nothing about it.[6] These findings indicated the dark figure of crime was far larger than had been suspected, that law enforcement agencies could be doing a much better job, and that a large part of the needed improvement for law enforcement lay in public relations and in instilling more public confidence in the police.

The value of the early victimization surveys was immediately recognized by academics and public officials. These surveys helped to remedy the two main deficiencies of the UCR. For one thing, a nationwide survey of households did not depend upon the political vagaries of 18,000 law enforcement agencies voluntarily submitting crime data to the FBI; and, more importantly, it shed light on the dark figure of crime, exposing a wealth of details of which criminologists and law enforcement authorities had been only vaguely aware. By 1973, the Bureau of Justice Statistics (BJS) took on the responsibility of conducting annual (now biannual) nationwide victimization surveys, known as the National Crime Victimization Survey (NCVS). Today, the NCVS has become a very important source of data for criminological analyses. Unlike the UCR, which focuses on uniformity and needs to coordinate reporting among thousands of agencies, the NCVS has become relatively flexible and can be modified to include crimes that have only recently become of interest to criminologists, such as identity theft and school crime. It also includes a wealth of information that can be very valuable for the criminological understanding of crime. The types of data collected by the NCVS are listed as follows on the BJS website:

> For each victimization incident, the NCVS collects information about the offender (e.g., age, race and Hispanic origin, sex, and

victim-offender relationship), characteristics of the crime (including time and place of occurrence, use of weapons, nature of injury, and economic consequences), whether the crime was reported to police, reasons the crime was or was not reported, and victim experiences with the criminal justice system.[7]

In that it accounts for the dark figure of crime, criminologists are more inclined to rely on the NCVS to understand trends in crime rates, while the news media often give more emphasis to the UCR.

The strengths of the NCVS notwithstanding, it does suffer some deficiencies worthy of note. For one thing, victimization surveys rely on the respondent's memory. Some may not remember their victimization, especially if it were minor, while others may remember a crime that lies outside of the question's time frame. Sometimes victims may be confused about events in question and, for example, report a lost purse as a stolen purse. Some respondents may over-exaggerate a possible criminal event while others might under-exaggerate, or simply not report a crime for fear of embarrassment. And, lastly, like most surveys, the results are only as good as the sampling method itself. In that respondents participate in the survey voluntarily, there is a strong chance that some types of people are more likely to agree to participate than other types of people. This would create a systematic sampling bias that may taint the survey's results. As this book goes to press, for example, immigration is a volatile political issue and it is quite possible that large numbers of undocumented immigrants are avoiding the authorities, even those who administer victimization surveys. If these people are not included in the sample, then a substantial swath of crimes cannot be included in related criminological analyses.

Self-report surveys

One of the more interesting *and* problematic sources of crime data are self-report surveys. These employ questionnaires that ask respondents about the crimes they themselves have committed. It is, of course, critical to the utility of this method that respondents be assured of the anonymity of their responses and that there will be no negative consequences to their admission of crime. These are often administered to groups of people who are "captive" populations—especially, high school students and prisoners. Self-report surveys in the 1960s and 1970s received a lot of attention because they seemed to reveal important discrepancies in the official crime data. Namely, the UCR indicated substantial differences in the commission of crime between blacks and whites, between poor youth and affluent youth, and between men and women. Self-report studies suggested that these differences were greatly exaggerated, calling into question whether the official data were biased.

Subsequent studies of the self-report methodology suggest that it may have its own biases. Teenagers and prisoners, if they believe the assurances that their responses will remain anonymous, may be boastful and over-exaggerate or lie about their criminal involvement. If they do not believe these assurances, then they may lie and conceal their criminal activity. Research has also shown that different socio-demographic groups may be more honest about their criminal activity than others,[8] perhaps suggesting that certain groups are less likely to believe assurances of anonymity than others. Another concern deals more specifically with the administration of these surveys in high schools. What about the students that are not present the day the survey is administered? These absentees may be disproportionately represented by students who are chronically truant; these are the students criminologists may be most interested in understanding and their absence would introduce systematic bias to the sample. These criticisms, together, suggest that self-report surveys may be more useful in assessing the incidence of minor crimes and misdemeanors and far less useful in gauging the incidence of serious felonies.

Unlike the UCR and the NCVS, which are collected and published by government agencies, self-report surveys are usually conducted by individual criminologists for the purpose of theory testing. As such, they have no official standing and they are not published at regular intervals.[9] When they are administered to high school and college populations, they reveal that a great majority of respondents have engaged in criminal activity. With this as a typical result, self-report surveys are often used as a pedagogical tool to bust popular stereotypes of crime and criminals and to demonstrate to students that, in Philip Reichel's words, "The criminal is not the large-eared, beady-eyed, hulking stranger hiding in the alley. Instead, he is the person sitting next to us in class, or looking back at us from the mirror."[10]

COMPARATIVE CRIMINOLOGY

Sociologists who study crime may do so not just to understand crime itself, but also to understand the broader contours of society. Rules, or codes of conduct, or "norms" are what hold a society together. From the earliest months of life, we are being socialized to follow the norms. These norms are so pervasive that we learn to take them for granted, fail to notice them, and follow them automatically. Often, it is only when a norm is violated that we become aware of its existence. For example, we do not think about the norm of eating spaghetti with utensils until maybe we witness someone eating it with their fingers. Thus, by studying violations of the norms—i.e., deviance and crime—we can come to understand a society better.

Researchers are engaged in *comparative criminology* when they are comparing and contrasting matters related to crime in different societies. Such research can yield valuable insights into both crime and society. One of the earliest efforts in the field of comparative sociology was Emile Durkheim's classic investigation into suicide, published in 1897.[11] Durkheim found that suicide rates remained relatively constant within countries, but varied substantially between countries. The same can be said of crime rates today. For example, look at the murder rates in the United States (which has one of the highest rates among advanced industrialized countries) and Japan (which has one of the lowest rates) depicted in Table 1.2.

In the case of suicide, Durkheim demonstrated that what would seem to be the ultimate individual or psychological act (to kill oneself) could be better explained sociologically than psychologically. Likewise, the data in Table 1.2 clearly suggest that something is going on at the societal level that explains the differences between murder rates in the United States and Japan. Part of the explanation may have to do with the high value American culture places on individualism and independence, which makes shaming a less effective means of social control; whereas the value Japan places on conformity and the collective well-being makes shaming a very effective deterrent (see Braithwaite, p. 65). More research would be needed to confirm this explanation; but comparative criminology can reveal very interesting insights into crime and society.

Despite its potential to contribute to our understanding of crime, comparative criminology is fraught with methodological problems. All of the problems utilizing criminological data that were discussed earlier in this chapter are compounded by the fact that we are not dealing with data limitations in just one country, but in multiple countries. Different countries may define crimes differently and compile their data differently. For example, for burglary rates, one country may record every burglary arrest, while another country records every burglary conviction; or, in one country, victims may be more likely to report burglary to the police than in another; in either case, comparison of the two countries' burglary rates could be problematic. Marvin Wolfgang summed up the problems of using

TABLE 1.2 Homicide rates per 100,000 population		
	United States	Japan
2014	4.4	0.3
2013	4.5	0.3
2012	4.7	0.3

Notes
US data obtained from Crime in the United States, 2015, FBI, https://ucr.fbi.gov/crime-in-the-u.s/2015/crime-in-the-u.s.-2015/tables/table-1. Japanese data obtained from "Japan – Homicide Rate," World Data Atlas. Knoema, https://knoema.com/atlas/Japan/Homicide-rate.

cross-cultural data as involving "cultural variations in the definition of crime, sentiments of severity, degrees of reportability, probabilities of discovery, types of penalties, and the methods of collecting criminal statistics."[12] These problems are not insurmountable, but the comparative criminologist needs to be aware of them and proceed cautiously.

A CAUTIONARY NOTE

The American public tends to react to crime news on a more visceral level than a rational level. The media take advantage of and encourage such an emotional response to crime because it helps to sell more newspapers, attract more online readers, and boost advertising revenues. The fear of crime is also fueled by politicians who have found, throughout history and throughout the world, that such fear can often win supporters and sway elections.

While the vast majority of crime consists of property crime, the news media focus on violent crime. From the earliest days of broadsides and then newspapers, news journalists have been aware that crime news sells. The more unusual, fantastic, outrageous or gory the news, the better it sells. Or, as the old news adage goes, "If it bleeds, it leads."

An event is "news" immediately after it happens, and that is when criminal events get reported. However, it often takes days, weeks, or months of investigation to understand the reasons for a crime. In other words, crime news is presented out of context. Crime statistics are also reported out of context. Constant coverage and the lack of context makes criminal violence appear to be both pervasive and random. As such, the public is led to believe that being violently victimized is something just waiting to happen to everybody, and that often extraordinary precautions are necessary. The distribution of information about crime is a very serious matter because the precautions people take to avoid crime can severely impact their quality of life. Such precautions range from people avoiding strangers, to locking themselves in their homes, to carrying concealed weapons, to sacrificing civil liberties and to accepting higher taxes to afford tough-on-crime measures.

It does not take much criminological training to understand that crime is a very complicated phenomenon that needs to be understood in its context, and that the public's understanding of crime—as promoted by the media and our political leaders—is often very simplistic. So far, we have focused our attention on criminologists' complicated efforts to define and measure crime. Next, we will discuss their efforts to explain crime.

NOTES

1 Arson is not included in the FBI's composite report of property crime because the agency has determined that it is not reported consistently enough to be a reliable indicator.

2 Dean Scoville, "What's Really Going on with Crime Rates?" *Police*, October 9, 2013, www.policemag.com/channel/patrol/articles/2013/10/what-s-really-going-on-with-crime-rates.aspx. Retrieved June 7, 2017.

3 John A. Eterno and Eli B. Silverman, "The NYPD's Compstat: Compare Statistics or Compose Statistics," *International Journal of Police Science and Management*, vol. 13, no. 3. 2010. http://nylawyer.nylj.com/adgifs/decisions/011311eterno_silverman. pdf. Retrieved June 7, 2017.

4 Federal Bureau of Investigation, "National Incident-Based Reporting System (NIBRS)", www.fbi.gov/services/cjis/ucr/nibrs. Retrieved April 20, 2020.

5 Federal Bureau of Investigation, Crime Data Explorer, "Improving Access to Crime Data." https://crime-data-explorer.fr.cloud.gov/. Retrieved April 20, 2020.

6 Gresham M. Sykes, *Criminology*. New York: Harcourt Brace Jovanovich, 1978.

7 "Data Collection: National Crime Victimization Survey (NCVS)," Bureau of Justice Statistics, www.bjs.gov/index.cfm?ty=dcdetail&iid=245. Retrieved June 9, 2017.

8 Terrence P. Thornberry and Marvin D. Krohn, "Comparison of Self-Report and Official Data for Measuring Crime" *from Measurement Problems in Criminal Justice Research: Workshop Summary*, J. Pepper and C.V Petrie, eds., National Research Council of the National Academies, Washington, DC: The National Academies Press, 2003. www.nap.edu/read/10581/chapter/4. Retrieved June 11, 2017.

9 One self-report survey that is conducted and published annually is the Monitoring The Future survey which is administered to high school students with the primary purpose of tracking trends in substance use among teenagers. For more information, see http://monitoringthefuture.org/.

10 Philip Reichel, "Classroom Uses of a Criminal Activities Checklist," *Teaching Sociology*, vol. 3, no. 1, October 1975, p. 83.

11 Emile Durkheim, *Suicide: A Study in Sociology*, translated by J. Spaulding and G. Simpson, New York: Free Press, 1951[originally published 1897].

12 Marvin Wolfgang, "International Criminal Statistics: A Proposal," *Journal of Criminal Law, Criminology and Police Science*, vol. 58, no. 1, 1967, p. 65.

CHAPTER 2

Biological, psychological, and classical theories of crime

All crimes are different and all criminals are different. Consequently, there is not one theory that explains all crime, and not one theory that explains all criminals. Likewise, there is no one academic discipline that has or should have a monopoly on the understanding of crime. While biologists and psychologists have influenced the thinking of criminologists and criminal justice professionals today and in the past, sociology has had a far more prominent influence; and the preponderance of our theoretical discussions will consider the contributions of sociology to the understanding of crime and criminals. However, to understand the history of criminology, we need to delve into some biological and psychological theories of crime. In this chapter, we will also be considering some classical/rational theories of crime. These theories have had considerable influence on criminal justice policy on-and-off for centuries.

BIOLOGICAL THEORIES: LOMBROSO, FIRST AND STILL EMBLEMATIC

Biological theories were very much in vogue in the latter decades of the nineteenth century and into the first part of the twentieth century. These early biological theories were seriously flawed and have fallen into ridicule. More recent biological theories have some definitional and methodological problems; but they are often not as easily dismissed as their predecessors. Today, biological theories are quite controversial, in part, because of the racist and xenophobic implications that have pervaded biological investigations of the past. A look at the history of these investigations will reveal why many of today's criminologists are leery of research connecting biology and crime.

Without a doubt, the most familiar name in the history of biology and crime is Cesare Lombroso. Lombroso had been a doctor in the Italian army in the mid-nineteenth century when he noticed that the misfit soldiers, the troublemakers, often had similar physical features. He pursued this observation more systematically in subsequent posts as a physician in various Italian lunatic asylums. Based on post-mortem examinations as well as his observations of soldiers, lunatics, and prisoners, he concluded that criminality is inherited and that those born with criminal tendencies could be identified by unusual physical features, or "anomalies." The ear typical of the criminal, for example, is described as "often of large size; occasionally also it is smaller than the ears of normal individuals. Twenty-eight per cent of criminals have handle-shaped ears standing out from the face as in the chimpanzee: in other cases they are placed at different levels."[1] The more physical anomalies a person had, the more likely he was to be a "born criminal." Lombroso argued that such anomalies were indicative of a primitive reversion, or "atavism." He considered criminality, insanity, and genius to exist on a continuum, with criminals being the most atavistic of the lot.[2] Influenced by the then-recently published works of Darwin, Lombroso was arguing that criminals are not as highly evolved as the rest of us, essentially like "savages" living in the modern world.

Lombroso's work was very influential. Before him, most intellectual endeavors into the field of crime were focused on the law and legal philosophy (see, for example, Beccaria, in this chapter). Following Lombroso, criminologists began to turn their attention away from the law and to focus on the scientific study of the criminal. The legitimacy of the law and its application were implicitly taken for granted. The problem of crime had little or nothing to do with society or the environment, but resided in the biological constitution of criminals. Public antipathy towards criminals was already commonplace; but now there was scientific justification for considering them and treating them as biologically inferior or defective beings. If they are not as highly evolved, then there is little hope of reforming them; and standards of humane treatment are less relevant since criminals are less human.

As criminality has long been perceived to be concentrated among poor and minority populations, Lombroso established a "scientific" justification for treating criminals—and by implication, minorities and the poor—as biologically inferior. However, as with much subsequent research linking biology and crime, Lombroso only studied the criminals and deviants who had been caught and—in the case of prisoners—arrested, prosecuted, convicted, and incarcerated. He did not take into account all of the criminals who did *not* get caught, arguably, the vast majority of the population (see "self-report surveys" in Chapter 1). Poor people and minorities are more likely to penetrate the depths of the criminal justice system because of discrimination on the part of police, prosecutors, and jurors; and wealthy people/criminals can minimize their penetration into the system through bribery, their influential connections, and/or their ability to pay for a competent legal defense. Thus, sampling biases that are pervasive in the history of biological research resulted in the legitimation of prejudice and discrimination inside and outside of the criminal justice system.

Lombroso and his work were very well regarded in intellectual circles throughout Europe and America and the notion of the heritability of criminality influenced not only the behavioral sciences, but also politics and public policy. In the early twentieth century the belief that negative behavioral traits could be passed from generation to generation gave rise to the *eugenics movement*. With so-called "scientific" research to back them up, programs and policies were put into place to isolate and/or sterilize "undesirable" populations. The vast majority of those being so treated were poor, minorities, and immigrants. The eugenics movement was quite strong in the United States in the first half of the twentieth century; but it found its ultimate expression with the extermination of millions of "undesirables" during the Nazi Holocaust.

It is with this history in mind that biological research into crime has become very controversial. Nonetheless, biological research has continued, with many theories falling by the wayside, some maintaining interest for decades, and new ones in development. Some biological theories implicate genetics; some implicate diet or environmental contaminants; and some implicate defects in the brain.

Twin and adoption studies

Two popular subgenres of biological research on criminality are twin and adoption studies. *Twin studies* examine similarities in behavior ("concordance") among monozygotic (identical) twins, comparing them to similarities in behavior among dizygotic (fraternal) twins. If there is a genetic contribution to behavior, we should expect more concordance among identical twins because they share 100 percent of the same genes, whereas fraternal twins only share 50 percent of the same genes. Indeed, researchers frequently do find more concordance among identical twins. However, critics of twin studies point out that this research has not come up with a sound method for disentangling the effects of genes and the environment. Since monozygotic twins are identical, their environments are more similar and the ways people treat them are more similar. In fact, they are often dressed alike and people cannot tell them apart. Hence, greater concordance among identical twins could well have far more to do with similarities in their environment than similarities in their genetic makeup. Summarizing research on twin studies, Katherine Morley and Wayne Hall write,

Recent twin studies show persuasive evidence that both genetic and environmental factors contribute to antisocial behavior. However, the genetic evidence indicates that there is no single gene, or even a small number of genes, that predict an increased risk of antisocial behavior. Where there have been some effects, the increased risk associated with antisocial behavior is modest.[3]

Research on twins continues with the goal of developing better methods of separating genetic from environmental effects.

Like twin studies, *adoption studies* also look at the heritability of criminality. A typical adoption study would examine children of biological parent(s) with a record of criminal or antisocial behavior who are adopted by parents without such a record. Are these children more likely to grow up to display criminal or antisocial behavior than adoptees whose biological parents did not have criminal records? In such a research design, the biological parents would be considered the "genetic parents" while the adoptive parents would be considered "social parents;"[4] and the goal of the research is to determine the relative contributions of each to criminality. These studies have been called "natural experiments in which the effects of genetic and rearing influences may be separated to a relatively high degree."[5] The most often cited adoption studies were conducted separately in the mid-twentieth century, examining criminal and adoption records in Iowa, Denmark, and Sweden. These studies found a significant heritable contribution to criminality. Critics of these studies, however, have noted a number of confounding factors. One is that the social parents may have been informed of the genetic parents' criminality; thus, biasing their interactions with their adopted children. Another problem is that adoption agencies do not randomly select adoptive parents; instead, they apply selective criteria and personal prejudices in the placement of an adoptive child, and these may bias the results. Lastly, any amount of time the soon-to-be adopted child spends with his or her genetic parents would surely confound the separation of heritable effects from environmental effects; and the later the adoption, the more problematic the parent–child attachment can be.[6] Such criticisms do mitigate the conclusions that can be drawn from adoption studies; but they do not warrant a complete dismissal of their results. We can expect to see more research in this area.

XYY chromosomes

An example of theories fallen by the wayside came from bio-criminological research in the 1960s and 1970s linking the anomalous XYY sex chromosomes in some males to criminal behavior. (Females typically possess XX chromosomes and males are usually XY; hence those possessing the XYY-type were sometimes referred to as "supermales.") Research on inmates in prisons and mental institutions linked XYY to aggressive behavior. This research has since been cast into doubt; but let us assume for the moment that there is a link between XYY and aggressive behavior. Aggressive behavior can be a positive or a negative trait, depending upon its context (place to place, time to time, and culture to culture). In one context, it can make people criminals; in another, it can make them war heroes, CEOs, and presidents. XYY had also been associated with being unusually tall; and it could be that tall people with behavioral problems were perceived to be more menacing than people of normal stature with behavioral problems and, therefore, more likely to be convicted of crimes or committed to mental institutions. Thus, in both the cases of aggression and height, the link between XYY and crime is correlative and not causative. Nevertheless, experts such as geneticist Bentley Glass, the former president for the American Associations for the Advancement of Science, hailed the findings of research into XYY and "look[ed] forward to the day when a combination of amniocentesis and abortion will help to 'rid us of sex deviants of the XYY type.'"[7] Furthermore, some institutions for juvenile delinquents were screening boys for the extra Y chromosome and at least one institution in Maryland was treating boys who tested positive with female hormones.[8]

Biological researchers that focus on convicted criminals are implicitly relying on a legalistic definition of crime (see "mala prohibita" in Chapter 1), allowing the law to define criminal behavior, whereas those who lean toward a *male in se* definition of crime argue that there is nothing inherent in a behavior that makes it a crime. Law-making is a political process. Behaviors legally defined as criminal vary from place to place, time to time, and culture to culture. Thus, since there is nothing inherent in crime that makes it a crime, critics of biocriminology argue, there can be nothing inherent (or biological) in a person that makes him or her a criminal. Furthermore, when biological researchers look at crime, they usually focus on the kinds of crimes that poor people are more likely to perpetrate. That is, they are more likely to look at violent street crime and not embezzlement, fraud, or medical malpractice. Criminologists Walter DeKeseredy and Martin Schwartz address this issue,

> If the cause of crime is low IQ, bad genes, the wrong physical type, or similar problems, how do we account for people who steal millions of dollars; pollute our rivers, air, and land; perform dangerous, unnecessary surgery to gain more fees; create unsafe working conditions that can injure or kill dozens of people at a time, or take bribes in public office. Thus far, clinical criminologists have offered only the most unsatisfactory of explanations.[9]

Thus, critics argue that biological research tends to reinforce popular stereotypes about crime more than shed light on its causes.

More importantly, as for ethical considerations, we need to ask, if there were a connection between biology and crime, to what remedies does that lead us? Sterilization? Abortion? Chemical or surgical intervention? Annihilation? Whatever the remedy the biologist might have in mind is not necessarily the remedy that will be taken up policymakers; and the remedy adopted in one country will not necessarily be the one adopted in others (for example, the American eugenic remedies versus the Nazi remedies.). These considerations are not to deny the possibility of biological connections to criminality, but such research needs to be pursued with great caution; and resistance to biological theories should be understood within its historical and sociological contexts.

The medicalization of deviance

With the sociological and ethical concerns surrounding biological theories of crime in mind, let us take a look at a related phenomenon. Deviant behaviors, which were once explained in terms of moral failings or environmental or psychological deficiencies, are increasingly being explained in terms of biological defects or differences.

Every decade, for at least the past century, has brought well-publicized advances in the biological sciences; and the public has become receptive to proclamations of new advances in the biology of human behavior. What many fail to recognize is that so-called advances in the biological understanding of human behavior do not come close to advances in other branches of biology. Nevertheless, there is large arsenal of medications for a wide variety of psychiatric disorders that millions of people take on a daily basis. Most of them believe their doctors when they say that their "disorder" stems from a biological source or defect. As the biomedical establishment proclaims psychiatric truths, more behaviors, thoughts, and moods that deviate from the norm are subject to medical treatments. Sociologists call this change in the conceptualization of deviance the "medicalization of deviance."

For decades, doctors have told their patients that their mental, emotional, or behavioral disorder is caused by a biological defect or a chemical imbalance and the medications they are being prescribed help correct that defect or will bring those chemicals into balance. Yet, the biomedical establishment has not identified what biological defect(s) is responsible or what a healthy chemical balance would look like; and diagnoses of these disorders are rarely, if ever, based on biological or biochemical tests.

An example familiar to most of us is attention deficit disorder (ADD). Critics of the medicalization of deviance do not deny the possibility of the existence of a biological basis for ADD. However, without biological tests, there is no way to determine how many of the millions of children who have such a diagnosis actually have the biological condition that their diagnosis assumes. The drugs prescribed for this disorder are powerful amphetamines that are similar in structure to cocaine.[10] Yet, as there are no biochemical tests involved in diagnosis, the line between disordered and normal is blurred. It cannot be proven that what all people with a diagnosis of ADD have in common is a biological defect. Critics of the medicalization of deviance argue that what they all do have in common is that they had difficulty functioning within the norm before their diagnosis.

No doubt, many of those who carry psychiatric diagnoses suffer without their medications; and, arguably, they should continue taking them. However, we should be mindful of several facts: (1) just because medications alleviate their suffering does not mean the source of their problems is biological (sociologists make the case that very often the source of suffering is in the patient's environment and interpersonal relationships);[11] (2) many psychiatric medications come with serious side effects, including withdrawal and addiction; (3) many psychiatric medications work no better than a placebo; and (4) many psychiatric treatments of the past were considered effective, but later fell into disrepute.

The brain is an extraordinarily complex organ and scientists know only a tiny fraction of what needs to be known to understand most psychiatric disorders. Current explanations for why certain psychiatric medications work fall mostly within the domain of speculation and conjecture. To quote David Rosenhan, whose pioneering work is often cited in the literature on the medicalization of deviance, "Whenever the ratio of what is known to what needs to be known approaches zero, we tend to invent 'knowledge' and assume that we understand more than we actually do."[12]

Critics of the medicalization of deviance see it as a form of social control, that is, as a means of keeping people within normative boundaries. The social control function of the psychiatric establishment is most obvious in cases of involuntary commitments to mental hospitals. These used to be very common; but the "deinstitutionalization movement" of the early 1970s brought about numerous restrictions that limited the use of involuntary commitment to cases where the patient/defendant can clearly be demonstrated to be a danger to him or herself or others. As dangerousness is hard to predict, involuntary commitment remains a controversial issue today.[13]

Thomas Szasz—a psychiatrist himself, a prolific writer, and an outspoken critic of the medicalization of deviance—was more concerned about forms of medicine as social control that are more subtle than involuntary commitment. He believed, for example, that kids are naturally distractable and, at times, unruly; but when they cross some unknown boundary in the classroom—that varies from teacher to teacher—some kids find themselves referred to a doctor who diagnoses them as having ADD. Szasz spent his career warning the public that psychiatry has emerged as an agency of social control, enforcing the lesser norms, while the police and the courts enforce the norms that are codified into law.[14]

PSYCHOLOGICAL EXPLANATIONS FOR CRIME

Like their biological counterparts, psychologists are fundamentally concerned with how criminals are different from non-criminals. Psychologists answer this question in terms of intelligence, learning, childhood development, personality, or mental illness. Early in the twentieth century, the psychological focus was on intelligence, with criminologists attributing criminality to "feeble-mindedness" and low IQ. Frequently arguing that these traits are inherited, these theorists, along with the biocriminologists, played a major role in the eugenics movement. Later in the twentieth century, it was demonstrated that IQ tests had a strong class bias, with questions that had little relevance to lower class lifestyles; and people came to consider that some criminals were often highly intelligent, possessing, at least, a good deal of "street smarts."

Freudian theory

Freudian—or psychoanalytic—theory was very influential in the mid-twentieth century among psychologists and college educated Americans, in general. Sigmund Freud asserted that there are three components to the personality: the id, the ego, and the superego. The *id* represents our biological drives (for food, sex, and sleep, for examples); the *ego* is the socially reasonable part of our personality; and the *superego* is the conscience. For most of us, we are constantly trying to satisfy our biological drives (id) while conforming to the social rules (ego); and, if we violate social conventions, we feel guilty (superego). These components of the personality are shaped by experiences early in life; and our individual personality is a reflection of the balance between the three.

For Freud, the individual and society are always in conflict because society could not function if we were always satisfying our biological drives whenever and wherever we wanted; therefore, in order for us to function in society, we must learn to repress our id and satisfy our drives only within the constraints of social convention. Generally speaking, the criminal is a person who, because of early childhood experiences, has an underdeveloped superego and fails to feel guilty when he or she satisfies their biological drives in socially inappropriate ways. There are endless permutations of Freudian explanations for crime, however. Rather than criminality being caused by an underdeveloped superego, an overdeveloped superego could cause a person to repress their biological drives, creating an anxiety-ridden pressure cooker-effect, with the individual ready to explode into an id-releasing crime spree at any time. Or, an overdeveloped superego could lead to a person constantly feeling guilt and a need for punishment. Such an individual may commit crimes in order to get the punishment she or he feels they deserve.

Freudian theory provides an interesting conceptual framework that can be used to explain virtually any and all behaviors; but there is little evidence to back up these explanations. The id, the ego, and the superego cannot be directly observed and, therefore, assertions about their effects represent little more than conjecture. Nonetheless, Freud had an enormous impact on psychology and popular culture during and after his lifetime. Certainly, thousands of psychoanalysts in the 1950s, 1960s and 1970s would have sworn to the validity and utility of Freudian theory.

Kohlberg's moral development theory

Another branch of psychological theory that emerged in the mid-twentieth century focused on the child's cognitive and moral development. Developmental theory asserts that normal childhood, adolescent, and even adult development proceeds through a number of stages. These stages have a specific sequence and one must master the cognitive or moral skills in one stage to get to the next. Lawrence Kohlberg's moral development theory asserts that people proceed through a number of stages in the development of their ability to determine right and wrong. Kohlberg identified six stages of moral development, occurring in three levels. In the early level, the child's concept of right and wrong centers on the avoidance of punishment. Right behavior is behavior that does not incur punishment. This level is guided entirely by the child's self-interest. In the next level, children's ideas of right and wrong are guided by their concern for what family and friends might think of them. Right behavior is behavior which receives approval. In the last level, the behaviors of late teens and adults are guided by more abstract universal moral principles. In other words, they do the right thing because they believe it is the right thing, regardless of the expected reactions of others. In this level, they learn to distinguish legally established right and wrong from morally principled right and wrong.

Kohlberg posited that antisocial and criminal behavior is more likely to be performed by people who have not proceeded as far through these stages of development as non-criminals. Indeed, as we will see in Chapter 3, the most crime-prone years for most violent and property criminals occur in the late teens and early twenties; that is, among people who have not made to it the final level of moral development. Furthermore, studies have indicated that criminals are more likely to be "stuck" in early stages of moral development than non-criminals.

While the amount of research into moral development is impressive and still growing, it does lend itself to tautological thinking or circular reasoning where one can reason that since crime is immoral, then, of course, criminals are not as morally developed as the rest of us. Also, we might point out that even those who have reached the highest stages of moral development do not make all of their decisions based on the highest moral principles; instead, we might think of these stages as representing the *capacity* of individuals to make such decisions.

Psychopathic personality disorder

It was mentioned earlier that some critics of biological explanations for crime argue that there is nothing inherent in crime that makes it a crime; but perhaps some of the worst criminals possess one quality that distinguishes them from the rest of the population: a lack of empathy for others. Such a deficit explains the criminal's disregard for the harm he or she causes to their victims. Some psychologists suggest that this quality is indicative of a "psychopathic personality disorder."

The term "psychopath" has been around since the 1800s. One of the more famous descriptions of the psychopath, however, comes from psychiatrist Harvey Cleckly's book, *The Mask of Sanity*, published in 1941. He lists the following key features of psychopathy:

Superficial charm
Manipulative
Above-average intelligence
Absence of psychotic symptoms
Absence of anxiety
Lack of remorse
Failure to learn from experience
Egocentric
Lack of emotional depth[15]

IMAGE 2.1
Ted Bundy: Serial killer who fit the classic description of a psychopath. Known for his intelligence, charm, and ruthlessness.

The concept of psychopathy piqued the public imagination in the 1980s and 1990s when serial killers pervaded the news media and popular culture. The ultimate expression of the psychopath was probably best expressed in the character of Hannibal Lecter from the 1991 film *Silence of the Lambs*. Lecter was charming, brilliant, egomaniacal, brutally calculating, and totally lacking in regard for the suffering of his victims. Since the serial killer scare of the 1980 and 1990s (see Chapter 4), such characters have become a staple in the crime thriller genre.

Lecter was, of course, an extreme and fictionalized psychopath. It is estimated that one percent of the population could be classified as psychopaths. They are disproportionately represented in prison populations, especially among repeat offenders.[16] However, not all psychopaths are criminals; and not all criminals are psychopaths. The traits that characterize the psychopath may also be ones that enable its possessors to succeed in the often ruthless worlds of business, politics, and war. Journalist Jon Ronson writes of his meeting with "Chainsaw Al," a corporate executive who moved from the helm of one company to next in the 1990s, hired by their boards to fire employees by the hundreds or even thousands and cut labor costs, and, in the process, devastating cities and towns that were dependent on those jobs.

> I was researching a book about psychopaths and had come to meet Al Dunlap, a merciless cost-cutter and the onetime CEO of Sunbeam, a man who seemed to actually, unlike most humans, enjoy firing people. He'd made his reputation closing down plants on behalf of Scott, America's oldest toilet-paper manufacturer, and I thought he might fit a theory I'd heard: that some of our best CEOs are actually psychopaths. That maybe what got us into this global financial crisis wasn't just hubris but a string of rampant psychopaths.
>
> Looking around Dunlap's foyer, I noticed a lot of gold. I was prepared for this, the gold, having recently seen a portrait of him sitting on a gold chair, wearing a gold tie, with a gold suit of armor by the door and a gold crucifix on the mantelpiece. "Well," said Al, "gold is shiny."
>
> He pointed at a sculpture of four sharks encircling the planet. "Sharks," he said. "Their spirit will enable you to succeed."[17]

Indeed, Robert Hare, one of the leading authorities on psychopathy and developer of the often-used Psychopathy Checklist (PCL), turned his attention to the issue of successful psychopaths late in his career with the book he coauthored, *Snakes in Suits: When Psychopaths Go to Work*.[18]

Thus, like the XYY chromosome type (see page 18), psychopathy can be either good or bad, depending on the context. Some contexts require dispassionate decision-making that may have adverse effects on the wellbeing of others; and the psychopath may be well-suited for such situations. But unlike XYY—which either you have or you don't—most everyone shares some traits with the psychopath, at least, some of the time. Psychopathy lies on a continuum with non-psychopathy and there is not clear consensus as to where to draw the line between the two. Furthermore, as an explanation for crime, psychopathy lends itself to tautological thinking, as anyone who commits a horrendous series of crimes, for example, can obviously be said to be lacking a conscience and is, therefore, a psychopath.

CLASSICAL AND RATIONAL CHOICE THEORIES

Beccaria and Bentham

Cesare Beccaria was born into the Italian aristocracy and sent off for Jesuit training at the age of eight. He resented the stifling and inflexible education among the Jesuits. Later, he went on to the University of Pavia, where his performance was less than impressive. According to one biographer, "All that these years seemed to create in the frustrated young man was lethargy and discontent."[19] He lived in poverty for a brief period when, over a dispute, he lost his father's financial support. Before the publication of his treatise, *Dei delitti e delle pene* (*On Crimes and Punishments*) in 1764, Beccaria did little to distinguish himself from his contemporaries and was likely considered something of a ne'er-do-well. When he did dedicate himself to his writing project, he spent a mere nine months working on it and he produced one of the most important documents in the history of Western jurisprudence.

On Crimes and Punishments was a tightly argued attack on the use of the criminal justice system as a means of political oppression by European aristocracies of his time. The law of his day was used by kings, popes, and magistrates to torture, vanquish, and annihilate their enemies, and to intimidate their would-be political foes. Little or no evidence was required and there was little or no judicial oversight. Because of these conditions, it was actually quite daring of Beccaria to publish his work; and it was initially published anonymously. Upon publication, however, when his name was revealed, Beccaria became an overnight sensation, hailed throughout European society as the guiding light of criminal justice reform.

Beccaria's treatise reflected the works of social contract theorists before him, especially that of the seventeenth century Scottish philosopher Thomas Hobbes. Social contract theorists had been interested in the question "why is there government?" This is a timelessly interesting question because where there is government (that is, everywhere), the people are not free; they are *governed*. So why do people allow themselves to be governed? According to Hobbes, without government, life would be "solitary, poor, nasty, brutish and short." That is, without government, people would be tearing at each other's throats, trying to survive or get ahead. So government arose to protect each person from every other person. A contract involves each party giving something in order to receive something in return from the other. In this case, each individual member of a society gives up a portion of his or her freedom to form a government in order to receive protection from that government, as depicted in the Figure 2.1.[20]

The total sum of those freedoms equals the power of the state and, according to Beccaria, the social contract stipulates that the government can only use that power in order to protect each person from every other

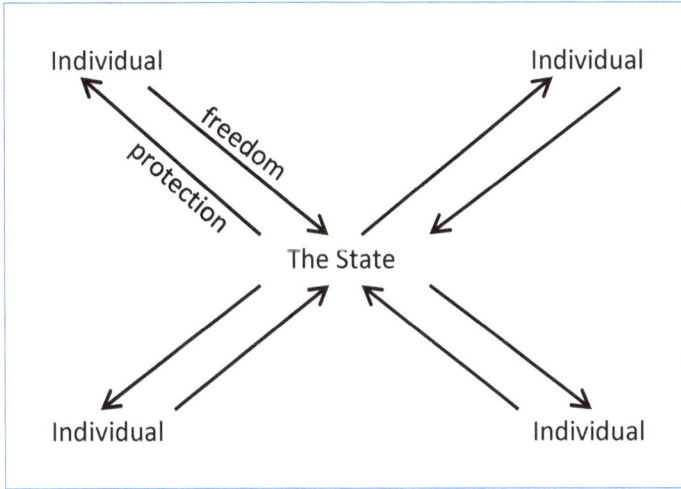

FIGURE 2.1
Thomas Hobbes's social contract.

person. Any other use of that power constitutes a violation of the social contract. Thus, when government officials use their power to suppress their opponents, their actions represent a violation of the social contract. Following this logic, Beccaria acknowledged the need for law and for punishments specified by the law, as these are needed to protect each person from every other person. But these need to be applied equally because we have all given equally of our freedom to form a government.

Beccaria is recognized as being a member of the *classical school of criminology*. The classical theorists viewed humans as rational beings who mentally weigh the benefits and the costs of their actions. If the benefits of illegal activity outweigh the costs, then crime will be the result. According to Beccaria, then, the state should apply only enough punishment to make crime irrational; any more than that is a violation of the social contract. In this sense, he advocated for milder forms of punishment than were prevalent in his time. Beccaria writes,

> Can the shrieks of a wretch recall from time, which never reverses its course, deeds already accomplished? The purpose can only be to prevent the criminal from inflicting new injuries on its citizens and to deter others from similar acts. … For punishment to attain its end, the evil which it inflicts has only to exceed the advantage derivable from the crime; in this excess of evil one should include the certainty of punishment and the loss of the good which the crime might have produced.[21]

Punishments which are more severe than necessary to deter crime are not only a violation of the social contract, but they can also make crime rational as criminals "are driven to commit additional crimes to avoid punishment for a single one."[22]

Further, Beccaria argued punishment should be swift and certain because swiftness and certainty reinforce the automatic association between crime and punishment in the minds of the offender and of the public. By the same token, he opposed the granting of clemency and pardons (and by implication, probation and parole) because these weaken the association between crime and punishment. But, he notes, "As punishments become more mild, clemency and pardon become less necessary."[23]

Beccaria was a staunch opponent of torture and the death penalty, both of which were common at the time. With regard to torture, he writes,

> The fact of the crime is either certain or uncertain; if certain, all that is due is the punishment established by the laws, and tortures are useless because the criminal's confession is useless; if uncertain, then one must not torture the innocent, for such, according to the laws, is a man whose crimes are not yet proved.[24]

As for the death penalty, he argued that the intensity of punishment is less of a deterrent than its duration. The moment of death lasts just an instant and nobody knows what happens afterwards. Some even wish for death as evidenced by suicide rates, which are often higher than homicide rates. But nobody wishes for a lifetime of forced labor. The death penalty, he argued, sets an "example of barbarity" and encourages the exact behavior that it is supposed to discourage. It is absurd, he argued, to order a public murder in order to deter murder.

There are few ideas that are original in Beccaria's treatise, but he audaciously brought these ideas together under a framework of social contract theory, which appealed to his contemporaries and leading figures during the Enlightenment. John Adams opened his defense of the soldiers involved in the Boston Massacre with a passage from Beccaria's treatise. Given that *On Crimes and Punishments* was a must-read for political reformers of his day, there is little doubt that Beccaria provided both moral and intellectual inspiration behind both the American and French Revolutions; and his ideas are quite pronounced in the Bill of Rights of the U.S. Constitution with its emphasis on the rights of the accused. Centuries later, experts agree that Beccaria's work had "more practical effect than any other treatise ever written in the long campaign against barbarism in criminal law and procedure."[25]

When criminologists today talk about classical theorists, most often they are referring to the works of Beccaria and/or of his British contemporary, Jeremy Bentham. For Bentham, the purpose of punishment is to ensure security. In this context, "security," writes Pat O'Malley, "can be broadly defined as that condition in society in which the future is known in key respects, in particular with respect to the protection of life and property."[26] Informed by the writings of Adam Smith, Bentham believed that people are rational actors and need to be able to predict the consequences of their actions. The economy depends on such predictability; and, no matter, whether your business is competing with the best products at the lowest prices, criminal victimization could come along and destroy the fruits of your success, erasing the predictability needed for a smooth functioning economy. It is the state's purpose, then, to impose punishment to make crime irrational and thereby ensure a certain degree of security (predictability) in society; and Bentham agreed with Beccaria that any punishment exceeding this goal represented an abuse of the state's authority. Consequently, Bentham set out to "scientifically" determine which punishments best accomplished this goal. While Beccaria and Bentham worked upon the same assumptions about human nature and came to similar conclusions, Beccaria based his argument on social contract theory, and Bentham based his on economic theory.

Rational choice theory

Laypeople are often disturbed by all or most criminological theories because such theories downplay the existence of free will, and instead "blame" the individual's crime on his or her biological or psychological constitution, or on their environment. Rational choice theory often appeals to those who see other types of theories as somehow "excusing" the criminal for his or her behavior. Rational choice theory is a modern day extension of the classical criminologists who argued that humans choose their own actions based on a rational calculation of the costs and the benefits of such actions. Such an understanding of human behavior is prominent today in the field of "behavioral economics." Accordingly, if the rewards of criminal behavior are perceived to outweigh the costs, then crime will result. In the case of crime, "rewards" might be in the form of money, sex, power, or peer group status; "costs" might take the form of ostracism, shame, or prison time.

The thinking behind rational choice theory has been around for hundreds, if not thousands, of years; but it was articulated for modern criminology by Derek Cornish and Ronald Clarke in the 1980s. They write,

> Offenders seek to benefit themselves by their criminal behavior; that this involves the making of decisions and choices, however rudimentary on occasion these processes might be, and that these processes exhibit a measure of rationality, albeit constrained by the limits of time and the availability of information.[27]

So while criminal behavior may, at times, seem impulsive, and while some criminals may seem to have miscalculated the benefits and costs of their behavior, Cornish and Clarke would explain the seemingly irrational elements of crime in terms of "the limits of time" and misinformation.

Rational choice theory suffers in explaining why, when two people are confronted by the same configuration of rewards and costs of a given action, one might choose crime while the other one does not. Rational choice theorists would first explain that it is not the actual costs and rewards that determine choices, but the perception of rewards and costs. In which case, background factors—be they biological, psychological, or sociological—do come into play when we consider a person's perceptions and how they come to be involved in crime. By recognizing the influence of biological, psychological, or sociological factors, however, we return to the problem of downplaying the role of free will.

The focus of rational choice theory, however, is not on understanding *criminal involvement*, but on preventing the *criminal event*. As such, this theory has had practical applications for *situational crime prevention* (SCP). According to Freilich and Natarajan, "SCP focuses on why certain crimes happen and why they concentrate in time and space. The goal is to understand 'how' the crimes are successfully completed so as to find ways to prevent their occurrence."[28] Ronald Clarke and Pat Mayhew, give the example of suicide in England and Wales in the 1960s and 1970s. Realizing that 40 percent of all suicides were gas-induced, the authorities had carbon monoxide removed from the public gas supply and the number of suicides per year dropped from 5,700 to 3,700 between 1963 and 1975.[29]

A variation of SCP is *crime prevention through environmental design* (CPTED). The goal of CPTED, writes David Mackey, is

> to effectively arrange the physical environment, whether it is a neighborhood, a park, or a building, such as a school, to simultaneously give legitimate users more efficient access to the space and to let potential offenders know that risks and rewards are not in their favor in that particular location.[30]

An early example of CPTED was in the thirteenth century when the king of England had the roadways cleared of brush on either side so that would-be robbers could not hide while waiting for a carriage to pass. A more modern example would be locked foyers at the entrance to a school to prevent visitors with malevolent intent from entering.

Early critics of SCP were concerned that such efforts would only lead to "crime displacement." That is, criminals would just go somewhere else to commit their crimes, or find another means to commit their crimes (or suicides). The suicide data mentioned above and numerous studies on SCP, however, have shown this not to be the case.[31]

Rational choice theory is perhaps most popularly expressed in the belief that the best way to tackle the problem of crime is to increase the severity of punishment (see "deterrence," p. 178). As such, rational choice theory provided much of the theoretical impetus for the crackdown on drugs and crime in the 1980s and 1990s, leading to an era of mass incarceration (see Chapter 7).

NOTES

1 Gina Lombroso-Ferrero, *Criminal Man: According to the Classification of Cesare Lombroso*. The Project Gutenburg Ebook, #29895. Release date: September 3, 2009 [originally published 1911], www.gutenberg.org/files/29895/29895-h/29895-h.htm. Retrieved June 15, 2018.

2 Paolo Mazzarello, "Cesare Lombroso: An anthropologist between evolution and degeneration," *Functional Neurology*, vol. 26. No. 2, pp. 97–101. www.ncbi.nlm.nih.gov/pmc/articles/PMC3814446/. Retrieved June 16, 2018.

3 Katherine Morley and Wayne Hall, "Is there a Genetic Susceptibility to Engage in Criminal Acts? Australian Institute of Criminality, September 2003. Australian Government. https://aic.gov.au/publications/tandi/tandi263. Retrieved December 14, 2019.

4 Callie Burt and Ronald Simons, "Pulling Back the Curtain on Heritability Studies: Biosocial Criminology in the Postgenomic Era," *Criminology*, vol. 52, no. 2, 2014.

5 Quoting Mednick and Kandel from Jay Joseph, "Is Crime in the Genes?" A Critical Review of Twin and Adoption Studies of Criminality and Antisocial Behavior," *Journal of Mind and Behavior*, vol. 22, no. 2, Spring 2001, p. 193.

6 The first two criticisms from Jay Joseph, the last from Burt and Simons.

7 Jon Beckwith and Jonathan King, "XYY Syndrome: A dangerous myth," *New Scientist*, vol. 14, November, 1974.

8 Ibid., p. 474.

9 Walter DeKeseredy and Martin Schwartz, *Contemporary Criminology*, Belmont, CA: Wadsworth, 1996, p. 191.

10 Richard DeGrandpre, *The Cult of Pharmacology: How America Became the World's Most Troubled Drug Culture*, Durham, NC: Duke University Press, 2010.

11 See Robert Heiner, "The Medicalization of Deviance," in *Deviance across Cultures: Constructions of Difference*, 2nd ed., Robert Heiner, editor, New York: Oxford University Press, 2014, pp. 347–349.

12 David Rosenhan, "On Being Sane in Insane Places," in *Deviance across Cultures: Constructions of Difference*, 2nd ed., Robert Heiner, editor, New York: Oxford University Press, 2014, p. 358.

13 Involuntary commitment is also controversial because many of the homeless in the United States are mentally ill; and critics argue it should be easier to commit them to a mental hospital for treatment, and for their own safety.

14 Szasz wrote many books and monographs, but the most famous of these was arguably *The Myth of Mental Illness: Foundations of a Theory of Personal Conduct*. New York: Harper, 1974. To see a brief presentation he gave summarizing his position on mental illness, go to www.youtube.com/watch?v=2Qegsqy HU2E.

15 D.A. Andres and Janes Bonda, *The Psychology of Criminal Conduct*, 5th edition, New York: Routledge, 2010. p. 207.

16 Danielle Egan, "The Psychopath and the Hare," *Discover*, June, 2016, vol. 37: 5, http://web.a.ebscohost.com.libproxy.plymouth.edu/ehost/detail/detail?vid=4&sid= 8b77efe2-930b-4ce8-af4b-a9cab49079cb%40sessionmgr4007&bdata=JnNpdGU9Z Whvc3QtbGl2ZQ%3d%3d#AN=114399067&db=aph. Retrieved July 4, 2018.

17 Jon Ronson, "Your Boss is a Psycho," *GQ*, December 18, 2015. www.gq.com/story/ your-boss-is-a-psycho-jon-ronson. Retrieved July 5, 2018.

18 Paul Babiak and Robert Hare, *Snakes in Suits: When Psychopaths Go to Work*. New York: HarperBusiness, 2006.

19 Elio Monachesi, "Cesare Beccaria," from *Pioneers in Criminology*, 2nd edition, edited by Hermann Mannheim. Montclair, NJ: Patterson Smith, 1972, p. 36.

20 What is being referred to in this figure as "the government" Hobbes called "the sovereign." While there are differences in meaning, "the government" better serves our purposes in understanding Beccaria's work.

21 Cesare Beccaria, *On Crimes and Punishments*, translated by Henry Paolucci. Indianapolis: Bobbs-Merrill, 1963. pp. 42–43.

22 Ibid., p. 43. Emphasis added.

23 Ibid., p. 58.

24 Ibid., p. 30.

25 Ibid., quoting a 1952 passage from Harry Elmer Barnes' and Howard Becker's *Social Thought from Lore to Science*.

26 Pat O'Malley, "Jeremy Bentham," from *Fifty Key Thinkers in Criminology*, K. Hayward, S. Maruna, and J. Mooney, eds., NY: Routledge, 2010, p. 11.

27 Derek Cornish and Ronald Clarke, *The Reasoning Criminal: Rational Choice Perspectives on Offending*, NJ: Transaction Publishers, 2014, p. 1, [originally published 1986].

28 Joshua Freilich and Mangai Natarajan, "Ronal Clarke," from *Fifty Key Thinkers in Criminology*, K. Hayward, S Maruna, and J. Mooney, eds., NY: Routledge, 2010, p. 238.

29 Ibid.

30 David Mackey, "Theoretical Foundations of Crime Prevention," from *Crime Prevention*, D. Mackey and K. Levan, eds., Burlington, MA: Jones and Bartlett, 2013, p. 7.

31 Freilich and Natarajan, "Ronald Clarke."

CHAPTER 3

Sociological theories of crime

SOCIOLOGICAL THINKING ABOUT CRIME

Biologists and psychologists typically think about crime on an individual level, asking how is the criminal different from the non-criminal? Sociologists, on the other hand, focus less on the individual and more on the environment, asking, how does the environment influence people's behavior? In an over-simplification, it is often said that sociologists study groups. This is because the groups to which we belong determine the environments to which we are exposed. Here, the word "group" often refers to the demographic group to which we belong, for examples, our social class, race, age, gender, religion, and the neighborhood or region in which we live.

With its focus on the group, sociologists are better able to explain aggregates, trends, and crime rates than are biologists and psychologists. For example, in the 1980s, it was estimated that there were 35 serial killers on the loose at any given time.[1] Thirty-five is a very small number relative to a population of more than 300 million; and one might better turn to the psychologist rather than a sociologist for an explanation of why does someone become a serial murderer. On the other hand, there were over 16,000 homicides in the United States in 2018; and the sociologist is better equipped to handle such questions as why are murder rates so much higher in Chicago than in Seattle, or why are murder rates so much lower today than they were in 1990, or which demographic groups are more likely to commit murder and why.

Sociologists are also concerned with societal reactions to crime. Criminal justice policies represent a set of societal reactions, as do the labeling of criminals, and public fears about crime. For example, while there were considerably fewer than 100 victims of serial murderers in any given year, in the 1980s, the FBI was reporting that there were many thousands of such victims; popular culture was inundated with accounts of serial killers; and the public's awareness and fear of serial killers rose exponentially.[2] So, while sociologists may not be so interested in why a person becomes a serial killer, they might be very concerned with why the FBI's and the culture's reaction to the phenomenon was so disproportionate to its actual incidence at that time (see Chapter 4).

The theories below are discussed in chronological order, more or less. When criminologists discuss theory among themselves, the name of the theorist often becomes shorthand for the theory itself. Thus, some of the theories below are introduced by the name of the theorist, while other times, the name of the theory is more familiar to criminologists. As the discipline of criminology is largely a "spinoff" from sociology, sociological theories had a profound influence on the development of criminology, and most of the theories discussed below are quite familiar to most American criminologists, whether or not they were trained in specifically in sociology.

KARL MARX (CONFLICT THEORY)

Karl Marx was born in Germany of Jewish parents in 1818. He studied law and philosophy at the University of Berlin. He began contributing articles on social and economic issues to a newspaper in Cologne and eventually became its editor. As he matured, his writing became decidedly revolutionary and Marx was banished from a number of European countries. He settled in London and devoted himself to his writing. His writing would go on to become among the most influential and controversial works in history, spreading revolutionary zeal among the working classes and fear among elites throughout much of the world. Marx had very little to say about crime, per se; but his ideas about the connections between politics and economics would be applied to the understanding of crime by many criminologists who followed him.

Marx saw the contours of history as reflecting the dynamics between competing interest groups. Writing in the early days of the Industrial Revolution, he was primarily interested in the conflict between the people who owned the factories and the people who worked for them (as discussed below); however, modern conflict theorists are concerned with the conflict between all interest groups: between rich and poor, men and women, blacks and whites, Christians and Muslims, etc.

According to Marx, in a capitalist economy, the difference between what the worker is worth and what the worker is paid is equal to profit. In other words, the employer makes a profit by paying his or her employees less than what they are worth. *Capitalism is based solely on exploitation and, according to Marx, such a system depends upon the maintenance of relatively high levels of unemployment.* When unemployment rates are high, workers compete more fiercely for jobs, making them willing to accept lower wages, and increasing the profits for their employers. A government that represented the interests of the people would ensure the welfare of the unemployed, but government provisions for the welfare of the unemployed would weaken the sting of unemployment, competition for jobs would become less fierce, wages would go up, and the profits of the bourgeoisie would go down. Instead, a government that represented the interests of the elite would ensure that the unemployed are allowed to suffer.

This is the jumping off point for many of the conflict criminologists who followed in the Marxist tradition, noting, for example, that most of the people in prison today were poor and unemployed before they got there. Many modern conflict theorists, or *critical criminologists*, focus their attention on the United States because it has one of the most capitalistic economies and does way less to moderate the pains of poverty and unemployment than most other industrialized nations, ostensibly because such moderating policies constitute "interference" in the free market economy. Consequently, the United States has relatively high rates of inequality and poverty, *and* the highest incarceration rate in the world (see Chapter 7).

When an economy requires high rates of unemployment, there is need to deal with the millions of "surplus" population. This population, according to Steven Spitzer,[3] falls into two categories: social junk and social dynamite. *Social junk* is made up of the elderly and disabled as well as millions of unemployed people who accept current economic arrangements and are biding their time until a new job comes along. *Social dynamite* is made up of those who do not accept current economic arrangements and, therefore, pose a threat to the status quo. The United States spends tens of billions of dollars a year to neutralize the social dynamite through its criminal justice system, in particular, its system of incarceration; and tens of billions more are spent through its welfare system, providing financial assistance to the social junk, just enough to prevent them from transforming into social dynamite. All of this time, money and effort are spent to control the unemployed and preserve the status quo, which benefits elite interests to the detriment of the working class.

Not only do the elite dictate the terms of the relationship between employers and their employees, but they also have substantial influence over the crafting of legislation, that is, in defining what is "criminal" and who gets punished and how. This is where the study of white collar crime comes into play. Until Edwin Sutherland introduced the concept of the "white collar criminal" in 1940[4] (see "Sutherland," in this chapter), criminologists focused all of their attention on crimes committed by the poor. Sutherland, instead, demonstrated that many, if not most, of the largest, most reputable corporations in the United States routinely engaged in criminal activity with virtual impunity. Since then, critical criminologists have frequently argued that the harms done by corporations and white collar criminals far outweigh the harms done by poor criminals. This goes for both financial harm (tax evasion, insider trading, collusion, and the financial maneuverings that led to trillions of dollars in losses during the Great Recession starting in 2008) as well as physical harm (pollution, the sale of dangerous products, unsafe working conditions). And yet, the law has been crafted in such a way that the crimes committed by the elite do not fit a legal standard for "crime;" or they are dealt with in civil or regulatory courts where the punishments are less severe; or, when they do receive criminal convictions, white collar criminals are often sent to minimum security prisons where the pains of imprisonment are less severe.

Lastly, the elite have substantial influence over the dissemination and content of the information that we receive. Through their ownership of media outlets, they can exercise such control. In addition to their control through ownership, the elite can influence media content through their control of advertising dollars, because advertising makes up most or all of the revenue for most media outlets. That is, news media outlets do not want to run afoul of elite interests because, if they were to do so, their advertising revenue would vanish. Therefore, given prevailing patterns of news coverage, the public comes to perceive that the real threat of crime is posed by the poor and not by the rich. We are also led to believe the poor are slovenly and inclined to take advantage of welfare assistance. *According to the critical criminologists, the real "enemy" of both the lower and middle classes is the disproportionate influence that elite interests have over their living conditions. But the fear and distrust of the poor propagated by the media prevents the oppressed classes from realizing their common interests and uniting to fight for a fairer and more just society.*

Conflict theory is elaborated by Richard Quinney later in this chapter, and it is reflected in much of the discussion of criminal justice throughout this book.

EMILE DURKHEIM (FUNCTIONALISM)

Emile Durkheim became the most influential proponent of a branch of sociology called *functionalism*. Before Durkheim, the British philosopher Herbert Spencer compared society to a living organism, a system of interdependent parts, evolving and struggling to maintain stability. Durkheim did not take the living organism analogy literally, but he did make extensive use of the logic of that analogy; that is, *in order to understand a given social phenomenon, we must understand how it contributes to the functioning of society as a whole.* Just as with the human body, one cannot understand the spleen unless one understands how it *functions* for the body as a whole. If we do not understand what the liver does for body, we do not understand the liver.

In *The Rules of the Sociological Method*[5] (1895), Durkheim applied this logic to crime. He noted that since crime occurs in all societies throughout the world and throughout history, it cannot be seen as pathological, or as a sign that there is something wrong with a society. Since crime is universal, it must contribute to the well-being of society. He argued that *crime contributes to the essential function of social cohesion.* Without social cohesion, there would be no such thing as society; we would simply be a number of isolated individuals with nothing in common; but crime brings us together in our mutual abhorrence of the criminal and his/her crime. Still today, there are few things that we have more in common with our neighbors than our fear and hatred of crime and criminals. Crime unites us by providing us with a common enemy.

Following Durkheim, many have noted other functions of crime. Most obviously, crime provides for millions of jobs both inside and outside of the criminal justice system, including police officers, district attorneys, defense attorneys, judges, bailiffs, probation officers, parole officers, prison guards, as well as those who build and supply the prisons, those who sell theft insurance, those who design and manufacture guns and security devices; and the list goes on. Less obviously, functionalists have noted the role organized crime has played in American history in allowing persecuted minorities to move into the mainstream of American society.[6] Beginning with the Irish in the middle of the nineteenth century, then the Jews just after the turn of the twentieth century, and then the Italians in the 1930s—when each group of immigrants arrived, they were persecuted, with few legitimate opportunities for success available to them. When some Irish immigrants became successful at organized crime, money began to flow through the Irish community and more opportunities became available for law-abiding Irish immigrants. The same can be said for the Jews and the Italians. Thus organized crime functioned, according to Daniel Bell, as "a queer ladder of social mobility."[7] Supplying illegal goods and services still functions as a means of upward mobility for many ethnic groups.

In a classic extension of Durkheim's functionalist analysis of crime, Kai Erikson argues that crime is necessary in maintaining the moral boundaries of the community.[8] For a community to maintain a sense of identity, it must establish boundaries that distinguish between those who are part of the community and those who are outside of it. This gives community members pride in their membership and a reason to follow the norms of the community. Deviance and reactions to deviance are crucial to this process. *A society needs deviance to publicize its moral boundaries.* Thus, for example, in eighteenth century England, when hundreds of offenses were punishable by death, public hangings were commonplace. People from the towns and countryside would gather around the gallows, cheering and jeering. This was akin to a rally around the flag, uniting people against a common enemy (according to Durkheim) and publicizing the community's moral boundaries. The message being conveyed to those present: "We are united in our mutual abhorrence; we are proud of being members of this community; and if you were thinking about stealing someone's cow, this is what will happen to you!" In the past, punishments—whipping, branding, tar and feathering, stocks, pillories, hangings, etc.—were performed in public to enhance the cohesive, boundary-maintaining effects of crime. Today, punishment takes place behind prison walls, but media coverage makes crime public and functions with the same effects.

Do we really believe that if we take a deviant (criminal), lock him up in a deviant environment (prison), with a concentrated population of deviants, and leave him there for years, he will come out *less* deviant? Erikson helps us to understand this paradoxical reaction to crime when he argues that the true purpose of prison is not to protect society, but to ensure a steady supply of deviants to "patrol" our moral boundaries. Thus, the high rates of reoffending among the ex-inmate population are not a sign of the system's failure, but of its success.

Durkheim's contribution to criminology extends to his discussion of the concept of "anomie." This concept was pivotal in Robert Merton's famous article "Social Structure and Anomie," which will be discussed later in the chapter.

SOCIAL DISORGANIZATION THEORY

Functionalist theory (see "Durkheim," above) views society as a system of interdependent parts and when one part changes, other parts must change as well. From this perspective, social change can have disruptive effects as the social system struggles to align its various parts with one another. Social disorganization theory, which employs the same logic, emerged from the University of Chicago in the early twentieth century to explain how the momentous social changes of the era were contributing to rising crime rates. The sociology department at the University of Chicago played an instrumental role in the development of American criminology and it has hence become known as the *Chicago School of Criminology*.

Today, people throughout the industrialized world have come to expect social change; but the kinds of social changes that were taking place in Chicago in the first decades of the twentieth century were far beyond what people of that era had come to expect. Chicago became a world leader in industrial production. Factory jobs, initially, required few skills, little experience, and they paid relatively well. Often, to get these jobs, applicants did not even have to know English. Consequently, people migrated by the millions from rural America and rural Europe to Chicago and other urban city centers in the United States.

According to social theorists in the Chicago School, the combination of the immense forces of industrialization, immigration, and urbanization produced a condition of social disorganization. Sociologists W.I. Thomas and Florian Znanecki defined social disorganization as "a decrease of the influence of existing social rules of behavior upon individual members of the group."[9] Thus, with massive immigration from rural America and rural Europe, traditional rural values and norms were losing their relevance and the emerging urban values and norms were in a state of flux. In such conditions, with the norms losing their hold on large sectors of the society, crime and delinquency should not be an unexpected result.

Thorsten Sellin used the term "culture conflict" to describe a variant of social disorganization. He was referring to the multiplied impacts of the clash between rural American values and urban American values, *and* between American values and the values of immigrants coming from other parts of the world. Sellin writes, "How much greater is not the conflict likely to be when Orient and Occident meet, or when the Corsican mountaineer is transplanted to the lower East Side of New York."[10] Where there exist so many clashes between rural and urban, native and foreign, culture and subculture, the laws will not reflect the values of large segments of the population and crime and delinquency will result.

Perhaps the most famous and influential of the social disorganization theorists were Clifford Shaw and Henry McKay. In their often cited research, Shaw and McKay took a map of Chicago and drew a series of concentric zones, with the city's factory zone at the center of the map. Moving out from the center was the zone in transition, then the working class zone, the residential zone, and the suburbs, as depicted in Figure 3.1 (these are not all the exact zone names coined by Shaw and McKay). Essentially, as we moved out from the factories, we moved from poor residential neighborhoods nearest the factories to wealthy neighborhoods farthest from the factories. Then Shaw and McKay pinpointed on the map the addresses of all the kids who came through Cook County Juvenile Court during the time frames that they studied. They found that the pinpoints grew denser as they moved toward the factories; that is, they were densest in the zone in transition. They concluded that delinquency is strongly correlated with one's geographic residence.

As the factory zone adds more industry, the zone enlarges its territory and expands outwards into the zone in transition. The landlords in the zone in transition, expecting to sell off their property to industry, allow

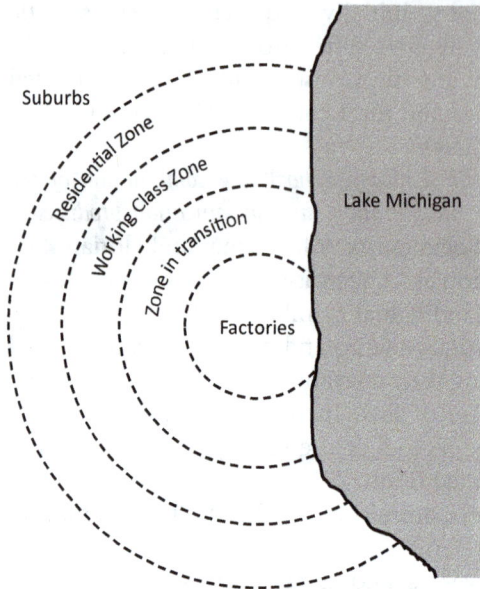

FIGURE 3.1
Shaw and McKay's division of Chicago into concentric zones.

their properties to deteriorate, and residents in the zone in transition live in substandard tenement housing.

The zone in transition had the highest delinquency rates and the highest poverty rates. This is the neighborhood where poor immigrants seeking jobs first settled. Once they could afford to move out, they did; hence, this zone consisted of transitional neighborhoods. With people moving in and out, they did not develop relationships with their neighbors and did not look out for each other's kids. The kids fell in with gangs and when they were brought into court, they were almost always brought in with other kids. This suggested that the zone in transition fostered a culture that was supportive of criminal values and behavior. This supported Shaw and McKay's initial belief that it was the environment, or the culture, that explained delinquency rather than the individual's moral deficiencies, race or ethnicity. Shaw and McKay's work came to be known as *cultural transmission theory*. They wrote, "This means that the traditions of delinquency can be and are transmitted down through successive generations of boys, in much the same way that language and other social forms are transmitted."[11]

Shaw and McKay also noted that different neighborhoods were dominated by different ethnic minorities at different times, and that delinquency rates remained relatively constant within a given neighborhood "no matter what group—German, Irish, Scandinavian, Polish, Italian—was living there; but rates for each group had gone down as its members gradually moved out toward the suburbs …"[12] This finding further bolstered their contention that *it was the geography and the environment which explained delinquency rather than the moral, ethnic or racial qualities of the individual.* With this finding, Shaw and McKay were among the first to contribute to the study of crime and place, an essential component of situational crime prevention, discussed in Chapter 2.

While social disorganization theory was usefully employed to relate crime and social change in the early decades of twentieth century America, it may still have its applications today in other parts of the world that are undergoing similar changes. Until very recently most people in the world lived in rural areas. However, in recent decades, as poor countries are developing industrial economies, tens of millions of people every year are moving from the countryside into already overcrowded—some would say "disorganized"—cities for a shot at those factory jobs. As their lifestyles are changing so rapidly, and as cities bring into close vicinity the clashing values and norms of different racial, ethnic, and religious groups, the social disorganization theorist sees the potential for rising crime rates in such environments.

To an extent, social disorganization theory foreshadowed the development of *"broken windows theory"* which asserts that *signs of social disorder act as an inducement to criminal behavior.* James Q. Wilson and George Kelling write,

> If a window in a building is broken and is left unrepaired, all the rest of the windows will soon be broken. This is as true in nice neighborhoods as in rundown ones. Window-breaking does not necessarily occur on a large scale because some areas are inhabited by determined window-breakers whereas others are populated by window-lovers; rather, one unrepaired broken window is a signal that no one cares, and so breaking more windows costs nothing.[13]

Broken windows are not the only inducement to crime, but other signs of social disorder—prostitutes, drugs users, porn shops—send a signal to potential offenders that the police are essentially off-duty and that they can commit crimes with impunity. When broken windows theory influences law enforcement policy, police are used to "clean up the streets" and officers may engage in questionable use of "stop and frisk" methods (see Chapter 5).

Social disorganization theory and, more generally, functionalist theory have conservative implications. A conservative is one who likes to "con serve" or hold on to the status quo and, thus, conservatives, as well as functionalists, tend to be leery of social change and see it as the source of numerous social problems. Commentators have also noted that many of the early adherents of social disorganization theory at the University of Chicago originally came from rural, racially and ethnically homogeneous areas and their work reflected a small-town, anti-urban bias, which may have been accompanied by racial and ethnic prejudices as well.

These objections notwithstanding, social disorganization theory and the methods employed by its proponents had an enormous impact on social scientists' understanding of urban crime for decades to come.

ROBERT MERTON

Robert Merton's classic article, "Social Structure and Anomie," published in 1938 in the *American Sociological Review*, may well be the most often cited article in the history of criminology, and among those most often cited in the history of sociology as well.[14]

Merton argued that people's desires are culturally induced, with different cultures setting different goals for their members. Thus, one society might set military heroism as a preeminent goal, another may set honoring one's family, another may set service to God; each society is distinctive in the goals that it sets. The United States, according to Merton, is distinctive in the preeminence it gives to the goal of achieving financial success. So important is the goal of financial success in the United States that Americans have even named this goal after their country—*the American Dream*. So important is the emphasis placed on the goal of financial success that it becomes a measure of people's success in life.

The American Dream is foisted on all Americans; they are told that it is achievable by all; and this claim is based on the presupposition that there is equal opportunity in the United States. Here is the first problem: there is *not* equal opportunity in the United States. The proof of that is simple and irrefutable. It is much more difficult to get rich if you are born poor than it is to stay rich if you are born rich. The notion that there is equal opportunity is, essentially, a lie. A related problem is that American institutions are simply not equipped to provide financial success to everybody. Thus, *while all well-socialized Americans are striving for financial success, tens of millions are being set up for failure—especially those in the lower rungs of the social hierarchy—because there is not equal opportunity and because society's institutions are not equipped to provide wealth for all.*

Not only do cultures specify the goals for which their members are to aspire, but they also specify the means by which they are to achieve them. In the United States, people are supposed to aspire for the goal of financial success by means of hard work and following the rules. Another problem identified by Merton is that American society places such enormous emphasis on the goal of financial success that the emphasis placed on the legitimate means of achieving success pales in comparison. Thus, it is not how you play the game, but whether you win or lose.

The norms that place so much emphasis on the goal of financial success and that tell us that it is achievable by all through hard work and following the rules are misaligned with reality. These norms are irrelevant to millions of Americans, especially those from the lower class who have worked hard and followed the rules and they are still poor. Or, they have seen their parents and grandparents who have worked hard all of their lives and who are still living in poverty. For them, the norms have lost their meaning. And since these norms that set our goals are so important, when they lose their meaning, other norms—such as it is wrong to lie, cheat, and steal—start to lose their meaning as well. The norms anchor us in society, and when they lose their meaning, we are cast adrift in a sea of meaninglessness. This is a condition Durkheim called "anomie," or, to use Merton's term, "normlessness."

In such a situation as that outlined by Merton, there are several possible "modes of adaptation." He depicted them graphically as seen in Table 3.1. Examining this table, a person engaged in conformity accepts the goal of financial success and accepts the means of hard work and follows the rules. This is what all well-socialized Americans are supposed to do. Someone engaged in innovation accepts the goal of financial success, but rejects the means and attempts to achieve success by breaking the rules. This mode of adaptation is the one of most interest to criminologists; it includes drug dealing, robbery, embezzlement and just about every criminal activity oriented toward financial gain. Someone engaged in *ritualism* has given up on the goal of financial success, but still goes through the motions and plays by the rules. Someone engaged in *retreatism* gives up on both the goals and the means and withdraws from the game prescribed by the norms. This category might include hardcore homeless alcoholics and drug addicts. Lastly, someone involved in *rebellion* rejects the goal of financial success and the means of following the rules and replaces them with his or her own goals and means. This might include someone who joins a monastery or a religious cult, or even a terrorist trying to overthrow the Western capitalist order.

TABLE 3.1 Merton's "modes of adaptation"		
Modes of adaptation	Goals	Means
Conformity	+	+
Innovation	+	−
Ritualism	−	+
Retreatism	−	−
Rebellion	±	±

The popularity and longevity of Merton's theory lies in the fact that it makes the connection between crime and poverty in a specifically American context. While his theory is specific to American society, it has implications for the understanding of crime in general. If there is a connection between crime and poverty, as has been postulated for centuries, why does the United States, the wealthiest country in the world, have some of the highest crime rates in the industrialized world? Merton's theory suggests that there are two interrelated answers to this question. First, while other countries may have higher rates of poverty, the correlation between crime and poverty is not as strong in those societies because the emphasis on financial success and the belief in equal opportunity are not as strong; therefore, it may well be that the frustration engendered by poverty is not as keen in those countries as it is in the United States.

Merton's theory also suggests that the higher rates of crime in the United States have to do not just with the misalignment between culturally prescribed goals and the institutional means of achieving those goals, but also to the particular configuration of that misalignment. If we lived in a society where the preeminent goal prescribed for us all was to honor our family, this is a goal that could theoretically be achieved by us and all of our fellow citizens; and, if we found our path to be blocked for some reason, breaking the law is not likely to help us bring honor to our family; it would quite likely do the opposite and bring them shame. Instead, Americans live in a society where the preeminent goal is financial success; millions of Americans are set up to fail in achieving that goal if they restrict themselves to legitimate means; but they may be able to achieve that goal through the commission of crime. In other words, the particular configuration of the misalignment between goals and means in the United States is such that achievement of the culturally prescribed goal can be brought about by the commission of crime. If the goal were different, that would not likely be the case.

EDWIN SUTHERLAND

There are few people as influential in the history of American criminology as Edwin Sutherland. His theory of *differential association* is one of the most recognizable theories in twentieth century criminology. But possibly more importantly, his influence extends from the fact that his book, *Principles of Criminology*, first published in 1924, was one of the best-selling textbooks in the field for many decades, with the 11th edition published in 1992. (Sutherland died in 1950 and the continuation of his book depended upon co-author Donald Cressey and later, David Luckenbill.) Through the remarkable longevity of his textbook, Sutherland played a major role in establishing criminology as a subdiscipline of sociology throughout most of the twentieth century and he influenced the range of subjects that would be included in the standard undergraduate criminology course. His theory of differential association made its first appearance in the 1939 edition of his textbook.

For Sutherland, criminal behavior is normal. By that, he meant that criminal behavior is learned the same way that all behavior is learned—through our social interactions, or "associations", with others in our environment. Hailing from the University of Chicago, Sutherland was influenced by social disorganization theory (see page 38); but he took issue with the term. High crime areas are not "disorganized;" in fact, they are often highly organized, as they must be when they include illegal drug networks, gambling operations, prostitution rings, extortion rackets, and the like. So, instead of characterizing high crime areas as disorganized, he said they were organized differently, or "differentially" organized. The way one's environment—or area, or neighborhood—is organized will determine the nature and quality of his or her associations; and those associations will determine what he or she learns. Sutherland's theory is depicted in Figure 3.2.

According to Sutherland, *people who live in high crime areas are likely to associate with others who have little respect for the law and, from them, they are likely to learn "techniques of committing the crime" and "definitions" which predispose them to criminal behavior.* "A person becomes delinquent," he writes,

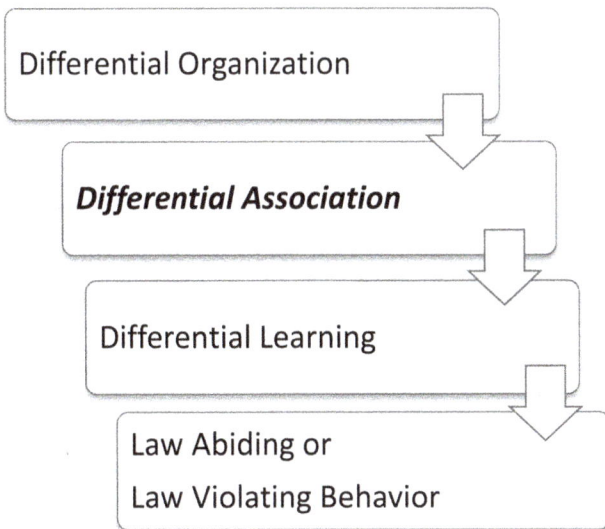

Differential Organization

Differential Association

Differential Learning

Law Abiding or
Law Violating Behavior

FIGURE 3.2
Sutherland's theory of differential association.

"because of an excess of definitions favorable to violation of law over defi-nitions unfavorable to violation of law."[15] To be more specific, he writes,

> In some societies an individual is surrounded by persons who invariably define legal codes as rules to be observed, while in others he is surrounded by persons whose definitions are favor-able to the violation of legal codes. In our American society these definitions are almost always mixed, with the consequence that we have a culture conflict in relation to the legal codes.[16]

On its face, differential association boils down to what parents have been telling their children for thousands of years: "hang around with bums and you'll become a bum." This analogy is, of course, an oversimplification because, by the word "association," Sutherland was referring to the process of communication and the content of that communication, and whether or not that content favors violation of the law. Thus, a problem we encoun-ter thus far might be called the problem of "differential response." Namely, some people hang around with criminals and do *not* become criminals, while some people who have not hung around with criminals *do* become criminals. Again, however, Sutherland was not actually referring to the criminal status of those we interact with, but to the content of our commu-nications with them.

To further address the problem of differential response, Sutherland delineated several dimensions or "modalities" of association: frequency, duration, priority, and intensity. "Frequency" and "duration," he writes, are dimensions of association that "are obvious and need no explanation." By "priority," he was referring to the stage in life when one begins his or her criminal associations; and by "intensity," he referred to the "emotional reactions related to the associations."[17]

While differential association theory was enormously influential in twentieth century American criminology, the theory has been impervious to empirical testing. Namely, it is impossible to measure the content of a lifetime of communications for just one individual, let alone a sample or class of individuals (i.e., criminals). Further, it would be very difficult to measure the modalities of association and to determine how they should be weighted. Sutherland, himself, writes,

> In the precise description of the criminal behavior of a person these modalities would be stated in quantitative form and a mathematical ratio be reached. A formula in this sense has not been developed, and the development of such a formula would be extremely difficult.[18]

Despite the problem of empirical verification, there are a number of factors that explain the popularity of differential association. Probably the most important factor has already been mentioned above, and that is that Sutherland wrote the textbook that became the standard in American criminology and he was able to promote the theory through his book. Further, the theory's appeal relates to the fact that it is a theory about the effects of bad parental and bad peer influence on bad behavior, and such effects have always been presumed by professionals and laymen alike. Sutherland articulated that influence in the language of sociology and gave it academic credibility. And lastly, the logic of differential association was employed or assumed in a number of important criminological theories that were to follow Sutherland, thus assuring the longevity of his theory.

Before leaving our discussion of Sutherland, another important contribution of his to criminology is worthy of note. He introduced the concept of "white collar crime" in his presidential address to the American Sociological Society in 1940. (According to one biographical sketch, it "was one of the few such addresses that received front-page publicity in the daily newspapers."[19]) *He defined white collar crime as "crime committed by a person of respectability and high social status in the course of his occupation."*[20] His recognition of white collar crime became a milestone in the history of criminology. Before this recognition, criminologists concerned themselves almost exclusively with crimes committed by the poor and with the "underworld" of crime. Sutherland paved the way for the study of crimes committed by corporations and by the elite and he made way for the study of the relationship between crime and work. (White collar crime will be discussed at more length in Chapter 4.)

ALBERT COHEN

Albert Cohen was one among several prominent sociologists in the 1950s and early 1960s who focused their attention on the formation and activities of lower class male gang delinquents. Cohen characterized the behavior of these gangs as being non-utilitarian, malicious, and negativistic. By *non-utilitarian*, he meant that their delinquent activities do not seem oriented toward a purpose. When delinquents steal, for example, they usually are not stealing anything that will be of use to them; instead, they seem to steal at random, take things they do not need, and often destroy those things. By *malicious*, he meant that they seem to take pride in being "just plain mean." And by *negativistic*, Cohen meant that these juvenile gangs seem to take the dominant middle class norms, turn them upside down, and do the opposite of what is expected of them. Cohen writes,

> The same spirit is evident in playing hooky and in misbehavior in school. The teacher and her rules are not merely something onerous to be evaded. They are to be *flouted*. There is an element

of active spite and malice, contempt and ridicule, challenge and defiance, exquisitely symbolized, in an incident described by writer Henry D. McKay, of defecating on the teacher's desk. ... The delinquent's conduct is right by the standards of his subculture, precisely *because* it is wrong by the norms of the larger culture. "Malicious" and "negativistic" are foreign to the delinquent's vocabulary but he will often assure us, sometimes ruefully, sometimes with a touch of glee or even pride, the he is "just plain mean."[21]

Much of Cohen's theory goes on to explain why the lower class male gang delinquent behaves as he described above.

According to Cohen, everybody seeks status. That is, we all want recognition; we all want to be held in the esteem of others because our self-esteem depends upon the esteem of others. Sociologists distinguish between ascribed status and achieved status. Ascribed status is essentially status that we are born with, whereas achieved status is status that we earn, that is the result of our actions. Kids born into lower class families are born with little or no ascribed status, so any chance they have of finding the esteem of others will have to be derived from achievement. The environment in which most kids achieve legitimate status is in the school system. Unfortunately, these kids are forced to compete for status against middle class kids in a middle class school system, with middle class administrators and middle class teachers who have middle class values and middle class prejudices. In other words, *these juveniles are born with little or no status and the deck is stacked against them when it comes to achieving status*. The normal avenues for feeling good about themselves are blocked.

Kids in this situation can adapt in one of several ways. Some will buckle down on their schoolwork, intent on going to college. To succeed, they will have to distance themselves from the influence of their lower class peers, and sometimes from their own parents and families who may place little value on academics. Other kids will give up and hang out on street corners with kids like themselves.

Another mode of adaptation involves the gang. *Often, these kids will gravitate toward one another and reward each other's status, based on their ability to offend the dominant middle class culture, which has blocked other avenues to status attainment.* They revel in their defiance of the middle class and its norms and values. Their defiance manifests itself in delinquent behavior. So why do their crimes appear non-utilitarian? Why are their behaviors so malicious and negativistic? Indeed, their crimes *are* utilitarian when one understands that their goal is to achieve status within their gang; and their behaviors are malicious and negativistic because these are the attributes which will win them status among their peers. The standards of the gang evolved as a reaction to the deprivation of status through legitimate means in the broader society.

One of the problems with Cohen's theory is that if it held true, one would expect the victim of the poor juvenile gang member would most likely be someone from the middle class, because it is the middle class that deprived him of the ability to achieve legitimate status. However, the victims of these crimes are most often other poor juveniles. Nonetheless, the theory still maintains its currency. So why would a modern gang banger perpetrate a drive-by shooting? According to Cohen, to achieve status within his gang—for street cred—in an environment in which there are few other avenues to achieve status.

GRESHAM SYKES AND DAVID MATZA (TECHNIQUES OF NEUTRALIZATION)

Sykes and Matza's article "Techniques of Neutralization" has been and continues to be a staple in any criminological education. The authors begin the article by taking issue with some of their contemporaries and asserting that the value sets of juvenile delinquents are much the same as those of the rest of us. Popular idols—movie stars and famous athletes—represent our values, and delinquents uphold the same idols as other kids their age. Furthermore, juvenile delinquents draw strong lines between those people who can and cannot be victimized; and sometimes, juveniles may feel guilty for their crimes. In other words, juvenile delinquents are aware of the wrongfulness of their acts. Having made this argument, *Sykes and Matza ask the very important question, why do people violate the rules in which they believe?* The answer lies in the fact that the rules are not stated as absolutes. In fact, one of the first rules that we learn is that there are exceptions to every rule. We learn, for example, that it is wrong to kill; but it is okay to kill in war. We learn that it is wrong to lie; but a "little white lie" to preserve a friend's self-esteem is okay. *The problem for juvenile delinquents is that they learn to recognize exceptions to the rules that are not recognized by the law.* Sykes and Matza call these exceptions that are recognized by juvenile delinquents "techniques of neutralization"—that is, techniques by which juveniles neutralize the wrongfulness of their acts—and they identify five such techniques.

The first technique is *denial of responsibility*. In this case, the juvenile denies responsibility for his actions, instead claiming, for example, that it was an accident, or blaming his actions on peer pressure or unloving parents. Here, the juvenile sees him- or herself as "more acted upon than acting."[22] The second technique Sykes and Matza identify is *denial of injury*. Here, the juvenile may explain auto theft as "just borrowing" the car; or, they may see vandalism or bullying as "just a prank." The next technique is *denial of the victim*. In this case, the juvenile, for example, may blame an assault on the victim, saying "they should know better than to come into our neighborhood." Here, they see the victim as "asking for it." The next technique is *condemnation of the condemners*. With this technique, the juvenile diverts the attention away from the wrongfulness of his or her behavior and onto that of her or his accusers. In this case, they see their behaviors as no worse than those of other kids, but "the teacher is always picking on me," or the "the cop is a racist." The last technique is *appeal to higher loyalties*. Examples of this technique might include: "he beat up on one of my buds," or "he called my sister a 'slut'." In this case, the juvenile does not deny the wrongfulness of his or her actions, but other loyalties take precedence.

According to the theory, these techniques should not be viewed as mere excuses or rationalizations. The juvenile actually believes in the logic of these techniques; such beliefs are present *before* the delinquent behavior takes place, and they pave the way for the delinquency. We all need to believe that we are right and that we are good people. It is the belief in these techniques that enables the juvenile to commit acts of delinquency and still feel good about him- or herself.

The influence of neutralization theory has extended far beyond the literature in juvenile delinquency. It has been used to explain such behaviors as deer poaching, soliciting prostitutes, entering children into beauty pageants, and many other behaviors, both legal and illegal.

LABELING THEORY

Labeling theory has quite an extensive theoretical pedigree. In large part, it is a specific application of a theoretical approach called *symbolic interactionism* to crime and deviance. In order to grasp the principles of labeling theory, it will be helpful to understand the concept of *the self* as it was developed by early symbolic interactionists.

According to Charles Horton Cooley, the self is made up of three components: (1) the imagination of our appearance to others, (2) the imagination of their judgment of our appearance, and (3) pride or shame.[23] In other words, our perception of our self is made up of our perceptions of other peoples' perceptions of us. (It is not made up of their actual perceptions because we cannot get into their heads and know exactly what they are thinking.) That is, if you think you are cool, it is because you think other people think you are cool; if you think you are fat, it is because you think other people think you are fat. In which case, "cool" or "fat" become part of your self. Another leading figure—actually *the* leading figure—in the development of symbolic interactionism was George Herbert Mead. *For Mead, people do not respond to reality, they, instead, respond to their perceptions of reality, and those perceptions are learned through social interaction.*[24] We all perceive, or interpret, reality differently because no two people have been exposed to the exact same series of human interactions. The interpretations that are most important in understanding human behavior are our *definition of the self* and our *definition of the situation* which, again, are both the product of social interaction. Figure 3.3 summarizes the essence of symbolic interactionism.

We will return to symbolic interactionism in a moment; but first we will discuss the distinction made by Edwin Lemert between primary and secondary deviance.[25] Primary deviance happens for any number of reasons that are of little or no concern to the labeling theorist; instead, the labeling theorist is concerned with secondary deviance. *Secondary deviance is deviance that results from having been labeled deviant; that is, a deviant label tends to act as a self-fulfilling prophecy.* There are a number of reasons that explain why this is the case. When someone is labeled deviant, he or she is being stigmatized, identified as different, singled out. The quality of their interactions with others is altered. The opportunity for "normal" interactions becomes more limited. Making the case that it is normal for teenagers to engage in mischievous behavior, Frank Tannenbaum describes how only some teens are singled out and their world changed in the process:

> There is a gradual shift from the definition of specific acts as evil to a definition of the individual as evil, so that all of his acts come to be looked upon with suspicion. In the process of identification his companions, hang-outs, play, speech, income, all his conduct, the personality itself, become objects of scrutiny and question.[26]

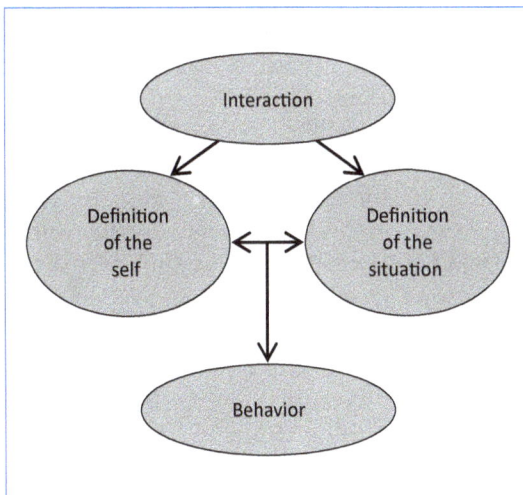

FIGURE 3.3
The symbolic interactionist model.

According to symbolic interactionism, our behavior is, in significant measure, a product of our definition of self, and our definition of self is derived from social interaction. Thus, *if people act toward us as though we are deviant, a deviant identity will be incorporated into our definition of self. Rejected by "normal" members of the community, someone so labeled will likely gravitate toward others who have been so labeled.* The teenager, for example, who has been labeled delinquent, says Tannenbaum, comes slowly to recognize that "the definition of him as a human being is different from that of other boys in his neighborhood, his school, street, community. This recognition on his part becomes a process of self-identification and integration with the group which shares his activities."[27]

We should note that labeling is a process, and to state that a deviant label is a self-fulfilling prophecy is an over-simplification. Instead, it is more accurate to say that someone who has been *successfully* labeled deviant is likely to engage in secondary deviance.

Another element of labeling theory is that its focus is often more upon the labelers (the "audience") and less upon the criminal and his or her behavior. Prior to the advent of labeling theory, the works of criminologists tended to assume that there was something inherent in the criminal that made him or her bad, or something inherent in the criminal activity that made it bad. Criminologists saw themselves as problem solvers and crime, they assumed, was inherently problematic. However, noting that the definitions of crime vary from time to time and place to place, in the 1960s sociologists began to question the meaning of the word "crime." Since it is difficult to identify any behaviors that are defined as crime in all cultures throughout history, it follows that there is nothing inherent in crime that makes it a "crime." Instead, to understand crime, we must examine the society, the culture, the laws, and the labelers.

On these points, labeling theory and conflict theory often converge. Remember that conflict theory (see "Marx" in this chapter) focuses on unequal power relations and on how different groups use their power to further their own interests. People and groups with power have the ability to affix deviant labels on people and groups without power and they do so to further their own interests. With this in mind, an examination of history reveals that drug legislation in the United States, for example, has had less to do with the control of inherently dangerous drugs than it has had to do with the labeling and control of various minority groups who have been perceived by those in power to be a threat. Thus, writes David Musto,

> The most passionate support for legal prohibition of narcotics has been associated with fear of a given drug's effect on a specific minority. Certain drugs were dreaded because they seemed to undermine essential social restrictions which kept these groups

under control: cocaine was supposed to enable blacks to withstand bullets which would kill normal persons and to stimulate sexual assault. Fear that smoking opium facilitated sexual contact between Chinese and white Americans was also a factor in its total prohibition. Chicanos in the Southwest were believed to be incited to violence by smoking marijuana. Heroin was linked in the 1920s with a turbulent age group: adolescents in reckless and promiscuous urban gangs. Alcohol was associated with immigrants crowding into large and corrupt cities. In each instance, use of a particular drug was attributed to an identifiable and threatening minority group.[28]

In other words, *minority group members are more likely to be labeled as drug offenders not because they use more drugs, but because of their minority group status.*

It is because of such analyses that labeling theory struck a chord and had a prominent influence in criminology and criminal justice during the civil rights movement in the 1950s and 1960s, and partly into the 1970s. Its influence was clearly on the downswing in the 1980s, due, in part, to a conservative backlash to the social justice reforms of the civil rights era.

TRAVIS HIRSCHI (CONTROL THEORY)

Most criminological theories start with the question, "Why did he or she commit the crime?" Travis Hirschi, instead, starts with the question, "Why doesn't everybody commit the crime?" Criminal behavior, after all, is not difficult to understand. Zach, for example, saw something in the store he wanted, but he did not have the money to pay for it. It just happened to be pocket-sized, so he stealthily slipped it into his pocket and left the store. Such behavior, according to Hirschi, is not difficult to understand. It is more difficult to understand why everybody does not put unpurchased merchandise into their pockets. Other criminological theories may ask the question, "What is present in the criminal's environment or psyche that makes him or her different from non-criminals?" Hirschi, instead, addresses the problem in terms of "What is absent?" The answer, in a word, is "controls." These controls take the form of bonds between the individual and society. *The criminal is a person for whom the bonds between him- or herself and society are weaker than normal.*

Hirschi's control theory is not the first of its kind. Freudian theory, as it is applied to criminal behavior, for example, represents a form of control theory. For Freud (see "Freudian Theory" in Chapter 2), the personality is made up of three components: the *id*, the *ego*, and the *superego*. The id constitutes one's biological or natural impulses; the ego is the socially reasonable side of the self; and the superego is the conscience, or the guilt that we feel when we express our id in socially inappropriate ways. Thus, for Freud, criminal behavior may result when the id is not adequately *controlled* by the ego or the superego.

Freud's theory of the personality concerns the absence of psychological controls. Hirschi's theory concerns the absence of *sociological* controls. *Hirschi identified four types of bonds between the individual and society which serve as social controls: attachment, commitment, involvement, and belief.* Attachment refers to the extent to which one is concerned about the desires and feelings of others. For example, a person may refrain from criminal behavior because he or she worries that being arrested would bring shame to their loved ones. Commitment refers to one's investment in conventional society that could be lost by engaging in criminal activity. If arrested, the individual could lose her job, her house, her kids. Involvement refers to the extent to which one is engaged in conventional society. Hirschi writes,

> The person involved in conventional activities is tied to appointments, deadlines, working hours, plans, and the like, so the opportunity to commit deviant acts rarely arises. To the extent that he is engaged in conventional activities, he cannot even think about deviant acts, let alone act out his inclinations.[29]

Lastly, belief refers to the extent to which an individual subscribes to conventional notions of right and wrong. When this bond between the individual and society is weak, the individual does not have "an attitude of respect toward the rules of society … and feels no moral obligation to conform regardless of personal advantage."[30]

As there is significant overlap between the different types of bonds between the individual and society that were identified by Hirschi, it is difficult to put his theory to the test. His theory most likely remains a classic in American criminology, though, because it so well explains why crime rates are so much higher in the United States than in so many other countries. The contrast is particularly striking, for example, when we compare American crime rates to those of Japan. Control theory suggests that crime rates are so high in the United States because of the premium its culture places on individualism; whereas Japan's crime rates are so low because of the value it places on collectivism.

Collectivist societies, such as Japan, often place a high value on honoring one's parents (attachment); in such societies, people's identity is strongly tied to their work or their workplace (commitment); in Japan, children often attend *juku* ("cram schools") after school or on weekends in preparation for their college entrance exams (involvement). Together, factors such as these are likely to strengthen the Japanese adherence to a common value system (belief).

By contrast, "individualism," by its very nature, suggests that the bonds between the individual and society are weak. Arguably, Americans might care less about shaming their parents than the Japanese; they have less to lose in terms of their group commitments; and, spending more time alone or at home, they are less involved in communal activities. According to control theory, the lack of such inhibitions promotes higher crime rates in the United States.

STANLEY COHEN (MORAL PANICS)

Crime can be a fearful phenomenon and it has captivated the public imagination for centuries, if not millennia. Kings, presidents, senators, police chiefs and mayors have raised the specter of crime to rally support behind them. From the broadsides of early eighteenth century, to the earliest days of the newspaper, to the modern crime novel, publishers have long known that crime "sells." With political leaders, bureaucrats and the media capitalizing on crime, it is not surprising that crime "waves" get blown out of proportion and people get the impression that the threat of crime is far greater than the reality it presents. While criminologists have long recognized this phenomenon, it was British sociologist Stanley Cohen who analyzed it systematically and popularized its identification as a "moral panic."[31]

In his book, *Folk Devils and Moral Panics*, Cohen analyzed an incident occurring in the beach resort town of Clacton on a holiday in 1964. Two groups of youths—later to be known as the Mods and the Rockers—bored because it was too cold to enjoy the beach that day, engaged in acts of mischief. Cohen describes their behavior, "Those on bikes and scooters roared up and down, windows were broken, beach huts were wrecked and one boy fired a starting pistol in the air."[32] The incident made national headlines, depicting it as though it were an invasion of violent biker gangs marauding the seaside. "Words and phrases such as 'riot,' 'orgy of destruction,' 'battle,' 'attack,' 'siege,' 'beat up the town,' and 'screaming mob'"[33] were deployed in the reporting of the incident. Politicians decried the state of England's youth, creating the impression that this was the first of many such incidents to come. Police throughout the country were put on high alert. Indeed, such an incident did follow in Whitsun and, even though it was *less* disruptive than the one in Clacton, it was also characterized by the media with the same alarmist rhetoric as the incident in Clacton. One media outlet characterized the participants in Whitsun as "long-haired youngsters with knives indulging in an orgy of hooliganism."[34]

Cohen points out that all news agencies have to be selective in the information that they distribute—because all of the information in the world simply cannot be distributed through the news—and certain subjects are far more likely to make it through the news filter into the public imagination. Crime and deviance figure prominently among those subjects. Cohen writes,

> It is not that instruction manuals exist telling newsmen that certain subjects (drugs, sex, violence) will appeal to the public or that certain groups (youth, immigrants) should be continually exposed to scrutiny. Rather, there are built-in factors, ranging from the individual newsman's intuitive hunch about what constitutes a "good story," through precepts such as "give the public what it wants" to structured ideological biases, which predispose the media to make a certain event into news.[35]

Such news reportage *sensitizes* the public, and other issues come to be seen as related to the original disturbance and symbolic of deeper problems in the society. The deeper problem in Cohen's analysis was the popular perception that England's younger generation was undisciplined and out of control. Thus, with the Clacton incident having resonated so well among the media, politicians, and the public, other issues that might be only slightly related to the theme of undisciplined youth suddenly became newsworthy, further fueling the moral panic. Kenneth Thompson writes,

> As a result of sensitization, incidents that might have been written off as "horseplay" or a "dance hall brawl" were interpreted as being part of the Mods and Rockers phenomenon. Public nervousness increased and there was pressure for more police vigilance and stronger action from the forces of law and order. The police then reacted by stepping up patrols and increasing their interventions in potential trouble spots—seaside towns, dance halls, fairs and other public events. Court proceedings reflected the sensitization.[36]

The moral panics literature suggests that *the public is more susceptible to being misled by alarmist reports of crime during periods of momentous social change. Such change creates uncertainty and anxiety, and the issue which is the focus of the moral panic comes to symbolize the threat of social change.* Jeffrey Victor calls the moral panic a "collective nightmare,"[37] just as nightmares purportedly are a symbolic representation of anxieties we may have experienced during the day. The moral panic over the Mods and the Rockers had to do with the immense social changes taking place in post-World War II Britain. Life had been hard for the British during the Depression and got even harder during the war. By 1964, conditions had improved enormously and the older generation was sensing that the youth were getting by too easily; they were not learning the lessons that come from hardship;

they were spoiled and had no moral compass. A nerve had been exposed, and the incident at Clacton tapped into these fears.[38] Such are the makings of a moral panic.

Another classic moral panic took place in the United States in the 1980s. This had to do with the panic over "satanic ritual abuse" alleged to be taking place in day care centers around the country. It began with hundreds of allegations of sexual assault at the McMartin Preschool in California in 1983. These led to a trial lasting more than two years, and costing more than any trial in the U.S. history up to that point. There were no convictions; but the "cultural response to the McMartin case," writes Mary deYoung,

> had all of the characteristics of what sociologists call a moral panic: it was widespread, volatile, hostile, and over-reactive … From Texas to Tennessee, New Jersey to North Carolina, Maine to Michigan, hundreds of local day care centers were investigated for satanic ritual abuse and scores of day care providers, as many males as females, were arrested and put on trial. From the witness stand, their accusers, the three- and four-year-old children once entrusted to their care, accused them of sexual abuse during satanic ceremonies that included such ghastly practices as blood-drinking, cannibalism, and human sacrifices. Despite the absence of evidence corroborating the children's accounts, many of the day care providers were convicted, and to the cheers and jeers of their deeply divided communities, were sentenced to what often were draconian prison terms.[39]

deYoung's description of the children's allegations in the 1980s may strike the reader as reminiscent of the notorious witch trials in Salem, Massachusetts in the late seventeenth century; and indeed, that series of events had the qualities that mark a moral panic.

According to deYoung, the social change that made the public susceptible to misleading information in the 1980s was the massive movement of women into the workplace. Almost all of a sudden, millions of parents began leaving their young children in the care of virtual strangers. This created anxiety, exposing a nerve, and the McMartin case "proved" parents' worst fears. They became sensitized to the issue and, all over the United States, parents began to suspect their children's caretakers. Sensitization had occurred to the extent that bed-wetting, for example, was taken as a sign that a toddler was possibly being victimized at day care. Allegations, trials, and convictions ensued. Even those who were not convicted had to deal the shame and disgrace of being accused in the first place. Thus, while moral panics are rooted more in the public imagination than in reality, their consequences can be very real.

Identifying a moral panic while it is going on can be a morally and politically fraught endeavor. Those that did so during the child molestation panic were accused of lacking empathy for the victims and siding with child molesters. To call out the witch trials in Salem, Massachusetts invited the accusation that you were in league with the devil. Likewise, to suggest that the fear and fervor surrounding the issue of undocumented immigrants in the United States in 2018 amounted to a moral panic invites the accusation of political bias, or worse. It may be that only with the advantage of historical distance—perhaps generations—that large sectors of the public come to recognize that something akin to a moral panic has taken place. Indeed, many scholars are critical of the concept of moral panic because of the political and controversial factors involved in the identification of a moral panic.

FREDA ADLER AND THE EMERGENCE OF FEMINIST THEORY

Before the publication of Freda Adler's book *Sisters in Crime: The Rise of the New Female Criminal*,[40] criminologists paid little attention to female criminality. Those that did address the subject often started with the question "what is it about female criminals that makes them more like men?," suggesting that crime is masculine behavior. Therefore, sexuality became the main feature explaining women's criminality. That is, early treatments of the topic tended to attribute women's criminality to disturbances in their sexuality, whereas discussions of male criminality rarely implicated the perpetrator's sexuality (unless, of course, the topic had to do with sex crimes).

Published in 1975, *Sisters in Crime* was one among many now-classic feminist treatises published in numerous fields in the 1960s and 1970s. Adler argues that there are essentially no biological differences between men and women that account for their differential involvement in crime. Instead, the essential factor accounting for the differences in men's and women's participation in crime had to do with differences in societal expectations of men and women. Girls, the saying went, were made of "sugar and spice and everything nice," while boys were made of "snakes and snails and puppy dog tails." This is not what the two sexes were "made of" by nature; but what they were "made into" by the gendered nature of their socialization. Boys were raised to be aggressive, competitive and mischievous, while girls were raised to be passive, compliant, and nurturing. Boys were raised to get into trouble; girls were raised to stay out of it. Although the idea that differing rates of criminal activity among the sexes is due to their socialization and not their biological make-up may seem obvious to those of us in Western society in the twenty-first century, it was not so obvious before the 1970s. In this sense, Adler's book was ground-breaking and historically significant.

Noting that crime rates among women were accelerating faster than crime rates among men, Adler further argued that the crime-gender differential was not only explained by gender-role socialization, but also by differential access to criminal opportunities. Here she employed *opportunity theory* developed by Richard Cloward and Lloyd Ohlin (1960).[41] Cloward and Ohlin suggest that in understanding criminal behavior we have to take into account whether the opportunities for crime exist. Just as, at certain times in certain places, there may be a scarcity of legitimate opportunities in the form of jobs, there may be a scarcity of illegitimate opportunities in the form of crime. In areas where there is nothing to steal, for example, there are likely to be few acts of theft.

Adler introduced her version of opportunity theory as it applied to women and it is sometimes called *emancipation theory*. In the first half of the twentieth century, with women largely confined to the home by gendered role expectations, they had little opportunity to engage in criminal activity. *With the women's movement and the emancipation of women, as women began to have more opportunities to move from the home to the workplace, women gained more opportunities to commit crime.* Such, she argues, is what had happened during World War II. Men went off to war, women moved into the workforce to replace them, and crime rates among women increased faster than those among men. When the men returned from the war and replaced the women, sending them back home to be mothers and homemakers, the differences in the growth in crime rates diminished. Moving to the modern era, Adler states, "with the emancipation of women … girls are involved in more drinking, stealing, gang activity and fighting—behavior in keeping with their adoption of male roles."[42]

The publication of *Sisters in Crime* caused quite a sensation. Adler became something of a celebrity, interviewed often by the news media, and appearing on television talk shows. While few criminologists would deny that Adler helped usher in the new field of feminist criminology, her book was heavily criticized, even by feminists. Written in the midst of the women's movement, some critics were concerned that Adler's book legitimated conservative fears of the changing roles of women by suggesting that "women's liberation" would lead to more crime. Another criticism centered on the data. When *Sister's in Crime* was published—and since—crime rates among women were indeed accelerating faster than those among men; however, the absolute number of crimes committed by women was still only a small fraction of those committed by men; and, even though the proportion of women in the workplace today nearly equals that of men, changes in the rates of crime committed by women, relative to men, are hardly commensurate with changes in women's participation rates in the workforce.

However, the data do not disprove Adler's theory because her work emphasizes *both* gender-role socialization *and* increased access to criminal opportunities. It is the interplay between the two that may give rise to increasing rates of female criminality. While women's increased access to legitimate opportunities over the past half century has increased their access to illegitimate opportunities, gender-role socialization has not changed as fast as women's participation in the work force.

As we see girls raised with traits traditionally assigned to the male role, crime rates among women, relative to those among men, could begin to rise faster than they have been. This could be even more likely because, as women are being raised to be more aggressive in roles outside of the home, men are being raised to be more nurturing in roles inside the home. These trends, together with women's increased access to criminal opportunities, could well culminate in further changes in the crime-gender differentials.

The contrast in "criminologies" before and after the emergence of feminist theory is quite remarkable. Although women made up half of the population, before the 1960s, criminology paid little or no attention to women's issues in crime and criminal justice. During and after the women's movement, criminology became much more inclusive and criminologists turned their attention to issues such as spousal violence, rape (including date rape and marital rape), stalking, sexual harassment, and the conditions of women's prisons. (Intimate partner violence is discussed at length in Chapter 4.) In more recent years "queer criminology" has turned our attention to the ways society forces us into the binary categories of female and male, feminine and masculine, with little tolerance for those who fall outside of these categories. Consequently, members of the LGBTQ community suffer various forms of bullying, harassment, and violence from bigots at large, in the schools, at work, and from the police.

RICHARD QUINNEY (CLASS, STATE, AND CRIME)

With his earlier work focused on the differential treatment of white collar criminals versus street criminals, Richard Quinney turned his focus to the relationship between capitalism and crime. According to Marx (see "Marx" in this chapter), capitalism is an economic system whereby the labor of the working class is exploited by the elite class which owns and controls the means of production in society. The injustice inherent in such an unequal system of production necessitates the kind of force that can only be applied by the criminal justice system to maintain that system. *The criminal justice system, Quinney argues, was developed and is controlled by the elite class for the purpose of justifying and maintaining the unequal relations between the elite and the subjugated working class.*[43] It is the elite's control of the criminal justice system that explains why behaviors perpetrated by the elite, the corporate elite in particular, that, while they may be injurious to vast numbers of people, are not defined as "criminal." Or, if they are considered criminal, their perpetrators are treated less severely than poor people who commit crime.

Take climate change for example. Weather conditions are becoming more extreme throughout much of the world, ocean levels are rising, and vector-borne diseases are shifting their geographic boundaries. Hundreds of thousands of people have already been displaced by climate cata-strophes; millions more could be displaced by rising ocean levels. It could be that the whole of humankind will be adversely affected by the end of the century. Untold numbers could lose their livelihoods, even their lives as a result of climate change. What crimes committed by working class people could wreak this much devastation?

There are few among thousands of scientists who argue that corporate emissions do not significantly contribute to climate change. Those few that do are likely to be on corporate payrolls. The corporate elite have mar-shalled forces—namely through political campaign contributions and through their influence on mass media—to effectively deny the reality of climate change. James Hansen, the Director of NASA's Institute for Space Studies who first alerted the public to the potential devastation of global warming in 1988, says the CEOs of major fossil fuel companies "should be tried for high crimes against humanity and nature."[44] Instead, they reap millions in salaries and stock options and, meanwhile, the prisons in the United States and in other capitalist countries are filled almost entirely with poor people. Quinney would argue that such injustices are due to the fact that the elite class is able to use the criminal justice system to defend its own interests at the expense of the working class. This applies not only to the law, but to the state itself. Quinney writes,

> The state exists as a device for controlling the exploited class, the class that labors, for the benefit of the ruling class. ... Contrary to conventional wisdom, law instead of representing community custom is an instrument of the state that serves the interests of the developing capitalist ruling class.[45]

Based on the perpetrators' relationship to the means of capitalist produc-tion, Quinney lays out a typology of criminal activity. Those crimes com-mitted by the ruling elite, or on behalf of their interests, he calls *crimes of domination*. This category includes crimes of control, crimes of government, and crimes of economic domination. Crimes of control are those carried out by agents of the criminal justice system in the forms of laws such as police brutality and the denial of the civil rights of the accused. Crimes of government are those committed by elected and appointed government officials, such as taking bribes or permitting torture in the name of national security. And crimes of economic domination are those committed by the corporate elite for the purpose of furthering the accumulation of capital, such as price fixing, insider trading and environmental pollution. The activities of the CEOs of fossil fuel companies that contribute to global warming and obstruct its remediation (mentioned above), though not considered "crimes" by the ruling elite, would fall into this latter category.

Quinney calls the crimes committed overwhelmingly by members of the working class *crimes of accommodation and resistance*. These are crimes that are a reaction to the conditions of exploitation, unemployment, and poverty that are endemic to capitalism. Crimes of accommodation include predatory crimes and personal crimes. Predatory crimes are para- sitical in nature and are oriented toward financial gain, such as burglary, robbery and drug peddling. These are crimes that threaten the capitalist order because the participants are not engaged in capitalist production and such crimes demonstrate that wealth can be gained in activities that do not contribute to the interests of the ruling elite. Personal crimes are committed by poor people against poor people, such as murder, assault, and rape. These are acts of frustration committed by people "who have already been brutalized by the conditions of capitalism."[46] Lastly, crimes of resistance are "direct reflections of the alienation of labor."[47] Accord- ing to Marx, all members of the working class are alienated from their work because they are paid less than what they are worth and the profits from their labor go to their employers, thereby increasing their employ- ers' wealth and power and enabling them to further exploit their workers. Crimes of resistance include sabotage and organizing illegal strikes. Quinney argues that there will be more such crimes of resistance in the future because "increased economic growth necessitates the kind of labor that further alienates workers from their needs."[48] Indeed, in the modern economy, as digital automation is replacing workers throughout the workforce, job security has become more and more tenuous, thereby increasing employers' leverage over their employees. Increased alienation is the likely result.

Thus, Quinney is notable among a number of criminologists who employ Marxist theory to explain the relationship between poverty, unem- ployment, and crime in capitalist societies. Like other criminologists in the Marxist tradition, Quinney examines the role of power in the definition and treatment of crime. In the conflict between the haves and the have- nots, those with power have the ability to define crime in such a way as to further their own interests. Those without power are the victims of an unjust system and find themselves impoverished and often incarcerated. As wealth and power concentrate in fewer and fewer hands, the legitimacy of such a system becomes increasingly difficult to sustain and, therefore, many Marxist thinkers expect either the state will become increasingly repressive, or capitalism will fall.

LAWRENCE COHEN AND MARCUS FELSON (ROUTINE ACTIVITIES THEORY)

Writing in the late 1970s, Lawrence Cohen and Marcus Felson[49] addressed their work to the apparent paradox between improving indicators of societal well-being and rising crime rates. Crime rates in the United States had been going up rather dramatically since the early 1960s and, yet, by the end of the 1970s, problems frequently associated with crime—such as unemployment, median family incomes for both black families and white families, and the percentage of kids dropping out of high school—had been improving. Even the most prominent explanation for rising crime rates—the growth in the proportion of males in their crime prone years (ages 15 to 24)—was losing its relevance as this growth began to level off as the baby boom played itself out. Yet crime rates continued to climb.

Cohen and Felson attributed the rising crime rates to broader social changes taking place since the end of World War II that affected the *routine activities* of everyday American life. They argued that,

> Structural changes in routine activity patterns can influence crime rates by affecting the convergence in space and time of the three minimal elements of direct-contact predatory violations: (1) motivated offenders, (2) suitable targets, and (3) the absence of capable guardians ...[50]

When these three elements converge, crime is more likely. If any of these elements is missing, crime is far less likely. Unlike other criminological theories which often focused on the criminal's motivation, Cohen and Felson took the element of "motivated offenders" as a given, and focused their attention on "suitable targets" and the "absence of capable guardians."

Crime is more likely to occur when there is an absence of capable guardians. In the decades following World War II, routine activities shifted away from the home. Increasing numbers of women left the home and went into the workplace and higher numbers of young women went off to college. These trends left more households unattended, without capable guardianship. "Daily work activities," Cohen and Felson write, "separate many people from those they trust and the property they value."[51] In the 1960s and 1970s, the proportion of people living alone began to climb as people waited longer to marry and as divorce rates rose. This higher proportion of single-adult households increased the likelihood that homes would be left unattended. Increased automobile ownership meant people could leave the house often and travel longer distances for longer intervals. Victories in collective bargaining meant more time off from work and more vacations away from home. Not surprisingly, as routine activities shifted away from the home, burglary rates climbed faster than rates for most other categories of crime.

Changes in production and technology also changed routine activities, especially with regard to both guardianship and suitable targets. As leisure time was increasing in the 1960s and 1970s, people were purchasing more electronics to fill that time with entertainment—more televisions, more radios, more stereos, etc. So, while guardianship was compromised by more people working and away on vacations, when people were not at work or away on vacations, more of them were home at night watching television and listening to music. This reduced the number of people who were out at night communing with their neighbors. This reduced "natural surveillance," or the number of capable guardians keeping an eye out for trouble and deterring criminal activities. Motivated offenders could violate the law away from public scrutiny.

A society so dependent on mass consumption inevitably produces massive quantities of suitable targets. More importantly, technological innovation was making these devices smaller, lighter, and more portable—things more easily removed from unattended homes by motivated offenders.

While Cohen and Felson took the element of motivated offenders for granted, we might surmise that young people fall disproportionately into this category. Their routine activities are generally less structured than those of their adult counterparts, especially when they are out of school. Further, it is well known that teenagers often go out of their way to absent themselves from capable guardianship. These factors increase the likelihood of a convergence among motivated offenders, suitable targets, and an absence of capable guardians.

Cohen and Felson admit the theory of routine activities is hardly new. We see elements of opportunity theory (see "Adler" in this chapter) in that the presence of suitable targets and the absence of capable guardians create the opportunity for crime. We also see some elements of control theory (see "Hirschi" in this chapter) in that the motivation to commit crime is assumed and a good deal of the focus is on a lack of controls on the offender or his/her environment (i.e., lack of capable guardians). However, Cohen and Felson should be credited with bringing a together a disparate body of literature on how crime rates are affected by social change and changing lifestyles under the umbrella of routine activities theory. We might also note a convergence of routine activities theory with rational choice theory (i.e., situational crime prevention – see Chapter 2). Both take motivated offenders for granted, and focus instead on suitable targets and capable guardianship.

JOHN BRAITHWAITE (REINTEGRATIVE SHAMING)

All societies have ways to ensure that their members follow the rules (or "norms"). Sociologists call these ways "social controls," or "social control mechanisms." Societies can employ both formal mechanisms of control and informal mechanisms. *Formal social controls* include positive sanctions (e.g., a medal, or an award) and negative sanctions (e.g., after school detention, a fine, banishment, or imprisonment). *Informal social controls* also include positive sanctions (e.g., a pat on the back, a look of approval, or popularity) and negative sanctions (e.g., rumor, gossip, or ostracism). The informal mechanisms of control are more effective because they cause us to *internalize* the norms, to incorporate them into our personality; that is, most of us follow the rules of our society because we believe in them. It is only when informal means of control fail that formal negative sanctions come into play.

From the perspective of the labeling theorist (see "Labeling Theory" in this chapter), negative sanctions such as those described above—whether formally or informally applied—are accompanied by a certain degree of shaming; and the self-fulfilling nature of a shameful label can have only deleterious effects. According to John Braithwaite, however, shaming is a necessary mechanism of social control. Crucial to his argument is the contention that certain types of shaming reduce the likelihood of criminal behavior while other types of shaming increase its likelihood. Braithwaite writes,

> The first step in productive thinking about crime is to think about the contention that labeling offenders makes things worse. The contention is both right and wrong. The theory of reintegrative shaming is an attempt to specify when it is right and when wrong.[52]

Specifically, shaming can have a reintegrative effect and reduce crime; or it can have a disintegrative effect and exacerbate crime. Reintegrative shaming is applied more informally and is commonplace in more communitarian societies where people are more interdependent and enmeshed in an intricate network of social relationships. Disintegrative shaming is applied more formally and is common in less communitarian societies where people are more individualized and less dependent on one another. It is best to think of these concepts as falling on a continuum, as depicted in Figure 3.4.

Communitarian societies, such as those found in many parts of Asia, are characterized by strong ties of interdependence between the individual and the community. Not only is the individual dependent on the community,

Communitarianism   Individualism
Reintegrative Shaming ◄─────────────────────► Disintegrative Shaming
   (e.g., Japan)   (e.g., United States)

FIGURE 3.4
Braithwaite's reintegrative and disintegrative shaming.

but the community is dependent on the individual. It is not in the best interests of the community to have the individual indefinitely incapacitated as a result of his or her rule breaking. In these societies, rule breaking is met with reintegrative shaming. Justice is meted out by the community with the goal of restoring both the victim and the offender. The violator is frequently shunned; but there is an understanding that he or she will be reintegrated back into the community in due time. Eventually, he or she will be forgiven, often after they have undergone some ritual of redemption, perhaps involving restitution or public apology. There is a beginning and an end to the shaming process.

In Western industrialized countries with weaker communitarian traditions and fewer interdependencies, individualism rules. In these societies, justice is removed from the victim and meted out by the criminal justice system. There is little to no concern about the rule breaker's reintegration into society; and there are no rituals to facilitate his or her redemption. The stigma that results from shaming becomes an endless roadblock to reintegration. A prison record, for example, makes it difficult to attain decent employment and all the more difficult to establish relational ties to the community. The problem is made worse by the fact that the people who undergo this process are more likely to be people with weaker relational ties in the first place: young, unmarried, unemployed males. Isolated, stigmatized and deprived of access to legitimate activities, these people gravitate towards one another and develop norms and values that are likely to contribute to further rule breaking.

Braithwaite's theory represents an impressive synthesis of a number of classic theories covered in this chapter. The emphasis on the relational ties that serve as inhibitors to rule breaking is reminiscent of Hirschi's control theory; the distinction between good shaming and bad shaming is a refinement of labeling theory; Albert Cohen's thesis is incorporated when Braithwaite argues that those offenders who have been stigmatized and deprived of access to legitimate opportunities will gravitate towards one another to form deviant subcultures.

The theory of reintegrative shaming has become the theoretical underpinning for the *restorative justice movement* in the criminal justice system (see Chapter 7). Restorative justice programs are being implemented in hundreds of locales throughout the United States to either replace or supplement the more traditional punishments meted out by the criminal justice system. Often at the core of such programs are efforts to bring the victim and the offender together. At the resulting meetings, the offender learns first-hand how his or her behavior has impacted the victim's life, and the two of them may work out a plan to best restore the victim to his or her original state. Such meetings are intended to involve the victim and make him or her feel part of the justice process; they are also believed to have a greater impact on the offender's moral sensibilities than incarceration; and, lastly, they offer the offender a chance at redemption, which will better facilitate his or her reintegration into the community.

DEVELOPMENTAL AND LIFE-COURSE THEORIES

It has been well established in many parts of the world that the rate at which people commit crime begins to climb rapidly in their mid- to late-teens, peaks in their early 20s and then begins to fall off sharply in their 30s.[53] (In fact, a great many of the sociological theorists discussed in this chapter focus their attention on adolescent delinquency.) Delinquent or anti-social behaviors are not so unusual for teenagers; and most offenders age out of crime by their late 20s, a phenomenon criminologists call "desistance."

However, developmental theorists often note that the official crime data only capture a small part of the picture. These represent only the people who are caught. For example, one study that incorporated self-report data found that respondents had committed an average of over 30 offenses for every one conviction.[54] Kids often engage in fighting, but are rarely arrested for assault; sometimes they are caught stealing from their parents, but they are not charged with larceny. Furthermore, there is a large variety of antisocial behaviors that may or may not be criminal. If we were to take into account such behaviors, according to developmental theorists, we would find a good deal of continuity in antisocial behavior over the deviant's lifetime. David Farrington writes,

> Most longitudinal researchers investigate not only violence and property crime but also many other topics—including drug use, alcohol use, drunk driving, reckless driving, smoking, gambling, sexual behavior, relationship problems, employment problems, educational problems, and mental and physical health. Many researchers have concluded that offending is only one element in a larger syndrome of antisocial behavior that tends to persist from childhood to adulthood and from one generation to the next.[55]

In other words, developmental theorists often see desistance as an artifact of the criminal law and our reliance on official crime data. From this perspective, an extensive history of antisocial behavior in childhood is the best predictor of anti-social/criminal behavior later in life.

While the developmental theorists are generally concerned with *continuity*, life-course theorists are generally concerned with *change*. That is, *life-course theorists are concerned with the forces that explain desistance and those that explain why some people do not age out of crime.* Terrie Moffitt distinguished between two types of offenders: the *adolescence-limited (AL) offenders* and the *life-course persistent (LCP) offenders*. AL offenders include normal adolescents who engage in minor crimes and then desist in their late teens or 20s; the LCP offenders consist of those who exhibit antisocial behaviors throughout their lives, people who are sometimes called "chronic" or "career" criminals. According to Moffitt, those who become persistent offenders start off in life with some combination of neuro-psychological deficit and environmental disadvantage. People with neuro-psychological impairments are not as easily socialized as the rest of us and they can be difficult for their parents and caretakers. They can be born into disadvantaged environments and/or their impairments can alter their environment in deleterious ways, having negative effects on parent–child bonding, peer relationships, and interactions with authority figures (e.g., teachers, the police). These people can become "ensnared" in the consequences of their antisocial behavior. Moffitt writes,

> Personal characteristics such as poor self-control, impulsivity, and inability to delay gratification increase the risk that antisocial youngsters will make irrevocable decisions that close the doors of opportunity. Teenaged parenthood, addiction to drugs or alcohol, school dropout, disabling or disfiguring injuries, patchy work histories, and time spent incarcerated are *snares* that diminish the probabilities of later success by eliminating opportunities for breaking the chain of cumulative continuity. Similarly, labels accrued early in life can foreclose later opportunities; an early arrest record or a "bad" reputation may rule out lucrative jobs, higher education, or an advantageous marriage.[56]

Fortunately, life-course persistent offenders are the exception, while adolescent-limited offenders are the rule. Adolescents are in a stage of their lives between the dependence of childhood and the independence of adulthood. In this stage, it is expected that many or most will engage in behaviors that test the limits of their newly emerging freedom.

Robert Sampson and John Laub[57] note that everyone goes through a series of *transitions* in life; and adolescents are on the verge of a number of significant transitions. As they age and finish high school, they typically find employment or go to college, or join the military, get married, and start a family. Employment, the military, college, marriage, and the family—these are institutions that often have a stabilizing influence on the young adult. It is not so much the transitions themselves that mitigate antisocial behavior, but "the quality or strength of the social ties" that are formed as a result of these transitions. On the other hand, some people may forego these transitions; or they may undergo other transitions that are not likely to lead to desistance, such as incarceration or joining a gang; or they may fail to develop the quality relationships necessary in the otherwise normalizing transitions.

Life-course theory has become quite prevalent in criminological research today. Its focus is not so much on why people commit crime, but on why they stop or continue committing crime. As such, many criminologists believe such theories offer a great deal of promise with regard to developing strategies to interfere with the *trajectory* of those on the path to a life of crime.

CONCLUSION

The theories outlined above are known to virtually all American criminologists. All of these theories have their drawbacks and limitations; and no one theory explains all or even most crimes or criminals. However, all of these theories have survived, or are well on their way to surviving the test of time because each of them provides some important insight into matters related to crime; and taken together, they explain a great deal of crime.

NOTES

1 Philip Jenkins, *Using Murder: The Social Construction of Serial Homicide*, New York: Aldine de Gruyter, 1994.
2 Ibid.
3 Steven Spitzer, "Toward a Marxian Theory of Deviance," *Social Problems*, vol. 22, no. 5, June 1975.
4 Edwin Sutherland, Presidential address to the American Sociological Association in 1940. Then he published *White Collar Crime*, New York: Dryden, 1949.
5 Emile Durkheim, *The Rules of the Sociological Method*, translated by S. Soloway and J.H. Mueller, edited by G. Catlin. Chicago: University of Chicago Press, 1938.
6 Francis A.J. Ianni, "Ethnic Succession in Organized Crime: Summary Report," Law Enforcement Assistance Administration, U.S. Department of Justice, December 1973.
7 Ibid.
8 Kai Erikson, *Wayward Puritans*. New York: Macmillan. 1966.
9 Thomas, W. and F. Znaniecki. *The Polish Peasant in Europe & America*, vol. 4. Boston: Gorham, 1920.
10 Thorsten Sellin, *Culture Conflict and Crime*, Bulletin No. 41, (New York: Social Science Research Council), 1938, p. 63.

11 Clifford Shaw and Henry McKay, *Juvenile Delinquency and Urban Areas*. 1942. Reprinted in *The Chicago School of Criminology 1914–1945*, Piers Beirne, editor, Routledge, 2006, p. 168. Emphasis added.

12 James Bennett, *Oral History and Delinquency: The Rhetoric of Criminology*. Chicago: University of Chicago Press, 1981, p. 170.

13 Wilson, James Q., Kelling, George L. (March 1982), "Broken Windows: The police and neighborhood safety", *The Atlantic*. www.theatlantic.com/magazine/archive/1982/03/broken-windows/304465/.

14 Francis Cullen and Steven Messner, "The Making of Criminology Revisited: An Oral History of Merton's Anomie Paradigm," from *The Origins of American Criminology, Advances in Criminological Theory*, Volume 16, Francis Cullen, Sheryl Lero Jonson, Andrew Myer, and Freda Adler, editors. New Brunswick, NJ: Transaction Publishers, 2011.

15 Edwin Sutherland and Donald Cressey, *Principles of Criminology*, 7th edition. Philadelphia: J.B. Lippincott, 1966, p. 81.

16 Ibid.

17 Ibid., p. 82.

18 Edwin H. Sutherland; Donald Cressey and David Luckenbill, *Principles of Criminology*, 11th edition. Lanham, MD: General Hall, 1992, p. 89.

19 Howard W. Odum, *American Sociology: The Story of Sociology in the United States through 1950*. Quoted on the American Sociological Associations web page: www.asanet.org/about/presidents/Edwin_Sutherland.cfm.

20 Donald Cressey, "The Poverty of Theory in Corporate Crime Research," from *Advances in Criminological Theory*, Volume 1. Willima Laufer and Freda Adler, editors. New Brunswick, NJ: Transaction Publishers, 1987, p. 37.

21 Albert Cohen, *Delinquent Boys: The Culture of the Gang*. Glencoe, IL: The Free Press, 1955, p. 28.

22 Gresham Sykes and David Matza, "Techniques of Neutralization: A Theory of Delinquency," *American Sociological Review*, vol. 22, 1957, pp. 664–670.

23 Charles Horton Cooley, *Human Nature and the Social Order*. Scribner's, 1902.

24 George Herbert Mead, *Mind, Self and Society: From the Standpoint of a Social Behaviorist*, edited by Charles Morris. Chicago, IL: University of Chicago Press, 1954. (Original work published 1934.) See also Herbert Blumer, *Symbolic Interactionism: Perspective and Method*. Englewood Cliffs, NJ: Prentice-Hall, 1969.

25 Edwin Lemert, "Secondary Deviance and Role Conceptions," from *Social Deviance*, edited by Ronald Farrell and Victoria Lynn Swigert. New York: J.B. Lippencott, 1978, pp. 94–97. (Original work published 1951.)

26 Frank Tannenbaum, "Definition and the Dramatization of Evil," from *Deviance Across Cultures: Constructions of Difference*, 2nd edition, edited by Robert Heiner. New York: Oxford University Press, 2014, p. 57. (To his credit, Tannenbaum wrote this in 1938, long before "labeling theory" entered the lexicon.)

27 Ibid.

28 David F. Musto, *The American Disease: Origins of Narcotic Control*. New York: Oxford University Press, 1987, p. 244. See also Troy Duster, "The Legislation of Morality: Creating Drug Laws," in D. H. Kelly (ed.), *Deviant Behavior*, 3rd ed. New York: St. Martin's, 1989, 29–39.

29 Travis Hirschi, *The Causes of Delinquency*. Berkeley, University of California Press, 1969, p. 22.

30 Ibid., p. 25.

31 Stanley Cohen, *Folks Devils and Moral Panics: The Creation of the Mods and Rockers*. London: MacGibbon and Kee, 1972. Cohen was actually born and raised in South Africa, but trained and conducted most of his work in England.

32 Cohen, *Folk Devils*, p. 29.

33 Kenneth Thompson, "The Classic Moral Panic," from *Deviance Across Cultures*, 2nd edition, edited by Robert Heiner. New York: Oxford University Press, 2014.

34 Ibid. Vintage television news report posted on YouTube, www.youtube.com/watch?v=5Rj-OHCusEI.

35 Cohen, *Folk Devils*, p. 45.

36 Thompson, "The Classic Moral Panic," p. 120.

37 Jeffrey Victor, *Satanic Panic: The Creation of a Contemporary Legend*. Chicago: Open Court, 1993.

38 Cohen, *Folk Devils*.

39 Mary DeYoung, "The Devil Goes to Day Care: McMartin and the Making of a Moral Panic," from *Deviance Across Cultures*, 2nd edition, edited by Robert Heiner. New York: Oxford University Press, 2014, p. 125. Emphasis added.

40 Freda Adler, *Sisters in Crime: The Rise of the New Female Criminal*. New York: McGraw Hill, 1975.

41 Richard Cloward and Lloyd Ohlin, *Delinquency and Opportunity*. Glencoe, IL: Free Press, 1960.

42 *Sisters in Crime*, p. 95.

43 Richard Quinney, *Class State and Crime: On the Theory and Practice of Criminal Justice*. New York: Longman, 1977.

44 "James Hansen: "Try Fossil Fuel CEOs For 'High Crimes Against Humanity,'" *Environmental Leader*, June 24, 2008. www.environmentalleader.com/2008/06/24/james-hansen-try-fossil-fuel-ceos-for-high-crimes-against-humanity/#ixzz3ihAu45zL.

45 *Class State, and Crime*, p. 45.

46 Ibid., p. 54.

47 Ibid., p. 55.

48 Ibid.

49 Lawrence E. Cohen and Marcus Felson, "Social Change and Crime Rate Trends: A Routine Activity Approach," *American Sociological Review*, vol. 44 (1979), pp. 588–608.

50 Ibid., p. 589. Emphasis added.

51 Ibid., p. 591.

52 John Braithwaite, *Crime, Shame and Reintegration*. New York: Cambridge University Press, 1989, p. 14.

53 When life-course theories emerged in the 1990s, the age–crime curve peaked in the early to late teens, rather than in the early 20s as depicted here. It could be that the likelihood of criminal activity peaks a little later than before because people are getting married later, and marriage, according to life-course theory, acts to inhibit crime. See U.S. Census, "Median Age at First Marriage; 1890 to Present," www.census.gov/content/dam/Census/library/visualizations/time-series/demo/families-and-households/ms-2.pdf. Retrieved July 17, 2018.

54 This was the Pittsburgh Youth Study recounted by David Farrington, "Developmental Criminology," in *The Routledge Companion to Criminological Theory and Concepts*, A. Brisman, E. Carrabine, and N. South, editors, London: Routledge, 2017, pp. 60–64.

55 Ibid., p. 61.

56 Terrie Moffitt, "Adolescence-Limited and Life-Course-Persistent Antisocial Behavior: A Developmental Taxonomy," *Psychological Review*, vol. 100, no. 4, p. 684, emphasis in original.

57 Robert Sampson and John Laub, "Crime and Deviance in the Life Course," *Annual Review of Sociology*, vol. 18, pp. 63–84.

CHAPTER 4

Patterns of crime

PART I: VIOLENT CRIME

Without a doubt, one of the most notable trends with regard to crime in the United States has been the precipitous decline in both violent and property crime rates. Crime rates have been trending downward for nearly three decades. Figure 4.1 depicts the decline in violent crime rates. Property crime rates have followed a similar trend.

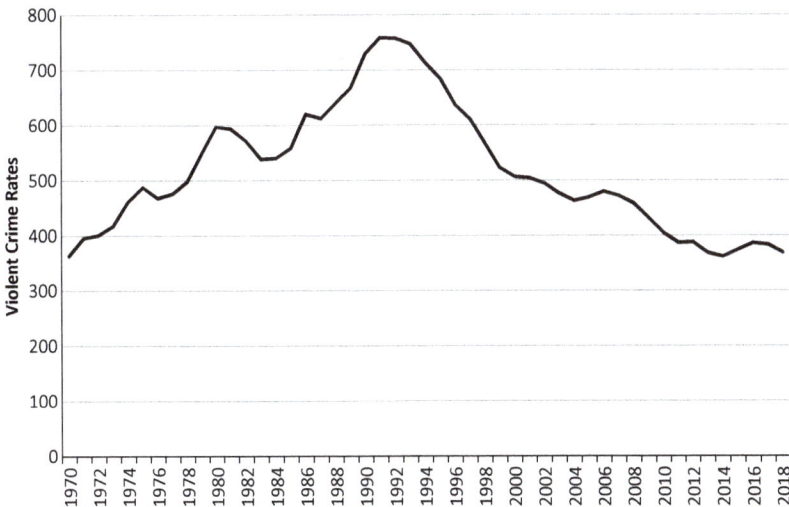

FIGURE 4.1
Number of violent crimes per 100,000 population by year.

Sources: Nathan James, Recent Violent Crime Trends in the United States, Congressional Research Service, June 20, 2018, https://fas.org/sgp/crs/misc/R45236.pdf; and Crime in the United States, 2018, https://ucr.fbi.gov/crime-in-the-u.s/2018/crime-in-the-u.s.-2018/topic-pages/tables/table-1.

As we noted in Chapter 1, homicide rates are the most reliable of the official crime statistics, and the homicide rates in the Unites States' five largest cities dropped remarkably between 1990 and 2009, as seen in Figure 4.2.[1] What factors brought about this remarkable decline? No answer has been put forward without its flaws; but we will mention a few of the more familiar explanations. Some say that with mass incarceration getting fully underway in the 1990s (see Chapter 7), so many violent offenders were getting locked up that there were fewer left on the streets to commit mayhem. Others point to the fact that federal grants made available in the 1990s enabled the hiring of more police officers and the expansion of police patrols, which served as an effective crime deterrent. Others have linked these changes in violent crime rates to the environmental regulations dealing with exposure to the chemical lead. Lead has been linked to impulsive, aggressive, and violent behaviors; and, until the 1970s, it was a basic ingredient in gasoline and house paint. Regulations eventually brought down levels of lead in the environment and violent crime rates declined roughly a generation later.[2] Still others point to birth rates and subsequent changes in the country's age distribution. That is, the steady rise in violent crime during the 1960s and the 1970s was, in part, a reflection of the post-World War II baby boomers reaching their crime-prone years (the mid-teens to the mid-20s);[3] and the drop reflects the decrease in the proportion of people in this age category in an aging population with declining birth rates.

Valid criticisms have been applied to all of these hypotheses. One criticism, common to most of them, has to do with timing. That is, increases and decreases in crime rates began or ended either sooner or later than the

	1990	2009	DECREASE
NEW YORK	30.7	6.8	−78%
LOS ANGELES	28.2	8.1	−71%
CHICAGO	30.2	16.1	−47%
HOUSTON	34.8	12.6	−64%
PHILADELPHIA	31.7	19.5	−38%

FIGURE 4.2
Homicide rates per 100,000 in five largest US cities, 1990–2009.

Source: Raw data from Franklin Zimring's, "The City that Became Safe: New York and the Future of Crime Control," Straus Institute Working Paper 09/11, p. 3. www.law.nyu.edu/sites/default/files/siwp/WP9Zimring.pdf. Retrieved April 10, 2020.

hypothesis would suggest. With this and other criticisms in mind, most criminologists would agree that it is unlikely that any one of these hypotheses, alone, explains a great deal of the crime drop; but some combination of these arguments may explain a substantial part of it.

On a final note, criminologist Tim Newburn suggests that that the crime drop is misleading in that the data do not incorporate most crimes committed on the internet. As teenagers and young adults are spending more time at home on their screens, they are spending less time outside committing the kinds of crime that account for crime rates as traditionally considered by law enforcement agencies and criminologists. If we instead accounted for the kinds of crimes committed on the internet, such as cyberbullying, fraud, and computer hacking, then the drop in crime rates discussed above would be less pronounced.[4]

Fear of crime

Despite the drop in crime that has been going on for most of three decades, during much of this time, a substantial proportion of the American population has been fearfully concerned that crime rates have been rising. In its annual nationwide survey, the Gallup Poll has asked respondents, "Is there more crime in the U.S. than there was a year ago, or less?" Every year since 2002, the majority of respondents have answered "more."[5] In fact, criminologists have found that the correlation between crime rates and the public's fear of crime has been historically weak.

So, if crime rates do not explain public fear, what does? This has been somewhat of a puzzle for criminologists; but, most often, politicians and the media are implicated. Politicians frequently attempt to muster support, campaigning with tough-on-crime platforms and promising to protect us from predatory crime. In so doing, they exploit and exacerbate public fears. Meanwhile, violence pervades entertainment media; and the news media have always devoted a large segment of their coverage to crime, especially violent crime, even though the vast majority of crimes are property offenses. Though people are increasingly getting their news online, we cannot overlook the following facts: senior citizens are more likely to get their news from television; local television news coverage is more likely than other news genres to focus on violent crimes; relative to their minimal risk of violent victimization, senior citizens are more likely to be fearful of crime; and historically, senior citizens are more likely to vote than their younger counterparts. Though most of the research on the connection between media consumption and fear of crime has focused on traditional media sources (e.g., newspapers and television), more recent research has found a correlation between social media consumption and fear of crime.[6]

While the media are an intuitively appealing explanation for the fear of crime, methodologically, it is difficult to prove. The problem is one of cause and effect. If we find, for example, that there is a correlation between the fear of crime and research subjects' exposure to television news, it may be that people who are more inclined to be fearful are more inclined to watch television news. In which case, watching television news would be the effect of fearfulness, rather than its cause.

While it is difficult to ascertain the real causes of the fear of crime, the effects of such fears are very real. When people are fearful of crime, they are more likely to bar their windows, buy security devices, and lock themselves in their homes; they are more likely to closely supervise their children and allow them less freedom to play outside and explore their neighborhoods; they are more likely to vote for politicians who pander to their fears and will spend their tax dollars on tough-on-crime measures; and they are more likely to tolerate government intrusions on their privacy—if they believe that such measures are what it takes to protect themselves from crime. In other words, the fear of crime has everything to do people's quality of life and their willingness to give up their civil rights.

Homicide

Despite the recent decline in violent crime rates, with the exception of Russia, the United States has the highest murder rate in the developed world.[7] According to World Bank data, the U.S. has a homicide rate of 5 per 100,000, while Australia and most Western European countries have a rate of 1 per 100,000; Japan and Singapore average less than 0.5 per 100,000.[8] However, comparisons of violent crime rates *other than murder* show that the United States does *not* stand out among its counterparts in the developed world.[9] In other words, the United States is not exceptionally violent; but it does have exceptionally high rates of violence resulting in death (see Figure 4.3). Criminologists have posited a number of possible explanations for this American phenomenon.

The availability of firearms in the United States is often cited as a reason for the high rate of lethal violence in the U.S. relative to other developed nations. The United States is a country founded in revolution; and victory in that revolution was in large part due to a well-armed population. Adam Lankford writes, "Americans do not simply want guns because they enjoy hunting or sporting activities; they still value firearms for their revolutionary potential."[10] One survey found that 65 percent of Americans agreed that the right to bear arms is there "to make sure that people are able to protect themselves from tyranny."[11] It is much easier to obtain a firearm (especially a handgun) in the United States than it is in most other parts of the world (and handguns are, by far, the most common weapon used in homicides in the United States).[12] A higher proportion of Americans own guns than anywhere else in the world. According to the Small Arms Survey (SAS) of the United Nations Office of Drugs and Crime, "With less than

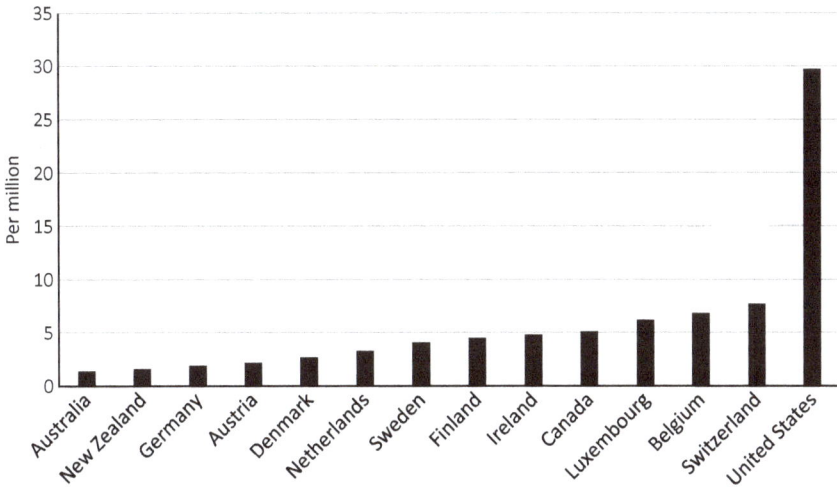

FIGURE 4.3
Homicides by firearms per one million population.

Source: Zach Beauchamp, "America doesn't have more crime than other rich countries. It just has more guns," Vox, February 15, 2018, citing data from the UNODC, Small Arms Survey. www.vox.com/2015/8/27/9217163/america-guns-europe. Retrieved January 5, 2019.

5% of the world's population, the United States is home to roughly 35–50 per cent of the world's civilian-owned guns."[13] According to the SAS, there are 88.8 firearms for every 100 people in the United States. This number far exceeds any other country. Yemen came in second, with 54.8 firearms per hundred people.[14]

Thus, the argument goes, the ease of access to firearms explains why the unremarkable rates of violence in the United States result in the remarkable rates of violent fatalities. This argument would engender little controversy in most parts of the developed world; but it is a very volatile issue in the United States, where a candidate's position on gun control can win or lose an election.

While the availability of guns cannot be extricated from the rates of gun-related murders in the United States, it is certainly not the only factor— because the vast majority of gun owners do not commit murder. In fact, even if we exclude all gun-related homicides, the United States still has a higher murder rate than the total murder rates for most other developed nations.[15] Thus, other criminologists have looked toward American *culture* as an explanation for the high rates of homicide in the United States. From the earliest days of slavery enforced by violence, to the forced relocation and extermination of Native Americans, to the gun-slinging lawlessness of the old West, to the widespread lynching of African-Americans in the

South, to the popular support of the death penalty in the modern day—America has always been and continues to be a violent culture.

An important part of culture has to do with the values of its people. As we have seen in Chapter 3, in his seminal work, Robert Merton identified the value that Americans place on financial success as the most distinctive feature of American culture. So important is this value that it has actually been named after the country: "the American Dream." Combine this value with the belief that "America is the land of opportunity," and the result is that Americans tend to blame poor people for their poverty. As substantial segments of the American population hold these beliefs, the United States tolerates higher levels of inequality (and poverty) than almost all other developed nations. Obviously, poverty, itself, does not cause people to murder others—because most poor people are not murderers. However, when such a high value is placed by the culture on financial success, failure to achieve it leads to higher levels of frustration experienced by the poor in the United States than in other cultures. It is easier for the poor to live an "honorable" lifestyle elsewhere in the world.

A great many homicides in the United States, if not the vast majority, involve the offender defending his or her sense of honor—that is, somebody retaliating against a perceived insult. David Luckenbill argues that the typical homicide involves a series of stages in which the would-be perpetrator interprets the actions of another as challenging his or her sense of "face."[16] This pertains to any number of situations, including a bar fight, a drive-by shooting, or even a parent killing a child. (In the latter case, the parent might interpret the child's refusal to comply with an order as an insult to his or her authority.) The would-be perpetrator then gives the victim-to-be a chance to back down or retract the insult. The would-be perpetrator then perceives the victim-to-be as not backing down, which is perceived to be a further insult; and the would-be perpetrator lashes out. (Note that the victim-to-be's behavior is not necessarily relevant. What is important is the would-be perpetrator's *perception* of insult.)

Honor-involved killings, says psychologist Martin Daly, are more likely to be perpetrated by the poor because they have so little to value other than their honor.[17] Journalist Maia Szalavitz writes,

> When someone bumps into someone on the dance floor, looks too long at someone else's girlfriend or makes an insulting remark, it doesn't threaten the self-respect of people who have other types of status the way it can when you feel this is your only source of value.[18]

As Daly explains, "If your social reputation in that milieu is all you've got, you've got to defend it."[19] Thus, the value one places on his or her honor, and the measures one is able and willing to take to defend that honor have much to do with social class, culture, and a society's willingness to tolerate high levels on inequality. While Americans may think of honor killings as being pervasive in some less developed countries in the world, the United States is no different in this regard.

The term "honor killings" is more typically used to refer to cases in India or the Middle East when a woman (or girl) ventures beyond her prescribed gender role, for example, by having sexual relations outside of marriage. In which case, the husband, or father, or brother may feel honor-bound to kill her. In the United States, patriarchal gender roles are also implicated in a great many homicides. Freda Adler called criminologists' attention to gender role socialization in the 1970s (see Chapter 3); and, in recent years, there has been increasing focus on the socialization of boys as a causative factor in the incidence of violent crime. The Uniform Crime Report has long revealed a striking difference in the rates at which men and women commit violent crimes, especially homicide. In 2017, for example, the number of homicides committed by males was more than seven times greater than those committed by females.[20] According to data compiled by *Mother Jones Magazine*, of the 111 mass shootings in the United States between 1982 and 2019, only three were committed by women.[21] Gender has been described as the "strongest single predictor of criminal involvement."[22] For the criminologist, the huge discrepancy between the numbers of killings committed by males and those committed by females begs for an explanation; but, to the layman, it needs no explanation because "everybody knows that males are more violent than females."

Throughout much of the world and much of history, physical prowess was often more important to success than mental prowess; and men maintained their dominance over women through the use of, or threat of, physical force. As societies developed, mental prowess became more important and women have been on the path of increasing parity with men. Cultures and traditions change slowly, though, and boys are still commonly raised to demonstrate their masculinity with a threatening physicality, which frequently manifests itself through violence. The term "toxic masculinity" has recently been popularized to describe masculinity that manifests itself in socially harmful behaviors. Masculinity has been implicated as a causal factor in violence as varied as mass shootings,[23] date rape,[24] domestic violence,[25] and gang shootings.[26]

The theory of *hegemonic masculinity* suggests that, as opportunities for men and women begin to equalize and the gendered power dynamics in the relationships between men and women diminish in society, some men fear their dominance being threatened and compensate for their loss of power with violence. Hegemonic masculinity is about power and refers not only to male-on-female violence, but also to male-on-male violence. Men and boys who occupy a socially marginal status (e.g., poor kids, kids who are bullied, unemployed men) are particularly prone to violence as they may feel a high degree of powerlessness.

A 2018 report from the American Psychological Association connects *masculinity ideologies* to the incidence of suicide, bullying, homophobia, violence, and a tendency to "externalize emotional distress."[27] Many people may find the APA's new critique of masculinity ideologies to be unsettling as it challenges the essence of what they feel it is to be manly. Journalist, Jerry Davich, writes,

> According to the [American Psychological] Association, conforming to the long-held social norms of this masculinity ideology can result in all kinds of emotional troubles for young boys. Such behavior can lead to the suppression of emotions, unhealthy risk-taking, inability to seek help, tendencies toward bullying and homophobic traits.
>
> In other words, everything that has defined manhood for centuries. Where was this warning in the 1960s and '70s during my impressionable adolescent years? I'll tell you where. It was being kicked to the curb by an endless army of risk-taking, bullying, homophobic men.
>
> "Traditional masculinity is, on the whole, harmful," the APA now warns us. Not only to women and to society, but also to us men.[28]

From the conflict perspective (see Chapter 3), the controversial nature of the criminological critique of male gender role socialization is easily understood. The criminologist's identification of gender role socialization as a contributor to violence amounts to a challenge to traditional hierarchies that have been taken for granted for millennia. Men have maintained their privileged status in large part through gender role socialization; and any critical appraisals of that socialization threaten to undermine male privilege. Traditionally, masculine roles and feminine roles have been viewed as part of the natural order of things; and traditionalists believe that efforts to change that order are dangerous or doomed to failure. Indeed, groups with a vested interest in maintaining traditional hierarchies—such as the ideology of white supremacy that legitimated slavery for centuries—have always felt that competing ideologies threatened to violate the natural order of things and were dangerous or doomed to failure. They did change, nonetheless; and the glaring contrast between the way boys and girls are socialized is changing too.

Intimate Partner Violence (IPV)

IPV is one of the more common forms of violence and it includes violence by a current or former intimate partner or spouse, by a person who is (or was) cohabiting with the victim, or by a person who shares a child with the victim.[29] According to the Centers for Disease Control, IPV includes the categories of (1) physical violence, (2) sexual violence, (3) threats of physical or sexual violence, and (4) psychological and emotional violence. (The latter category would usually not fit a legal definition of crime.) In addition, stalking is often considered a form of IPV.

Women are, by far, more often the victims of IPV than men. About a third of women who are killed are murdered by a current or former partner or boyfriend.[30] According to Jacqueline Campbell and her team of researchers, "When hand counts on medical record reviews correct for misclassifications in the Supplemental Homicide Reports, ... the percentage of women killed by an intimate or ex-intimate increases to 40% to 50%,"[31] whereas only about 6 percent of men who are killed are murdered by an intimate or a formerly intimate partner.[32]

In many parts of the world, throughout much of history, men were granted nearly absolute property rights over their wives. They could beat, and sometimes kill their wives with impunity. Sometimes that impunity was legally established; and, more recently, it was a matter of the police and the courts trivializing violence against women and failing to make an arrest or to prosecute a case. In the 1970s, feminist and progressive criminologists revealed IPV to be more extensive and leading to more deaths and injuries than many of the kinds of crimes that then occupied the public imagination; and IPV gained the attention of the public and criminal justice reformers.

Two somewhat contradictory, but not incompatible, hypotheses emerged with regard to IPV. The *amelioration hypothesis* suggested that IPV is the result of the unequal power dynamics between men and women and that, as women gained more equality in society, rates of IPV would decline; that is, women's progress would ameliorate the problem of male-on-female IPV. The *backlash hypothesis*, on the other hand, argued that, as women gained more equality, rates of IPV would go up, as men would resort to violence to compensate for their loss of power. While the backlash hypothesis employs much of the logic of our discussion of masculinity above and focuses on interpersonal relations, the amelioration hypothesis places IPV in a structural context and considers the effect of improved/improving status of women in general. That is, for example, as women gained more equality, they were able to influence the field of criminology itself, introducing feminist theory, and bringing professional and then public attention to the issue of IPV. As women gained more equality, they were able to affect public policy by drawing attention to sexist law enforcement and judicial practices. And more, importantly, as women entered the workforce, they were able to gain financial independence and leave their abusive partners. Indeed, due in large part to the empowerment of women, changes have occurred since the 1970s; including the establishment of more shelters and hotlines for abused women, policies of mandatory arrests and prosecutions in cases of domestic violence, increased use of restraining orders, primary care physicians trained to screen for domestic violence, the introduction of laws against stalking, and the recognition of marital rape as a crime.

Oddly enough, while the data show substantial reductions in the number of intimate partner homicides in the wake of these reforms, the largest reductions have been in the numbers of men being killed by their intimate partners; thus, making the ratio of female victims to male victims even greater than before the reforms. Campbell and her colleagues speculate that changes in society and the law have made it easier for women to leave abusive relationships—before they are driven to kill their partners in self-defense; thus, sparing their male intimates from becoming a mortality statistic.[33] The greater decline of male victims relative to female victims in recent decades remains an open question in criminology; and rates of violent victimizations of women within intimate relationships remain high. Unfortunately, while women have gained more equality and independence, their improved status in society does not guarantee their safety. In fact, women are at the greatest risk of dying from IPV in the first few weeks *after* leaving an abusive partner.[34]

As women's progress toward equality has been gradual, the amelioration process could be expected to take some time; but after some 50 years of "progress" since the "discovery" of IPV, backlash still appears to play a significant role in IPV.

When we note that intimate partner violence has been pervasive for hundreds or thousands of years, but was not recognized to be a problem until the rise of the feminist movement in the 1970s, we are moving in the direction of a theoretical perspective called *social constructionism*. That is, we are saying that while IPV has long been pervasive, it was not *constructed* as a social problem until feminists drew our attention to the phenomenon. Social constructionists often demonstrate that the degree of attention given to a social problem often bears little resemblance to objective harm caused by the phenomenon. (That is, IPV was not suddenly recognized to be a problem because it was getting worse.) Further, social constructionists argue that the construction of social problems is a political phenomenon. (That is, women were gaining political power and were/are fighting in the political arena for their right to be free from abuse.) When we reviewed Stanley Cohen's work on the Mods and

Rockers in Chapter 3, we were looking at an early contribution to social constructionism.

Social constructionism is often employed in conjunction with conflict theory. From this perspective, violence has been a means for men to maintain dominance over women; and, for men, IPV was not a problem, but a means to an end. It took the rise of feminism to challenge this position.

Less common, but greatly feared

Serial murder

Despite the prevalence of IPV, other kinds of violent crime which pose far less risk have been successfully constructed into far greater problems in the public imagination. Philip Jenkins' analysis of the serial killer phenomenon in the 1980s provides an excellent example of the kinds of insights that can be revealed through social constructionism.

In the 1980s and 1990s, serial murder came to occupy the public imagination in a big way. This was thanks largely to some highly publicized cases (e.g., Ted Bundy, Henry Lee Lucas, John Wayne Gacy, and later, Jeffrey Dahmer), as well as some very popular fictional books and movies (most notably, *Silence of the Lambs*). The FBI's Behavioral Sciences Unit was also highly instrumental in spreading fear of serial homicide. In the early 1980s, it estimated that approximately one-fifth of all American homicides were cases of serial murders; their estimates went as high as 4,000 or 5,000 cases per year. These estimates were based on the assumption that when the police reported an *unknown* circumstance in a homicide case, that case must have been the work of a serial killer. Phillip Jenkins writes:

> This interpretation of the data is quite unwarranted. In effect, it suggests that an *unknown* circumstance equates to *no apparent motive*, which in turn means that the murder is *motiveless*, or "with no apparent rhyme, reason, or motivation." This is unpardonable. All that can be legitimately understood from an *unknown* circumstance is that, at the time of completing the form, the police agency in question either did not know the exact context of the crime, or did not trouble to fill in the forms correctly.[35]

Nevertheless, in 1983, the U.S. Justice Department held a news conference about the alarming increase in the serial murder phenomenon. At the conference, Justice Department officials reiterated that there were likely several thousand cases of serial murder each year and "that there might be thirty-five such killers active in the United States at any given time."[36] The juxtaposition of these two figures—4,000 victims and 35 serial killers—meant that the average serial killer must have been responsible for over 100 killings per year. Interestingly, there is no confirmed case on record in which a serial killer was responsible for so many murders ever, let alone in one year. At least one of the two statistics was in need of serious readjustment.

According to Jenkins and, indeed, more recent FBI estimates, there may indeed be more than 35 serial killers operating in the United States at any given time; but the annual number of victims, rather than being in the neighborhood of 4,000, is more likely to be in the range of 50–70.[37] This latter estimate amounts to considerably less than 1 percent of all U.S. homicides. Writes Jenkins,

> In reality, serial homicide accounts for a very small proportion of American murders, and the claims frequently made in the 1980s exaggerated the scale of victimization by a factor of at least twenty. Moreover, such offenses are far from new, and the volume of activity in recent years is little different from conditions in the early part of the present century, while the phenomenon is by no means distinctively American.[38]

Misleading statistics and images concerning serial murders captured the public's attention and fostered a deeply ingrained fear of strangers among millions of Americans, even though statistically their chances of being murdered by an acquaintance or loved one were enormously greater than their chances of being murdered by a serial killer. In fact, 70 serial killings per year in a country of over 300 million people means that any person's chances of being murdered by a serial killer are infinitesimally small. One has to wonder the degree to which the fear of strangers among today's parents and children is a vestige of these misleading statistics propagated over a generation ago.

Thus, in the case of serial homicide, the perceived, or subjective, reality of the problem bore little resemblance to the objective reality. We can say, then, that serial homicide was a socially constructed problem. This leads us to the question, Why was this social problem so successfully constructed? Why were such misleading statistics accepted and internalized by so many? The answer, according to Jenkins' constructionist analysis, lies in the fact that a diverse number of interest groups found it to their advantage to perpetuate exaggerated statistics.

The FBI had an interest in perpetuating the myth that there were thousands of victims murdered by crazed killers who roamed the country. The FBI claimed part of the problem lay in the lack of communication between law enforcement agencies, as well as these agencies' inability to make the connections between similar crimes happening in very different locations. By exaggerating the extent of these crimes and the extent to which serial killers actually "roam" and by establishing themselves as the experts who could link these disparate killings, the FBI was able to enhance both its jurisdiction and its prestige. Prior to the serial homicide scare, the FBI's jurisdiction was quite limited, restricted to federal crimes and/or crimes that involved the crossing of state lines. However, thanks to the serial homicide scare, the Behavioral Sciences Unit managed to portray themselves as supersleuths, and the public and other law enforcement agencies came to welcome their help rather than resent the intrusion of federal powers, as they might have prior to the scare.

Jenkins argues that the serial killer scare also fit neatly into the ideological framework of the conservative Reagan administration. Conservative ideology places blame for society's problems on weak, immoral, or depraved individuals rather than on the social structure. The serial homicide scare diverted attention away from other crimes—the vast majority of crimes—that can be more readily associated with the social structure. The majority of homicides, for example, occurs within the lower class and can, therefore, arguably be linked with poverty and similar structural determinants. Serial homicides, on the other hand, are less readily linked to the social structure; they appear to occur randomly, and they seem to be committed by crazed, pathological, immoral individuals who are, quite simply, "evil." Consequently, by shifting society's focus on crime to serial killings, conservatives were able to perpetuate their view that crime has more to do with the moral breakdown of our society than with poverty, inequality, and the dismantling of social welfare programs.

Paradoxically, liberal groups also found an interest in perpetuating the inflated statistics. When the victims were black, as were many of Jeffrey Dahmer's and John Wayne Gacy's victims, black leaders could blame the problem on a lack of concern on the part of law enforcement agencies and their neglect of cases involving missing African Americans. When the victims were gay, similar complaints could be lodged by gay activists. When the victims were female, feminists could blame the patriarchal criminal justice system for its lack of concern for female victims, in which case serial homicide could be "contextualized together with offenses such as rape, child molestation, and sexual harassment."[39]

In short, the myths surrounding serial homicide were successfully constructed because many parties had an interest in perpetuating these myths and few had an interest in uncovering the truth.[1]

School and mass shootings

When school and mass shootings occur, they usually receive an enormous amount of media coverage and they ignite a great deal of impassioned political discourse. As a consequence, it becomes difficult to put these

---

1 This material, beginning with "In the 1980s" and ending here, was previously published in *Social Problems: An Introduction to Critical Constructionism*, fifth edition, by Robert Heiner, pp. 146–149. Copyright © 2016 by Oxford University Press. Reproduced with permission of the Licensor through PLSclear.

events into perspective. It helps to start with some definitions. These vary; but according to commonly accepted definitions, mass shootings are events in which at least four people are *injured or killed* by a firearm; and mass murders are events in which at least four people are *killed*. Of course, our definition (three or four? killed or injured?) will affect our understanding of the proliferation and causes of these events.[40] Mass murders are rare events, accounting for a fraction of one percent of all homicides. But they do get extensive media coverage and they appear to happen randomly. Thus, while the risk is small, we are all at risk. After all, "almost everyone goes to school, goes to work, or goes out in public."[41]

With such small datasets, it becomes difficult to make generalizations about mass murders. However, the public's need for an explanation often supersedes the experts' lack of knowledge. Popular understandings of school shootings often include the notions that the shooters "want to exact revenge on society for some harm that they have suffered (real or imaginary), commit suicide in a blaze of gunfire, and get national media attention for their last act."[42] Such assertions reflect the kind of tautological reasoning found in many psychological theories of crime (see Chapter 2), inferring that if someone kills numerous high school students, then, *of course*, they must be emotionally unstable, out for revenge, seeking media attention, and/or wanting to die in a blaze of gunfire. However, such understandings are either based on a small number of cases or upon no systematic review of the evidence at all. Based on his analysis of 343 "shooting events," David Paradice writes, "Few [shooters] have been diagnosed as emotionally unstable; most shooters are just angry about something. Twice as many shooters are arrested at or near the scene of the shooting as complete suicide. When asked why they did what they did, they rarely mention a desire for media attention."[43] As for mental illness as a causative factor, an FBI report concerning 63 active shooters between 2000 and 2013 observed that only 25 percent had ever been diagnosed with a mental illness.[44] America's worst mass shooting to-date took place on September 25, 2017 in Las Vegas, when a gunman opened fire from a hotel room overlooking an outdoor concert. The victims included 58 people who were killed and more than 850 who were injured. Following a 15-month investigation, the FBI, "did not find a 'single or clear motivating factor' for gunman Stephen Paddock's actions, but concluded he was in financial trouble and had difficulty coping with his age"[45]—which means the FBI did not understand much more about the underlying motivations for this attack than they do for most mass shootings. Psychiatry professors James Knoll and Ronald Pies write, "the ritualized hunt for the shooter's motive is usually an exercise in fruitless speculation and wasted resources."[46]

Part of the obsession with the mental fitness of the shooter has to do with the political fight over gun control. The political left favors more thorough background checks and more restrictions, if not outright bans, on assault weapons, high capacity magazines, and bump stocks; while representatives of the National Rifle Association and the political right are insistent that mass shootings have nothing to do with the ready availability of specialized guns and hardware, but have more to do with our inability to identify and treat or isolate the mentally ill. Further, they argue that if more people were armed, they would be able to stop mass shooters before they kill as many people as they do.

There are several counter-arguments to the NRA's position. First, as we noted above, the correlation between mass shootings and mental illness is problematic. Second, as we noted on page 76, guns are far more readily available in the United States and mass shootings are far more typical of the U.S. than of almost all other countries.[47] Finally, we should note that, in 1996, just 12 days after a mass shooting in which 35 people were killed, Australia passed a comprehensive gun control law, including a ban on rapid-fire guns. In the nine years before the gun ban, there had been four other mass shootings; and, as this book goes to press, almost 25 years later, there have been none since.[48] Arguing in support of the new gun laws, Australia's Prime Minister, John Howard, referenced the United States, saying, "I would dread the thought that this country would go down the American path so far as the possession of firearms."[49]

Just how much more pervasive mass shootings are in the United States than elsewhere is difficult to say. The difficulty lies in distinguishing between mass shootings, and shootings committed by terrorists and para-military forces. The problem of defining terrorism is discussed below; but, by most accounts, mass shootings by terrorists are more prevalent in other parts of the world than in the United States; and then there are countries wracked by insurgencies and counter-insurgencies wreaking havoc on civilian populations and engaging in mass shootings. Definitions that separate these phenomena are socially constructed and have political implications. Mass shootings at schools, on the other hand, are easier to separate from other mass shootings, and these do appear to be characteristically American.

Terrorism

The hijackings and attacks on the World Trade Center and the Pentagon on September 11, 2001, were, first and foremost, horrific crimes; and if ever there were an act of terrorism, those attacks would qualify as prime examples. However, the use of the word *terrorism* is quite problematic to many social scientists. The word has little or no social scientific value, as it has different meanings to different audiences in different contexts. The term describes a class of phenomena of which we do not approve, but it does not distinguish the objective reality of such phenomena from very similar phenomena of which we do approve. It usually, but not always, is used in reference to violence; but if a group happens to approve of the violence in question, then it is not likely to be considered "terrorism." Palestinian suicide bombers are often seen as martyrs by many Palestinians and people from some other Islamic groups who support the Palestinian goal of independence, whereas they are considered terrorists by most Israelis and by most Americans, who are less sympathetic to their goals. Hence, as the expression goes, "one man's terrorist is another man's freedom fighter," or, as an article that appeared in *The Economist* reads:

> Who is or is not a terrorist? The suicide bomber, the rebel guerrilla, the liberation front, the armed forces of the state? In practice, what act or person earns the label depends on who wants to apply it. To Ulster loyalists all IRA violence is terrorism; to Sinn Fein it is part of a legitimate war. To many Israelis, everyone from the suicide bombers in Jerusalem or Ashkelon to the Hizb ollah [*sic*] grenade-thrower in South Lebanon is a terrorist; to many Arabs during the 1982 Lebanon war, the worst terrorists in the Middle East were the—entirely legitimate, uniformed—Israel Defense Force.[50]

A commonly accepted definition of terrorism refers to violence perpetrated against innocent civilians to achieve a political objective. Very often, the term terrorist is used by powerful entities (i.e., representatives of powerful groups or countries) to refer to the violence perpetrated by entities with far less power. When a group (e.g., a racial, ethnic, or religious group) or a country has a grievance against a government that has far more political, economic, or military resources at its disposal, it may be quite rational and sometimes quite effective for that group to turn to violence. It may also be quite rational for the less powerful group to target innocent civilians because the group with which it has a grievance may have a tremendous military advantage; targeting only their military resources would lead to certain defeat. "Terrorism is the way that non-soldiers engage in war,"[51] and its victims are usually non-soldiers as well. At what point does a group's grievance justify war? And if their grievance does justify war, what do they do if they are at a severe military disadvantage? Acts that we consider "terrorism" may well be a reasonable and effective solution to the problem.

While political leaders inevitably claim that terrorism is a desperate and futile strategy that is doomed to failure, history has proven it to be a sometimes effective strategy. In 1948, for example, Zionists blew up the King David Hotel, the British headquarters in Palestine; this was a key event in forcing the British to leave and paving the way for the establishment of Israel. Subsequently, attacks on civilians by the Palestinian Liberation

Organization undoubtedly drew the world's attention to the plight of Palestinian refugees. While political leaders frequently state they will never negotiate with terrorists, they do indeed frequently negotiate with them. Gerry Adams and Yasser Arafat were leaders of alleged terrorist organizations, and both became prominent players in peace negotiations. Now deceased, Arafat is regarded by millions in the Middle East as a historical leader in international politics and a hero.

Such a critical perspective on terrorism does not legitimate such violence, but it does put it on par with violence perpetrated by military forces. During war, one or both sides has grievances with the other and turns to violence as a means of addressing such grievances. While military resources may be targeted, civilians are often killed and often killed knowingly. Eighty-four percent of those killed during the Korean War and 90 percent of those killed during the Vietnam War were civilians.[52] Of the seven million people who were killed in wars around the world between 1989 and 2003, 75 percent were civilians.[53]

Those who support the definition of terrorism given above would emphasize that acts of violence during wartime are distinguished from terrorist violence because the latter actually targets civilians, whereas in war, civilians are incidental casualties (or "collateral damage"). This distinction constructs an inflated difference between *intentionally* killing civilians and *knowingly* killing civilians. There are many shades of gray between the two, if they are not indeed two sides of the same coin. What about the hundreds of thousands of civilians killed in Hiroshima, Nagasaki, and Dresden during World War II? Were these acts of "terrorism?" (Would U.S. military objectives have been accomplished so effectively if so many civilians had not been killed?) In 1989, the United States aggressively bombed a well-populated, poor neighborhood in Panama in its effort to oust President Manuel Noriega, killing hundreds of civilians (some estimates go into the thousands). Was this an act of terrorism?

Your answer to these questions likely depends on whether you think these military actions were legitimate and whether you think the goals (grievances) being addressed by these actions were legitimate. Such a judgment is based upon your values and not upon the objective nature of these actions. The British Broadcasting Corporation—one of the most respected news agencies in the world—has a policy restricting the use of the word "terrorist" in its news broadcasts because to do so would imply that it is taking sides in a political conflict. The agency's editorial guidelines state, "Terrorism is a difficult and emotive subject with significant political overtones and care is required in the use of language that carries value judgements. We try to avoid the use of the term "terrorist" without attribution."[54] The language of this guideline reflects an understanding that the word terrorist is principally a term used by one side in a political conflict (usually the more powerful side) to demonize the enemy and delegitimize its tactics. The use of the word terrorist is an indicator of which side you are on in a political conflict.

Often when Americans use the term terrorism they are referring to attacks in which the perpetrators are Muslims. But the political nature of the term becomes apparent when liberals and conservatives disagree over whether attackers should be considered terrorists when they are white Christians. As the perpetrators of many recent mass shootings have been white supremacists, coming from the extreme right, political leaders on the right are often reluctant to call them terrorists, fearing the public will make a connection between right-wing ideology and violence.[55] On the other hand, right-wing ideologues are often quick to brand environmental activist groups such as Greenpeace and the Earth Liberation Front as "eco-terrorists," while those on the left of the political spectrum often applaud their efforts on behalf of the environment.[56]

In the days of American slavery, most southerners regarded the abolitionists Nat Turner and John Brown with the moral equivalent that we assign to contemporary terrorists. Today, we think of Turner and Brown in a different light because we have more sympathy for their cause. In 2014, the city of Charleston, South Carolina, unveiled a monument in honor of Denmark Vesey. Vesey was executed in 1822 for plotting to free the slaves of Charleston by burning down the city. No doubt, he was seen as the equivalent of a terrorist by the white population of his day; but today he is honored for his courage and conviction because a substantial part of Charleston's population has strong sympathy for his grievance against slavery.

Professor of law Paul Butler writes:

> The uncertainty about how to evaluate the morality of some terrorists (one might also think about the original American rebels) has two possible explanations: (1) we have a double standard about terrorism and morality depending on our sympathy for the terrorists' cause or (2) there may be some extreme cases in which the taking of innocent lives in pursuit of an urgent objective is warranted. If we accept the former explanation, the appropriate moral solution probably requires absolute condemnation in every case. If we endorse the second explanation however, there may be exceptions to the general rule that terrorism is immoral. These exceptions must be carefully delineated and then rigorously scrutinized to make sure they are not self-serving.[57]

Both of the explanations provided by Butler employ values and, therefore, relativity. Values determine our sympathy for the "terrorists' cause, and values determine whether we consider an objective as an urgent one that warrants the killing of civilians. While terrorism is spoken of in popular rhetoric in absolutist terms, though it might be distasteful, it is difficult to refute the argument that it is indeed a relative term that poorly reflects any objective reality. The use of the term in popular political discourse, at least, has corrupted its potential for any meaningful use in the social sciences.[2]

Theoretical connections

On page 51, we discussed "the self-fulfilling prophecy," an integral component of labeling theory. A corollary of the self-fulfilling prophecy is called the "Thomas Theorem," named after sociologist W.I. Thomas. It states that things perceived as real are real in their consequences. The fear of violent crime discussed earlier is a prime example of the Thomas Theorem. That is, though the fear of crime often bears little or no correlation to the risk of violent victimization, this fear does have real consequences in terms of reinforcing prejudices, and in terms of peoples' quality of life, their voting behavior, and how their taxes are spent. This applies not only to common crimes of violence, but to terrorism as well. Stanley Cohen's work on moral panics (page 55) also helps us to understand why politicians manipulate the fear of crime and how news outlets selectively tap into and reinforce this fear. To an extent, these insights apply to school and mass shootings as well. The mechanics of moral panics were also displayed in the discussion above concerning the serial murder phenomenon of the 1980s and 1990s. During this panic, various interest groups were able to use the serial murder phenomenon as a symbol for what is wrong with the country. This analysis also revealed where the moral panics literature and conflict theory converge in that the symbolism employed by these interest groups served to promote their own political interests and enhance their power (for examples, the panic enhanced the FBI's jurisdiction and served the Reagan administration by diverting attention away from away from poverty as a cause of violent crime).

While Robert Merton's theory of anomie is more often used to explain property crime rather than violent crime, it does shed light on the connection between poverty and violent crime in the United States. The levels of frustration experienced by the poor is especially acute, given the enormous emphasis American society places on the goal of financial success. This frustration manifests itself as a disregard for the norms, and crime (both violent and property crime) can be the result (see pages 42–44). Conflict theory (pages 34–35) has been discussed in terms of the use of violence as

---

2 This material, beginning with "The hijackings and attacks" and ending here, was previously published in *Social Problems: An Introduction to Critical Constructionism*, fifth edition, by Robert Heiner, pp. 185–187 (edited). Copyright © 2016 by Oxford University Press. Reproduced with permission of the Licensor through PLSclear.

a means of maintaining men's domination over women. Those hypotheses explaining the crime drop with regards to higher incarceration rates and increased police presence reflect routine activities theory. Remember, this theory suggests that crime occurs with the convergence of willing offenders, suitable targets, and a lack of guardianship (see pages 63–64). The notion that violent crime rates dropped because more violent felons were locked up and off the streets emphasized a decline in the numbers of willing offenders; and the emphasis on increased police presence meant an increase in guardianship. Along the way, we have also talked about the role of honor as a contributor to violent crime. This discussion reflects symbolic interactionism's emphasis on the importance of self-definition in explaining behavior; and it corresponds to the importance Albert Cohen (pages 47–49) assigned to the lower class delinquent's need for status as it is achieved through crime.

PART II: NONVIOLENT CRIME

Property crime

While violent crime gets all of the headlines and elicits so much fear, the vast majority of crimes committed are property crimes. In fact, over 85 percent of all index crimes reported by the FBI in 2017 were property crimes.[58] As we have seen with violent crime, property crime has been trending downward for the past several decades. Between 1998 and 2007, the property crime rate dropped by 20 percent, and then by another 20 percent in the next 10 years.[59]

Burglary

The FBI defines burglary as the "unlawful entry of a structure to commit a felony or theft." The entry need not have been forcible and the theft or felony need not have occurred for the offense to be classified as a burglary. In that the "victim" of a burglary might be conceived of as a location, analysis of burglary particularly lends itself to Geographic Information Systems (GIS) analysis. "Crime mapping" has been used to identify potential "hot spots" where future incidents of crime are more likely to occur, and where law enforcement authorities might consider allocating greater resources. British researchers Bowers, Johnson, and Pease, for example, have found through GIS analysis that the "risk of burglary is communicable." That is, they found that properties within a 400-meter circumference of a burglary are at a greater risk of burglary for up to two months after the initial offense; further, they found that "space-time clustering is greatest in more affluent areas."[60] Armed with this knowledge, the local police may consider boosting patrol in an affluent neighborhood after a burglary occurs; and, if no more burglaries or arrests happen there within two months, then they can move their patrol resources elsewhere. Burglary also lends itself to efforts in Crime Prevention by Environmental Design (CPTED – see p. 30).

The flowchart in Figure 4.4 was developed by Scarr, Pinsky and Wyatt for the National Institute of Law Enforcement and Criminal Justice in 1973. At the time, burglary rates were nearly three times what they are today; but their breakdown of the offense into a cyclic pattern provides a systematic way of looking at the problem that may offer some solutions to burglary and other crimes today.

In the first stage, the would-be burglar has needs. He or she might need drugs, or cash, or peer approval, or any number of needs that might be met through the commission of a burglary. Next, they have some skill. "Skill" is used loosely here and it could include the ability to pick a lock, or throw a rock through a window. Next, they perceive the opportunity to commit a burglary: a house that looks unoccupied, overhearing someone at the barbershop saying they are going out of town, etc. Next, he or she makes the connection in their mind that burglary may be a path to meeting their

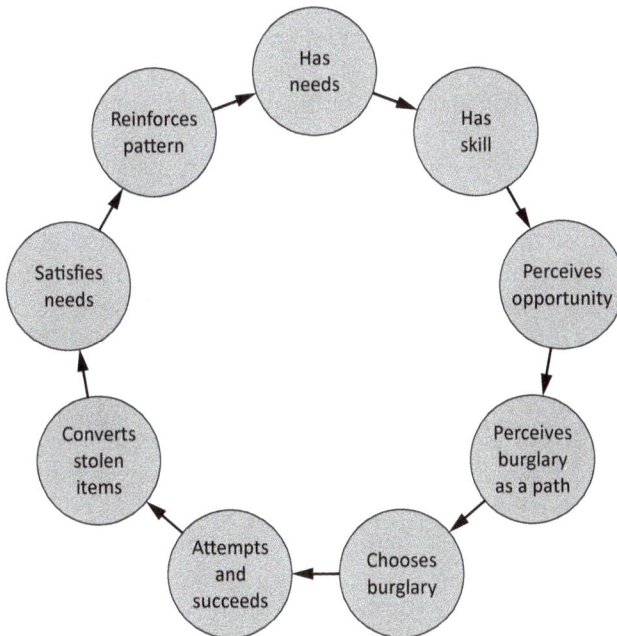

FIGURE 4.4
A specific-behavior cycle–burglary.

Source: H.A Scarr et al., *Patterns of Burglary*, U.S. Department of Justice, 1973, p. 116.

needs. Next, they choose to commit the burglary. Part of the attraction of burglary is that it is a *passive crime*. That is, if it is done right, you never have to confront the victim; there are no witnesses, and no violence. Next, they attempt the burglary and succeed. Then they convert the stolen items into need-meeting items: they sell the property to a fence or they buy their drugs from a dealer, or they show off among their peers and gain status. Thus, they satisfy their needs and this reinforces the pattern.

While this exercise may strike some as tediously obvious, it allows us to think about how and where this cycle may be broken. For example, at the "needs" stage, we might legalize drugs, provide job training, or guarantee a basic minimum income. At "perceives opportunity," we might increase police patrols, or establish a neighborhood watch, or educate residents about the need to lock their doors and to stop their mail delivery when they leave town. At "chooses burglary," we might heighten the severity of punishment for the crime in the hope it will deter people from making this choice. At "attempts and succeeds," we might run public service announcements on TV, telling viewers about signs of danger in their neighborhood and what to do when they see them. (For decades, advice-dispensing "McGruff, the Crime Dog," appeared on public service messages for more than a generation and was familiar to children and adults alike.) At "converts stolen items" we might crackdown on fences who buy stolen goods or on drug dealers. Thus, the seemingly tedious exercise can become a useful exercise in thinking systematically about crime prevention.

Larceny-theft

The FBI defines larceny-theft as the "unlawful taking, carrying, leading, or riding away of property from the possession or constructive possession of another. Examples are thefts of bicycles, motor vehicle parts and accessories, shoplifting, pocketpicking, or the stealing of any property or article that is not taken by force and violence or by fraud. Attempted larcenies are included. Embezzlement, confidence games, forgery, check fraud, etc., are excluded."[61]

This is the most common crime reported in the UCR, and its perpetrators vary across a wide range of demographics in terms of age, gender, race, and social class. There is a good chance that you, dear reader, have engaged in such crime. Some perpetrators may commit this crime once or twice in their lifetime, while, for others, it is their primary source of income throughout much of their lives.

The crime of shoplifting provides a good example of the variety of perpetrators. Kids, middle-aged, elderly, rich, poor, men and women are all common perpetrators of shoplifting. According to one study by Carlos Blanco and his associates, "Shoplifting occurred across all sociodemographic strata. However, it was more common among those with higher education and income, suggesting that financial considerations are unlikely to be the main motivator for shoplifting in most cases."[62] According to the National Association for Shoplifting Prevention (NASP), one in 11 people will engage in shoplifting during their lives; only one in 48 shoplifters are caught, and only half of these are reported to the police.[63] Shoplifting is likely to be one of the most under-reported of all crimes. As such, we know very little of the "typical" shoplifter because those who are detected/arrested are unlikely to be the typical shoplifter because the typical shoplifter is not caught.

It has been suggested that shoplifting may be on the rise globally for two reasons. The first is that the internet has made it easier to sell stolen goods; and the second is the emergence of self-checkouts, which have made it normal for customers themselves to put merchandise into bags to carry out of the store.[64] Estimates vary; but shoplifting probably costs retailers in the United States $10 to $20 billion annually. (Part of the difficulty of estimating the costs of shoplifting is separating them from the costs of employee theft, as both contribute to inventory "shrinkage."[65]) The costs of shoplifting are passed onto consumers in the form of higher prices on merchandise. The costs of added security—surveillance cameras, scanners, theft prevention tags, store detectives, etc.—are also passed onto consumers. Shoplifting can cost local communities in that those stores that lose lots of their inventory to shoplifting may relocate, taking jobs with them, leaving closed storefronts in their wake. Shoplifting also has costs for the environment because much of the non-recyclable plastic packaging filling up our landfills was designed to add bulk to merchandise (and/or to hide detection tags) to make it more difficult to shoplift.

Scams

Scams employ the use of deception by persons or groups without institutional connections for the purpose of financial gain. As they involve the use of fraud, they are not covered by the FBI's definition of larceny-theft. Traditionally, scams have been called "con games", or "confidence games," because the victims must have enough confidence in the perpetrator to give him or her control of their cash or assets. There are so many varieties of scams—and new ones are likely being developed every day—that it is impossible to characterize them in a few short pages; but most of us have been victims of actual or attempted scams. Scam "artists" may apply their trade traveling door-to-door (for example, posing as roof repairers), or using the phone (for example posing as a representative of the Internal Revenue Service), or using the internet (for example, posing as someone who needs help getting a large sum of money out of a foreign country). Box 4.1 contains a list of scams developed and disseminated by the Federal Trade Commission. For more examples, check out the website.

According to the FTC, romance scams are on the rise and cost victims $143 million in 2018, more than any other type of scam. In these scams,

Identity theft Your information is valuable. To you – and other people.		**Unwanted calls** You get a lot of unwanted calls. Many are from scammers.	
Imposter scams Someone calls to ask for money. Are they who they say they are?		**Tech support** **scams** **IRS imposter** **scams**	**Online dating** **scams** **Grandkid scams**
Health care scams You have a Medicare card, but a caller says you need a new one.		**"You've Won" scams** You won a prize! But you can't get it until you send money.	
Home repair scams Someone offers to repair your home. Cheap. For cash. Now.		**Money mule scams** Someone sends you money. Then asks you to send some of it to someone else.	
Work-at-home scams Ads promise big money working from home. For a fee.		**Charity fraud** Someone asks you to donate money to a charity. Today.	

BOX 4.1
Common Types of Scam

Source: Federal Trade Commission, "Pass It On," Consumer Information. www.consumer.ftc.gov/features/
feature-0030-pass-it-on.

perpetrators set up phony online profiles and cultivate relationships with their victims; once the relationship is firmly established they ask for money. They may claim a medical or financial emergency, or perhaps that they need money to come visit the victim. Victims may be strung along for a number of payments "for one crisis after another"; but eventually their online lover disappears without a trace. According to the FTC news release, "The median individual loss to a romance scam reported in 2018 was $2,600, about seven times higher than the median loss across all other fraud types." The highest rates of victimization involved people ages 40 to 69; but people 70 and older were taken for the highest amounts of money, with median losses at $10,000.[66]

People may have a certain admiration for scammers because they are clever, they do not use violence, and their victims are often seen as gullible and wanting to get rich quick. Even the term "con game" suggests a certain playfulness to the activity and trivializes the crime. There have been a number of popular movies in which con men and women are the prot-agonists; and their victims have been criminals or other unsympathetic characters.[67] However, scammers can be ruthless in their tactics, playing on their victims' emotional vulnerabilities, including loneliness, fear, despair, and desire for financial stability. Very often, victims will not report their victimization to the authorities or even tell their friends and relatives because they are embarrassed by their own gullibility and do not want to reveal their vulnerabilities. Elderly people, living alone on fixed incomes—that is, people who are most vulnerable and least able to afford financial victimization—are very often the targets of scammers. The American Association of Retired Person's provides a Fraud Watch Network; and financial exploitation—by both family and strangers—has been recognized as a form of elder abuse.[68] Medical researchers are suggesting that there might be a biological link—other than dementia—to "age associated financial vulnerability."[69]

In addition to the elderly, scammers are also attracted to victims of natural disasters. Scammers swoop in in the aftermath, offering fraudulent financial services, government assistance, and household repairs to people made desperate by hurricanes, tornados, floods, and wildfires. Recognizing the prevalence and seriousness of "disaster fraud," following Hurricane Katrina, the U.S. Department of Justice established the National Center for Disaster Fraud in 2005 to investigate and prosecute such cases. More recently, the Covid-19 pandemic drew out untold numbers of scammers, "offering free home testing kits, promoting bogus cures, selling health insurance, and preying on virus-related fears."[70]

Though scammers may be seen as more clever than other criminals, their crimes are not as benign as many people think; indeed, they are carefully calculated crimes, often preying upon the most vulnerable people in society.

Theoretical connections

Robert Merton's theory of anomie (page 42) is suited to the understanding of property crimes, as these are crimes oriented to the acquisition of financial or material gain. Recall that Merton implicates the American Dream and the emphasis that American culture places of financial success, so much emphasis that the rules (laws) pale in comparison. Burglars, shoplifters, scammers, and other property criminals all display a disregard for the law to avail themselves the opportunity for material gain. At the same time, many property offenders are able to avoid feelings of guilt and repeat their crimes because they are able to neutralize their criminal behavior (see techniques of neutralization, page 49). For example, burglars can tell themselves that they had no choice due to their drug addiction (denial of responsibility), shoplifters can tell themselves that they are doing no real harm (denial of injury), and scammers can tell themselves that their victims are motivated by greed (denial of the victim). Furthermore, scammers' positive definitions of themselves and their activities (see symbolic interactionism, page 51) are reinforced by the admiration for con artists that is reflected in American popular culture.

On the other hand, routine activities theory (page 63) assumes the presence of motivated offenders and looks instead at the availability of suitable targets and the presence or absence of effective guardianship. Burglary rates, for example, soared in the 1970s and 1980s when women left the home and went into the workplace, leaving homes without guardians for long periods of time. Also, during this time frame, televisions and other electronics became smaller and more portable, making targets more suitable for burglars to carry off. More security cameras and store detectives have increased guardianship in department stores; and bulkier packaging and theft prevention tags were developed to reduce the availability of suitable targets for shoplifters. Meanwhile, an aging population and an increase in natural disasters due to climate change are increasing the number of vulnerable ("suitable") targets for scammers.

Cybercrime

Cybercrime is an amorphous concept encompassing, among other activities, phishing, spamming, theft of services, denial of services attacks, ransomware attacks, identity theft, bullying, and distributing child pornography. The only element linking these crimes is that computers are used in their commission. Given the hundreds of millions of people in the United States who use a computer,[71] this is not a very distinguishing common element. Both perpetrators and victims of cybercrimes could be individuals, corporations, or even governments. Kirwin and Power note, "As with crime in general, most types of crime can be divided into 'property crimes' (such as identity theft, fraud and copyright infringement) and 'crimes against the person' (such as cybercrimes involving the sexual abuse of children)."[72] Further, Kirwin and Power distinguish between internet-enabled crime and internet-specific crimes. Internet-enabled crimes include those that could be committed without computers, such as distributing child pornography; and internet-specific crimes are those that can only be committed with a computer, such as distributing malware.[73] Very often, the perpetrators and the victims of cybercrime live in different countries, making it more difficult for law enforcement authorities to apprehend the perpetrator, and allowing perpetrators to operate with a good likelihood of impunity. As many cybercrimes involve fraud, they also fall into our discussion of scammers above.

Cyberbullying

There is a good chance that you are familiar with the phenomenon of cyberbullying, either because you have been a victim, or a perpetrator, or because your high school, like so many others across the country, mounted an initiative to educate their students about the phenomenon. In one recent survey, 30 percent of participating college students and 57 percent of high school students reported that they had recently been cyberbullied.[74] The numbers are similar in England, where over half of adolescents and teens reported being victims of cyberbullying.[75] Cyberbullying can include online harassment, posting naked pictures of the victim, publicly outing the victim, and a host of other threatening and humiliating activities, to which teenagers are particularly vulnerable.

Although, there is no physical contact between the perpetrator and the victim, Kirwin and Power would call cyberbullying a "crime against the person," and it can have serious physical and psychological consequences. Suicide rates have been rising in recent years and growth in suicide rates have been higher for girls than boys. Psychiatrist Joan Luby and psychologist Sarah Kertz implicate the role of social media and cyberbullying in these trends. They write,

> One reason for this sex disparity may be that compared with boys, girls' social media use may be more likely to result in interpersonal stress, a common factor associated with suicide attempts in youth. Compared with boys, girls use social media more frequently and are more likely to experience cyberbullying. Associations between social media use and mental health outcomes also differ by gender. Social media use is more strongly associated with depression in girls compared with boys, and cyberbullying is more closely associated with emotional problems in girls compared with boys. Other work shows that girls with depression elicit more negative responses from peers on social media compared with depressed boys. These findings suggest that increased social media use may have a more deleterious effect on girls, providing one potential explanation for why young girls may be increasingly vulnerable to suicidal thoughts and behaviors.[76]

All of the states have laws against bullying; some states specify cyberbullying, and some do not. There are no federal laws against cyberbullying unless patterns emerge indicating that race, religion, national origin, sex, or disability are a factor in targeting the victim(s). In which case, civil rights legislation requires that schools intervene.

The dark web

The "deep web," refers to online sites on the worldwide web that are not accessible to conventional search engines such as Google. Michael Bergman compares conventional search engines to a fishing net thrown across the surface of the water. What lies beneath the reach of the fishing net is the deep web. It is estimated that Google only accesses about 16 percent of sites on the worldwide web; most of the rest is deep web.[77] Access to the deep web requires special skills, encryption technology, passwords and/or identity verification. The deep web is an important tool for journalists and political dissidents to communicate through while avoiding reprisals from violent actors and repressive regimes. The part of the deep web, though, that involves criminal activity is called the "dark web" or the "darknet."[78] On the dark web, people deal in drugs, weapons, child pornography, stolen credit cards and stolen personal information. Terrorist organizations recruit and plan attacks on the dark web.[79] The gunmen in the November 2015 terrorist attacks in Paris were supplied their weapons through the dark web.[80] It is even alleged that murder for hire can be arranged on the dark web. It is also alleged that such assassination websites are just scams to cheat would-be conspirators out of their money.[81] (The latter is quite possible, given that the anonymity of the dark web would be very attractive to scammers, and would-be conspirators are not going to report having been scammed to the authorities.)

One notorious dark web operation was the Silk Road launched by the American Ross Ulbricht in 2011 as a "'free-market economic experiment' that focused on user anonymity."[82] The website operated similarly to Amazon's Marketplace where sellers could post their services and merchandise on the site; and it came to specialize in illegal drugs sales. Transactions were made in Bitcoin, a cryptocurrency that ensures a high level of anonymity for its users; and the website was accessed through TOR, a search engine that requires some technical skills to use and that routes signals anonymously through a series of servers worldwide. The operation was brought to the public's attention by an article published online by *Gawker* shortly after the site's launch, titled "The Underground Website Where You Can Purchase Every Drug Imaginable." The article opened with, "Making small talk with your pot dealer sucks. Buying cocaine can get you shot. What if you could buy and sell drugs online like books or light bulbs? Now you can: Welcome to Silk Road." The article continues,

> Here is just a small selection of the 340 items available for purchase on Silk Road by anyone, right now: a gram of Afghani hash; 1/8th ounce of "sour 13" weed; 14 grams of ecstasy; .1 grams tar heroin. A listing for "Avatar" LSD includes a picture of blotter paper with big blue faces from the James Cameron movie on it. The sellers are located all over the world, a large portion from the U.S. and Canada.[83]

Four days after the Gawker article appeared, Senator Chuck Schumer called for authorities to shut down the site. Ulbricht was arrested and the site was shut down in 2013; Ulbricht was convicted of drug and money laundering charges and sentenced to life without the possibility of parole in 2015.

THIS HIDDEN SITE HAS BEEN SEIZED

by the Federal Bureau of Investigation,
in conjunction with the IRS Criminal Investigation Division,
ICE Homeland Security Investigations, and the Drug Enforcement Administration,
in accordance with a seizure warrant obtained by the
United States Attorney's Office for the Southern District of New York
and issued pursuant to 18 U.S.C. § 983(j) by the
United States District Court for the Southern District of New York

IMAGE 4.1
The screen users would see this when looking for the Silk Road website after it was shut down by authorities.

Reliable data concerning illegal enterprises on such secretive online networks are difficult to obtain, but according to the Global Drug Survey (GDS) the percentage of drug consumers who reported having acquired drugs through the darknet has been on the rise in most countries. The GDS survey conducted in 2018 found that more than 28 percent of drug consumers in England reported having acquired drugs from the darknet over the past 12 months; and 12 percent in the United States did so.[84] Overall, more than 25 percent of consumers who reported having acquired drugs from the darknet were new initiates, having only done so for the first time in the past 12 months.[85] The survey did not distinguish between drug dealers and drug users. Since users would not necessarily know that their drugs were bought by their dealers through the darknet, the percentages of people using drugs acquired through the darknet would likely be much higher than those estimated in the GDS.

White-collar crime

As we mentioned in our discussion of Edwin Sutherland's contributions to criminological theory (pages 35 and 47), it was he who introduced the concept of "white collar crime" in 1940, defining it as "crime committed by a person of respectability and high social status in the course of his occupation." As with the terms "terrorism" and "cybercrime," there are problems with the term "white-collar crime" as well. For one, it is a very broad category of crime, the name of which is derived from the dress code of businessmen from decades passed. That is, scammers, hackers, and businessmen today may all be dressed alike; but laypersons as well as experts may disagree as to whether they are engaged in an "occupation." Indeed, criminologist Sally Simpson reports, "researchers have found that some so-called 'white-collar' offenders are unemployed at the time of their offenses, or have spotty employment records."[86]

It might also help in our conceptualization of white-collar crime to make a distinction between "occupational crime" and "corporate crime," where occupational crime is committed by the individual for his or her personal financial gain (e.g., embezzlement) and corporate crime is committed to advance the corporation's organizational goals[87] (e.g., cutting legal corners and dumping dangerous chemicals in violation of the Clean Water Act). Again, the distinction is not so clear when a CEO decides to dump dangerous chemicals to increase the value of the corporation in which he or she owns stock or is paid on the basis of corporation's profit margins.

Lastly, criminologists working from the conflict perspective take issue with the term white-collar crime in that it directs our attention only to the illegal activities of white-collar criminals. However, conflict theorists argue some of their most harmful and, in fact, deadly activities are only legal because the law serves the interests of the elite, and focuses its attention on crimes committed by the poor. If, instead, the law served the interests of society, then far more behaviors committed by the elite would be considered crimes. For Sutherland, crimes committed by corporations are morally equivalent to those committed by the poor, but criminal statistics are biased to obscure corporate crimes because the elite have the economic power to "influence the administration of justice in their own favor more effectively than persons of the lower socio-economic class."[88]

White-collar crime, with its orientation towards financial gain, is often discussed in the context of property crime. However, while the goal of corporate decision-making is profit, those decisions can put dozens, hundreds, or thousands of people at risk of physical harm or even death. According to the conflict theorist, it is only because of the elite's influence over the law and the media that the public and the authorities do not view these decisions as conspiracy to commit violence, or—when someone is injured or killed as a result—as assault or manslaughter. Ronald Kramer defines "corporate violence" as "corporate behavior which produces an unreasonable risk of physical harm to employees, the general public, and/or consumers, which is the result of deliberate decision-making."[89]

An often-cited example of corporate violence surfaced with the uncovering of the so-called Pinto papers. The Pinto papers were internal memoranda at Ford Motor Company that allegedly demonstrated that officials at Ford knew the Pinto automobile was dangerous; the papers indicated that they knew it tended to explode upon rear-end collision and that they estimated that about 180 people would die of burns incurred in such collisions and another 180 serious burn injuries could be expected. They also knew this problem in the Pinto could be fixed for about $11 per vehicle if they issued a recall. According to journalist Mark Dowie, to determine whether a recall was cost-effective, they proceeded to estimate the "cost" of a human life— that is, how much they could expect to settle with each victim's survivors— which came to just over $200,000. Using that figure, Dowie alleged that Ford officials determined that a recall would cost more than settling these cases and decided not to issue a recall for the Pinto. Dowie quotes a critic of Ford as saying, "One wonders how long Ford Motor Company would continue to market lethal cars were Henry Ford II and Lee Iacocca [the top Ford officials at the time] serving twenty-year terms in Leavenworth for consumer homicide."[90] (A very similar internal memorandum from General Motors, with allegedly very similar calculations pertaining to burn deaths, surfaced in the 1990s.[91] Consistent with their pro-corporate bias, this memo received very little coverage on the networks' evening news broadcasts.)

Tobacco has been linked to lung and heart disease and, even though tobacco use has been declining in the United States for the past two decades, it is still linked to over a hundred thousand deaths every year in the U.S. alone. Beyond these harmful physical effects of tobacco, the nicotine it contains is addictive. For decades, however, tobacco companies had denied the connections between tobacco and lung cancer and heart disease and addiction. However, internal memoranda and testimony from former employees cast serious doubt about what corporate officials had actually known for many years and about what they had been hiding. In other words, there is a strong case to be made that tobacco officials had been selling products they have long known to be deadly and that they had been covering up evidence of its deadliness. If this is true, then there is a substantial argument to be made that the acts of corporate officials in the tobacco industry *alone* cause more deaths and other physical and financial harm to society each year than street crime.[3]

Eventually, executives in the tobacco industry were called before Congress to account for their cover-ups, states sued the industry, and multibillion dollar settlements resulted. But there have been millions of tobacco-related deaths and these cases are settled in civil courts, not criminal courts. This is a distinguishing feature of white-collar crime. These cases are more often tried in civil courts where the penalties are financial. As a proportion of all criminal cases, rarely do white-collar criminals go to jail.[92] Again, the conflict theorist would argue that the laws are written by the elite and for the elite. However, there is another reason for the "excusability" of corporate crime. Corporations are integrated into the economy. If tobacco companies were ruled to be criminal enterprises and shut down, thousands of farmers would lose their livelihoods, factory workers would lose their jobs, the taxes the industry pays to cities and states would vanish, and the cities and towns that depend upon the tobacco industry would be economically devastated. The integration of bad acting corporations into the economy provides their executives with another level of impunity beyond the corruption of the law in favor of the elite.

---

3 This material, beginning with "An often-cited example" and ending here, was previously published in *Social Problems: An Introduction to Critical Constructionism*, fifth edition, by Robert Heiner, pp. 182–184 (edited). Copyright © 2016 by Oxford University Press. Reproduced with permission of the Licensor through PLSclear.

Drugs

The racist origins of drug control

Conflict theorists and historians argue that to understand the connection between drugs, crime, and justice, it is important to keep in mind that there were no laws banning any psychoactive substances throughout most of American history. This lack of drug laws was not because there were no psychoactive substances back when. Indeed opiates were pervasive in nineteenth century America. There were very potent tonics and elixirs laced with opium that were advertised in newspapers and were available at the general store and by mail, even in the Sears and Roebuck catalog. There were hundreds of thousands of drug addicts. One subset of these addicts was veterans of the Civil War who had been treated for their injuries with morphine. One popular opiate was a mixture of opium and alcohol, called laudanum, which was especially popular among upper class women, another segment of addicts prevalent at the time. A popular beverage during the latter part of the nineteenth century was Vin Mariani; this was a wine mixed with coca, the botanical source of cocaine, and it had been endorsed by Pope Leo XIII. Coca-Cola was originally laced with coca, hence its name. Heroin was developed by Bayer (as in "Bayer aspirin") and marketed as a cough suppressant and as a cure for cocaine addiction.

Despite the profusion of psychoactive drugs, the thousands and thousands of addicts, and the frequent overdose, there was little political activity organized to ban these substances. It has been suggested that the legal bans were the result of advances in chemistry when scientists were able to isolate the active principle in opium (morphine) and in coca (cocaine). The hypodermic syringe was also invented in the nineteenth century, which enabled these substances to enter directly into the bloodstream. Injection of these active principles made these substances much more potent, addictive, and lethal. It has also been suggested that the legal bans were put into place because of the mechanization of the workplace consequent to the Industrial Revolution. Stoned workers and heavy machinery made for a dangerous workplace and lowered productivity.

These explanations notwithstanding, historians have offered another compelling explanation for anti-drug legislation. They argue such legislation has been used as a powerful tool in the oppression and persecution of minorities in the United States; and history is rife with examples, beginning with the first drug laws and continuing through the more recent and ongoing "War on Drugs." While opiates pervaded American society, at the time, the only group that smoked it in significant numbers was the Chinese. The largest trade in the world, in the mid-nineteenth century, involved the British selling opium to the Chinese. The British forced the Chinese to open their ports and their markets to the opium trade. Many

Chinese, mostly single males, immigrated to the west coast of the United States bringing with them their opium addiction. They took jobs laying railroad track, one of the few jobs open to them because it was hard, back-breaking work that white workers avoided. Working long hours, these Chinese immigrants finished their day and retired to their preferred opium den. Few whites rallied to end this practice until the nation and California, in particular, were hit by an economic depression. Suddenly, modest stirrings of anti-Chinese sentiments were inflamed. The lack of job opportunities for whites was blamed on the Chinese. The first drug laws ensued. The very first drug law was passed in California in 1875 and it targeted Chinese immigrants. These laws targeted only opium smoking. "It was not the use of opium itself," writes Patricia Morgan, "but the smoking, a unique Chinese habit, which became a focal point for legislative action."[93]

Perhaps the convergence of these events may strike the reader as a coincidence; but much the same thing happened in the case of cannabis. In the first few decades of the twentieth century, few people smoked marijuana other than Mexican immigrants who brought their taste for the drug from their homeland. These immigrants worked largely as migrant labor, harvesting crops in the southwest United States. There was prejudice toward these laborers and a number of local and state laws banning marijuana. El Paso, Texas, for example, write law professors Richard Bonnie and Charles Whitebread, was characterized as a 'hot bed of marijuana fiends' where use of the drug was common not only among Mexicans, but among 'Negroes, prostitutes, pimps and a criminal class of whites.' In response, El Paso passed an ordinance banning the sale and possession of the drug in 1914.[94]

Anti-Mexican sentiments heated up during the Great Depression when those jobs working the fields suddenly looked good to whites. There was a flurry of newspaper articles linking the drug to the commission of violent crimes, particularly by Mexicans. Harry Anslinger, the head of the Federal Bureau of Narcotics made it his mission to rid the country of the marijuana menace. With hindsight, at least, his racist motivations are not difficult to detect. "[T]he primary reason to outlaw marijuana," he is quoted as saying, "is its effect on the degenerate races."[95] (The fact that most of us today refer to the drug as "marijuana" referring to its Mexican roots, rather than "cannabis," reflects one of the successes of the early anti-Mexican propagandists.) Indicative of the time, a letter from the editor of a newspaper in Alamosa, Colorado read,

> I wish I could show you what a small marijuana cigarette can do to one of our Spanish-speaking residents. That's why our problem is so great: the greatest percentage of our population is composed of Spanish-speaking persons, most of whom are low mentally, because of social and racial conditions.[96]

Eventually, in 1937, the Marijuana Tax Act was passed, making it all but impossible to legally acquire the drug and criminalizing those who used it. Psychiatrist and historian David Musto writes of the legislation, "When viewed from the narrow goal of placating fears about an 'alien minority,' the Act was serviceable for more than a quarter of a century."[97]

Following a similar pattern to laws targeting the smoking of opium and then cannabis, anti-black sentiments in the South helped to spur on laws against cocaine. Myths about blacks high on cocaine abounded in the South at the turn of the twentieth century. "The fear of the cocainized black," writes Musto, "coincided with the peak of lynchings, legal segregation, and voting laws all designed to remove political and social power from him."[98]

By the early twentieth century, the public had been educated about the addictive properties of opiates and cocaine. In 1906, the Pure Food and Drug Act required that products containing these ingredients be so labeled; and the manufacture and availability of these drugs dropped precipitously. The Harrison Act of 1914 banned the non-medical use of heroin and cocaine. Drug users were criminalized at the federal level and we now know that racism was a prime motivation behind various efforts at criminalization.

Continued racism

As we will see in Chapter 7, more recently, the United States embarked on the "War on Drugs" beginning in the mid-1980s and peaking in the first decade of the new millennium. Consistent with the racist origins of American drugs laws, African Americans and other minorities bore the brunt of the War on Drugs (WOD) and were disproportionately represented among those arrested, prosecuted, convicted, and sentenced for drug infractions. As we see in Figure 4.5, African Americans made up about 13 percent of illegal drug users, which happens to be their proportion in the general American population. In other words, at the height of the drugs war, African Americans were no more likely to be using illegal drugs than the general population; but they were nearly three times more likely to be arrested ($35 \div 13$), four times more likely to be prosecuted ($55 \div 13$), and almost six times more likely to be incarcerated ($74 \div 13$).

Enforcement data in various states and localities show even more striking disparities. For example, Georgia law allowed for a life sentence for a second drug offense and, as of 1995, this clause was applied in only 1 percent of second convictions for white offenders, but in 16 percent of cases where the offender was African American. "The result:" writes sociologist David Cole, "98.4 percent of those serving life sentences under the provision were black."[99] More astonishing figures from Baltimore—before and after the WOD was in full throttle—are seen in Figure 4.6.

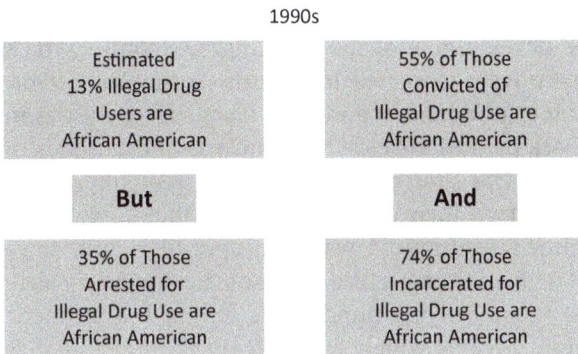

1990s

Estimated 13% Illegal Drug Users are African American	55% of Those Convicted of Illegal Drug Use are African American
But	**And**
35% of Those Arrested for Illegal Drug Use are African American	74% of Those Incarcerated for Illegal Drug Use are African American

FIGURE 4.5
African Americans involved in the criminal justice system.

Source: Data derived from "The Numbers Beyond the Bling," Ward Harkavy, *The Village Voice*, December 2004.

As if drug criminalization didn't wreak enough havoc on poor minority communities through mass incarceration (see more details in Chapter 7), the 1996 Welfare Reform Act denied welfare benefits to convicted drug offenders; the Anti-Drug Abuse Act of 1998 required the management at federally funded housing agencies to evict tenants involved in drug-related crimes; and the Higher Education Act passed that same year denied student aid to convicted drug offenders. Imagine a drug addict just released from prison, homeless, $50 in his pocket, and unemployed; it is a system that could not be better designed to ensure a return to drug use to escape the miseries of the real world and/or a return to drug sales to earn a living.

As this book was being written, the United States was being roiled by an opioid overdose epidemic. According to the National Institute on Drug Abuse, more than 130 people die every day from an opioid overdose;[100] and, according to the Centers for Disease Control (CDC), between 1999

	1980	1990
Number of *white* juveniles arrested for selling	18	13
Number of *black* juveniles arrested for selling	86	1,304

FIGURE 4.6
Arrests for drug sales, Baltimore, before and after the war on drugs was underway.

Source: Data obtained from David Cole, *No Equal Justice: Race and Class in the American Criminal Justice System*, The New Press, New York, 1999, p. 145.

and 2017 almost 400,000 people died from an opioid overdose.[101] This epidemic began with the development of the painkiller Oxycontin, which was aggressively and deceptively marketed to doctors in the mid-1990s. Doctors began prescribing it for a host of ailments, from sports injuries in high school athletes to back pain in the elderly. Hundreds of thousands of people became addicted to Oxy and other prescription painkillers and, when they could not get it from their doctors anymore, they took to the streets. On the streets, they found heroin was a cheaper high; but, since street drugs are often cut with adulterants, the purity of the drugs they were getting was unknown to them. Then, around 2010, fentanyl, a synthetic and far more potent opioid became widely available on the street, first as an adulterant, and then as a drug of choice. (Much of that fentanyl is being ordered on the darknet and is produced in, and sent from China.)

Two facets of the current opioid epidemic are particularly noteworthy to the conflict theorist. First, a sizeable, but unknown proportion of the millions of addictions, overdose deaths, and near-overdose deaths can be traced back to the deceptive marketing of prescription painkillers by pharmaceutical companies. Thus, large corporations bear considerable responsibility for much of the enormous amounts of personal and societal harms caused by opioids, arguably making this a white-collar crime of immense proportions. Yet we saw little progress in assigning criminal responsibility to these corporations until after hundreds of thousands of deaths had occurred. The other aspect of the opioid crisis that is of interest to the conflict theorist is that the face of the current crisis is white; whereas the face of the crack "epidemic" of the 1980s was black. The official response to the black crack epidemic was more severe—some would say "draconian"—criminal penalties; whereas the response to the white opioid epidemic has been a much more sympathetic swing toward treatment rather than punishment.

"Victimless" crimes

Crimes such as the possession of illegal drugs, gambling, prostitution, and a host of other offenses[102] are often referred to as "victimless crimes" because they involve willing participants who are harming no one else. When criminologists and policymakers refer to these offenses as victimless crimes, they often do so while arguing that one or more of these behaviors should be legalized. The arguments for legalization are multifaceted and compelling. One argument holds that criminalization leads to criminal markets and the emergence of organized crime. When drugs are made illegal, for example, legal suppliers are driven out of the market, prices go up; and higher prices incentivize criminal suppliers. Then criminal suppliers fight among one another to protect or increase their share of the market; and gangs and gang violence become a problem. This was the case with Prohibition in the 1920s; and it is still the case with the gangs and cartels surrounding the illegal drug industry today. Furthermore, the high prices of illegal goods incentivizes consumers (addicts, for example) to commit crimes in order to afford the goods; and the exorbitant profits to be made from illegal markets incentivizes bribery and the corruption of law enforcement officials (as was the case with Prohibition, and is the case with drug cartels in Mexico today).

It is on victimless crimes that problematic police behaviors are often centered. As there are no victims to report a case and see it though the criminal justice system, law enforcement officials can be paid—sometimes handsomely—to "look the other way" without being held accountable (a common plotline in many police/crime dramas). Also, because there are no victims to report these crimes, the police may use dubious or illegal tactics to uncover them, such as illegal wiretapping or entrapment. Thus, criminalization engenders more crime as well as the corruption of the police and other forms of police misconduct.

Lastly, many proponents of legalization argue that the state should not be meddling in people's private affairs, and that the state should not be legislating morality. Morality is constantly changing; and for some people, the laws that criminalize victimless behaviors are themselves immoral. Keep in mind that homosexuality was once criminalized; and cannabis is being gradually decriminalized in numerous parts of United States. Law enforcement resources, they argue, should instead be focused on more universally acknowledged crimes, that is, on crimes with victims.

Since every State has laws criminalizing certain behaviors that critics call "victimless," obviously, there are some compelling arguments for retaining such laws. For one thing, it could be argued that all laws represent the legislation of morality. We are morally offended by rape and murder, so we have laws banning these behaviors. Thus, in the case of victimless crimes, there is simply less consensus over whether these behaviors are morally offensive. More importantly, defenders of these laws argue that such behaviors do indeed have victims. The drug addict's victims include his or her family, which must cope with their behaviors and the lost income that often comes with addiction; society is also a victim of the lost productivity, which comes with millions of drug addicts who would work harder if they were not stoned so often; and taxpayers are victims when so much money is being spent on drug rehabilitation and social services that are afforded to drug addicts. The gambler's victims include his or her family who may be left destitute by their gambling losses. Lastly, the prostitute is often herself a victim of a pimp who is forcing her to engage in sex work and allows her only a small portion of the proceeds from such work.

Another argument in favor of retaining such laws is that these laws help to prevent other crimes with more certain victims. Violent and property crimes often flourish in the same neighborhoods where drug abuse, gambling, and/or prostitution flourish. Applying the "broken windows" theory (see page 41), high rates of drug abuse, gambling, and/or prostitution—especially in public—are an indicator that the police are neglecting an area and give criminals confidence that they can commit crime with impunity. Thus, by retaining these laws, police are able to clean up the streets, maintain order, and prevent other crimes.

Theoretical connections

Routine activities theory and conflict theory are particularly relevant to this last section on patterns of crime. The emergence of the internet as a critical element in most people's everyday routines has made available a wide variety of criminal activities. Social media has made cyberbullying common, with a large number of willing offenders, potential victims (targets), and a lack of guardianship (adult onlookers). Much the same can be said of the availability of child pornography, drugs, and weapons on the dark web. Social media, an aging population and the increasing frequency of weather-related disasters have each increased the numbers of susceptible targets for would-be scammers.

White collar crime and drug legislation are prime for the application of conflict theory. As we have discussed, white collar "crimes" can be far more destructive than street crimes; but with the laws being written by fellow elites, they are either not prohibited by law, or white collar criminals are able to avoid the severe penalties so often meted out to poor criminals. For most of the twentieth century and into the new millennium, those severe penalties have been eagerly meted out to poor minority drug users. However, when the stereotypical drug user became white, it has suddenly dawned on policymakers and the majority population that the severity of punishments for drug violations needs to be reconsidered. As we will see in Chapter 7, Michelle Alexander has made a compelling argument that drug enforcement in the United States is simply the most recent chapter in a long history of the oppression of the black minority.

The work of Joseph Gusfield on status politics and the American temperance movement sheds some light on our understanding of the status of victimless crimes. Gusfield suggests that, though the prohibition of alcohol in the 1920s was flagrantly disregarded and led to the rise of organized crime, the enactment of Prohibition represented a symbolic victory for teetotaling Protestants over newly arriving Catholic immigrants, showing them who was in charge.[103] Similarly, as justifications for the criminalization of victimless crimes are often rooted in biblical scripture, the retention of these laws represents a form of symbolic victory for fundamentalist Christians over secularists. Likewise, as these laws are struck from legal codes (as in the case of homosexuality and, increasingly, cannabis), this represents political inroads that are being made by secularists in various parts of the United States. Accordingly, decriminalization usually engenders great consternation from more devout Christians, not just because it violates their religious beliefs, but also because it signifies their loss of power in shaping the law. Gusfield's theory also represents a form of conflict theory as it concerns the power conflict between interests groups; that is, between fundamentalists and secularists.

NOTES

1 Data derived from Franklin Zimring, "The City that Became Safe: New York and the Future of Crime Control," working paper. www.scribd.com/document/48102346/Zimring-Journal-Article. Retrieved December 16, 2018. Decreases confirmed in Zimring's *The City that Became Safe: New York's Lessons for Urban Crime and Its Control*, Table 1.3, Oxford University Press, reprint edition, 2013, p. 16.

2 Rick Nevin, "How lead exposure relates to temporal changes in IQ, violent crime, and unwed pregnancy." *Environmental Research*, vol. 83, no. 1, 2000, pp. 1–22. National Public Radio, "Criminologist Believes Violent Behavior is Biological," April 13, 2013. www.npr.org/2013/05/01/180096559/criminologist-believes-violent-behavior-is-biological. Retrieved July 29, 2019.

3 Steven Levitt, "The limited role of changing age structure in explaining aggregate crime rates," *Criminology*, vol. 37, no. 3, 1999, pp. 581–97. Levitt argues that the baby boom can explain 10 to 20 percent of the rise in violent crime from 1960 to 1980, but that the age distribution of the population had or would have far less impact in subsequent years.

4 Tim Newburn, *Criminology: A Very Short Introduction*, Oxford: Oxford University Press, 2018.

5 Gallup Website, "Crime," https://news.gallup.com/poll/1603/crime.aspx. Retrieved December 17, 2018.

6 Jonathan Intravia, Kevin Wolff, Rocio Paez, and Bejamin Gibbs, "Investigating the Relationship between Social Media Consumption and Fear of Crime: A Partial Analysis of Mostly Young Adults," *Computers and Human Behavior*, vol. 77, December 2017, pp. 158–168.

7 "Industrialized world" is an important qualifier here. There are dozens of countries with higher murder rates than the United States; but, with the exception of Russia, these are all poorer countries, sometimes called "developing" or "Third World" countries, or countries in the "Global South" (view the data at https://data.worldbank.org/indicator/VC.IHR.PSRC.P5?year_high_desc=true). Retrieved January 2, 2019.

8 World Bank data at https://data.worldbank.org/indicator/VC.IHR.PSRC.P5?year_high_desc=true. WorldAtlas.com provides more detailed breakdowns, showing the U.S. at 4.88, and Singapore and Japan at 0.31 and 0.25, respectively, www.worldatlas.com/articles/murder-rates-by-country.html. Retrieved January 2, 2019.

9 James Lynch and William Pridemore, "Crime in International Perspective," from *Crime and Public Policy*, J.Q. Wilson and J. Petersilia, eds., New York: Oxford University Press, 2011.

10 Adam Lankford, "Public Mass Shootings: A Cross-National Study of 171 Countries," *Violence and Victims*, vol. 31, no. 2, 2016, p. 189.

11 Ibid. Lankford citing Rasmussen Reports, p. 189.

12 Handguns accounted for 47 percent of all homicides in the United States in 2016. Federal Bureau of Investigation, *Crime in the United States, 2016*. Expanded Homicide Data Table 4. https://ucr.fbi.gov/crime-in-the-u.s/2016/crime-in-the-u.s.-2016/tables/expanded-homicide-data-table-4.xls. Retrieved January 3, 2019.

13 "Gun homicides and gun ownership listed by country," *The Guardian*, www.theguardian.com/news/datablog/2012/jul/22/gun-homicides-ownership-world-list. Retrieved January 3, 2019.

14 Lankford, "Public Mass Shootings." These numbers were derived in 2007, before Yemen's civil war.

15 Steven Messner and Richard Rosenfeld, *Crime and the American Dream*, 5th ed., Belmont, CA: Wadsworth, 2012.

16 David Luckenbill, "Criminal Homicide as a Situated Transaction," *Social Problems*, vol. 25, no. 2, December, 1977.

17 Martin Daly, *Killing the Competition: Economic Inequality and Homicide*, New Brunswick, NJ: Transaction Publishers, 2016.

18 Maia Szalavitz, "Surprising factors driving murder rates: Income inequality and respect," *The Guardian*, December 8, 2017. www.theguardian.com/us-news/2017/dec/08/income-inequality-murder-homicide-rates. Retrieved January 6, 2019.

19 Ibid.

20 Federal Bureau of Investigation, Crime in the United States, Expanded Homicide Data, Table 3. https://ucr.fbi.gov/crime-in-the-u.s/2017/crime-in-the-u.s.-2017/topic-pages/tables/expanded-homicide-data-table-3.xls. Retrieved February 23, 2019. Data apply only to those homicides where the sex of the offender is known.

21 Mark Follman, Gavin Aronson, and Deanna Pan, "U.S. Mass Shootings, 1982–2019: Data from Mother Jones' Investigation," Mother Jones, updated February 15, 2019. www.motherjones.com/politics/2012/12/mass-shootings-mother-jones-full-data/. Retrieved February 25, 2019.

22 James Messerschmidt and Stephen Tomsen, "Masculinities, Crime, and Criminal Justice," Oxford Handbooks Online, February 2016.

23 Rachel Kalish and Michael Kimmel, "Suicide by Mass Murder: Masculinity, Aggrieved Entitlement, and Rampage School Shootings," *Health Sociology Review*, vol. 19, no. 4, 2010, pp. 451–464.

24 Dana Truman, David Tokar, and Ann Fisher, "Dimensions of Masculinity: Relations to Date Rape Supportive Attitudes and Sexual Aggression in Dating Situations," *Journal of Counseling & Development*, Jul/Aug96, Vol. 74, Issue 6.

25 Doug Schrock and Irene Padavic, "Negotiating Manhood," Contests over Identity in a Men's Anti-Battering Program," Conference Paper, American Sociological Association, Montreal, 2006.

26 Paul Stretesky and Mark Pogrebin, "Gang-Related Gun Violence," *Journal of Contemporary Ethnography*, vol. 36, no. 1, February 2007, pp. 85–114.

27 American Psychological Association, *APA Guidelines for Psychological Practice with Boys and Men*, August 2018, p. 3. www.apa.org/about/policy/boys-men-practice-guidelines.pdf. Retrieved February 25, 2019.

28 Larry Davich, "For most Males, "Toxic masculinity" is What Raised Us from Boys to Men," *Chicago Tribune*, January 21, 2019. www.chicagotribune.com/suburbs/post-tribune/opinion/ct-ptb-davich-toxic-masculinity-versus-decades-of-social-conditioning-st-0121-story.html. Retrieved February 29, 2019.

29 U.S. Department of Justice, Office on Violence Against Women, www.justice.gov/ovw/domestic-violence. Retrieved March 18, 2019.

30 Jacquelyn Campbell, N. Glass, P. Sharps, K. Laughon, and T. Bloom, "Intimate Partner Violence: Review and Implications of Research and Policy," *Trauma, Violence, and Abuse*, vol. 8, no. 3, July 7, pp. 246–269.

31 Ibid., p. 246.

32 Ibid.

33 Ibid.

34 Citing data from the Domestic Violence Intervention Program, Jennifer O'Neill reports "Women are 70 times more likely to be killed in the two weeks after leaving than at any other time during the relationship." In "Domestic Violence Statistics: The Horrific Reality," *Good Housekeeping*, February 24, 2016. www.goodhousekeeping.com/life/relationships/a37005/statistics-about-domestic-violence/. Retrieved March 19, 2019.

35 Phillip Jenkins, *Using Murder: The Social Construction of Serial Homicide.* New York: Aldine de Gruyter, 1994, 61.

36 Ibid. p. 64.

37 Ibid.

38 Ibid., p. 22.

39 Ibid., p. 17.

40 See Abené Clayton, "What Counts as a Mass Shooting?" *The Guardian*, December 13, 2019, www.theguardian.com/us-news/2019/dec/13/what-counts-as-a-mass-shooting-the-dangerous-effects-of-varying-definitions?CMP=Share_AndroidApp_Email. Retrieved December 13, 2019.

41 Lankford, "Public Mass Shootings," p. 188.

42 Quoted in David Paradice, "An Analysis of US School Shooting Data (1840–2015)," *Education*, vol. 138, no. 2, Winter 2017, p. 136. Original source: NE Nedzel, "Concealed Carry: The Only Way to Discourage Mass Shootings," *Academic Questions*, 27, 2014.

43 Ibid.

44 James, Knoll and Ronald Pies, "Moving Beyond Motives in Mass Shootings," *Psychiatric Times*, vol. 36, no. 1, January 2019.

45 Kieran Corcoran, Sinead Baker, and David Choi, "The FBI Has Closed its Investigation of the Las Vegas Mass Shooting …", Business Insider, January 29, 2019. www.businessinsider.com/timeline-shows-exactly-how-the-las-vegas-massacre-unfolded-2018-9. Retrieved April 1, 2019.

46 Knoll and Pies, "Moving Beyond Motives."

47 Lankford, "Public Mass Shootings."

48 Ibid.

49 Sean Rossman, "Australia Changed its Gun Laws after a 1996 Mass Shooting," *USA Today*, November 8, 2018. www.usatoday.com/story/news/nation-now/2018/11/08/thousand-oaks-shooting-australia-no-mass-shootings-since-1996/1934798002/. Retrieved April 2, 2019.

50 "What Is Terrorism," *The Economist*, March 2, 1996, 23.

51 Paul Butler, "Terrorism and Utilitarianism: Lessons from and for Criminal Law," *Journal of Criminal Law and Criminology*, vol. 93, no. 1, Fall 2002, 3.

52 Richard J. Goldstone, "International Law and Justice and America's War on Terrorism," *Social Research*, vol. 68, no. 4, Winter 2002, 1045–1054.

53 Dan Smith, *The Penguin State of the World Atlas*, 7th ed. New York: Penguin Books, 2003, 70.

54 "Language When Reporting Terrorism," British Broadcasting Corporation, Editorial Guidelines. www.bbc.co.uk/editorialguidelines/guidance/terrorism-language/guidance-full. Retrieved May 10, 2019.

55 Tom Malinowski, "America's Greatest Terrorist Threat? White Supremacists," *Washington Post*, May 3, 2019. www.washingtonpost.com/opinions/can-we-forget-politics-and-just-focus-on-keeping-people-safe/2019/05/03/d6cfe574-6d24-11e9-8f44-e8d8bb1df986_story.html?utm_term=.f3c8c138e84d. Retrieved May 10, 2019. Jonathan Chait, "Why Trump is Soft on White Supremacist Terrorism," *New York Magazine*, April 29, 2019, http://nymag.com/intelligencer/2019/04/trump-white-supremacist-terrorism-synagogue-mosque-shooting.html. Retrieved May 10, 2019.

56 See Paul Joosse, "Elves, Environmentalism, and Eco-Terror: Leaderless Resistance and Media Coverage of the Earth Liberation Front," *Crime, Media, Culture*, vol. 8, no. 1, April 2012, pp. 75–93.

57 Butler, "Terrorism and Utilitarianism," 10.

58 Federal Bureau of Investigation, Crime in the United States, 2017, Table 1, "Crime in the United States by Volume and Rate per 100,000 Inhabitants, 1998–2017. https://ucr.fbi.gov/crime-in-the-u.s/2017/crime-in-the-u.s.-2017/topic-pages/tables/table-1. Retrieved September 27, 2019.

59 First figure derived using the UCR Data Tool. Results from state-level crime estimates database. www.ucrdatatool.gov/Search/Crime/State/RunCrimeStatebyState.cfm. The second figure comes from FBI, 2017 Crime in the United States, Property Crime, https://ucr.fbi.gov/crime-in-the-u.s/2017/crime-in-the-u.s.-2017/topic-pages/property-crime. Retrieved May 14, 2019.

60 Kate Bowers, Shane Johnson, Ken Pease, "Prospective Hot-Spotting: The Future of Crime Mapping?" *British Journal of Criminology*, vol. 44, 2004, pp. 641–658.

61 Federal Bureau of Investigation, "UCR Offense Definitions," www.ucrdatatool.gov/offenses.cfm. Retrieved May 15, 2015.

62 Carlos Blanco, J. Grant, N. Petry, H.B. Simpson, A. Alegria, S-M Liu, and D. Hasin, "Prevalence and Correlates of Shoplifting in the United States, *American Journal of Psychiatry*, July 2008, pp. 905–913. www.ncbi.nlm.nih.gov/pmc/articles/PMC4104590/. Retrieved September 25, 2019.

63 Ibid.

64 "432,000 Shoplifters and Dishonest Employees Apprehended in 2017," *Security: Solutions for Enterprise Security Leaders*, vol. 55, no. 7, July 2018, p. 12. Alex Moshakis, "Nation of Shoplifters: The Rise of Super-Market Self-Checkout Scams," *The Guardian*, May 20, 2018. www.theguardian.com/global/2018/may/20/nation-of-shoplifters-supermarket-self-checkout. Retrieved May 15, 2019.

65 Katie Reilly, "Shoplifting and Other Fraud Cost Retailers Nearly $50 Billion Last Year," *Money*, June 22, 2017. http://money.com/money/4829684/shoplifting-fraud-retail-survey/. Retrieved May 15, 2019.

66 Federal Trade Commission, "Romance Scams Rank Number One on Total Reported Losses," *Data Spotlight*. February 12, 2019. www.ftc.gov/news-events/blogs/data-spotlight/2019/02/romance-scams-rank-number-one-total-reported-losses. Retrieved May 16, 2019.

67 For examples, *The Sting* (1973), *The Sting II* (1983), *The Grifters* (1990), *Confidence* (2003), *American Hustle* (2013).

68 See "Elder Abuse Resource Roadmap: Financial," Department of Justice, October 3, 2016. www.justice.gov/elderjustice/file/900221/download. Retrieved May 17, 2019.

69 Marck Lachs and S. Duke Han, "Age Associated Financial Vulnerability: An Emerging Public Health Issue," *Annals of Internal Medicine*, vol. 16, no. 11, Dec. 1, 2015.

70 Federal Communications Commission, "COVID-19 Consumer Warnings and Safety Tips." www.fcc.gov/covid-scams. Retrieved April 19, 2020.

71 Monica Anderson, Andrew Perrin, Jingjing Jiang, and Madhumitha, Kumar, "10% of Americans Don't use the Internet. Who are they?" Pew Research Center, April 22, 2019. www.pewresearch.org/fact-tank/2019/04/22/some-americans-dont-use-the-internet-who-are-they/. Retrieved May 19, 2019.

72 Grainne Kirwin and Andrew Power, *Cybercrime: The Psychology of Online Offenders.* New York: Cambridge University Press, 2013, p. 3.

73 Ibid.

74 Bahadir Eresti and Yavuz Akbulut, "Reactions to Cyberbullying among High School and University Students," *Social Science Journal*, March 2019, vol. 56, no. 1, pp. 10–20.

75 Martin Evans, "Cyber Crime: 1 in 10 People Now Victim of Fraud or Online Offenses, Figure Show," *The Telegraph*, July 21, 2016. www.telegraph.co.uk/news/2016/07/21/one-in-people-now-victims-of-cyber-crime/. Retrieved May 20, 2019.

76 Joan Lube and Sarah Kertz, "Increasing Suicide Rates in Early Adolescent Girls in the United States and the Equalization of Sex Disparity in Suicide: The Need to Investigate the Role of Social Media," *JAMA Network*, May 17, 2019. https://jamanetwork.com/journals/jamanetworkopen/fullarticle/2733419?resultClick=3. Retrieved May 20, 2019.

77 Gabriel Weimann, "Going Dark: Terrorism on the Web," *Studies in Conflict and Terrorism*, vol. 39, no. 3, 2016. Pp. 195–206.

78 Research on the Dark Web is fairly new and the terminology not yet agreed upon. Some people use "Dark Web" and "Darknet" to refer to both legal and illegal activities. Some capitalize the terms while others do not. The terms "darknet" and "darknet market" are also used.

79 Ibid.

80 Eric Jardine, "Privacy, Censorship, Data Breaches and Internet Freedom," *New Media and Society*, vol. 20, no. 8, 2018, pp. 2824–2843.

81 For murder for hire, see Andy Greenberg, "Meet the 'Assassination Market Creator' Who's Crowdfunding Murder with Bitcoin," *Forbes*, November 18, 2013. www.forbes.com/sites/andygreenberg/2013/11/18/meet-the-assassination-market-creator-whos-crowdfunding-murder-with-bitcoins/#798ed58c3d9b. Retrieved May 22, 2019. For assassination scams, see Jasper Hamill, "Dark web 'hitmen-for-hire' service EXPOSED: Inside the 'assassination marketplace' that's hiding a shocking secret," *The Mirror*, May 17, 2016. www.mirror.co.uk/tech/dark-web-hitmen-hire-service-7988693. Retrieved May 22, 2019.

82 Rebecca Campbell, "The Silk Road: A Story of Bitcoin, Drugs, and the Dark Web," Block Explorer News, December 1, 2018. https://blockexplorer.com/news/silk-road-timeline-bitcoin-drugs-dark-web/. Retrieved May 22, 2019.

83 Adrian Chen, "The Underground Website Where You Can Purchase Every Drug Imaginable," Gawker, June 1, 2011, https://gawker.com/the-underground-website-where-you-can-buy-any-drug-imag-30818160. Retrieved May 22, 2019.

84 Adam Winstock, et al., *Global Drug Survey*, 2019 Executive Summary, www.globaldrugsurvey.com/wp-content/themes/globaldrugsurvey/results/GDS2019-Exec-Summary.pdf. Retrieved May 23, 2019.

85 Ibid.

86 Sally Simpson, "Reimagining Sutherland 80 Years after White-Collar Crime," *Criminology*, vol. 57, no. 2, May 2019, pp. 189–207.

87 Ibid.

88 Edwin Sutherland, *White Collar Crime*, Hinsdale, IL: Dryden Press, 1949, p. 8.

89 Ronald Kramer, "A Prolegomenon to the Study of Corporate Violence," Humanity and Society, vol. 7, 1983, p. 166.

90 Mark Dowie, "Pinto Madness," in J. H. Skolnick and E. Currie (eds.), *Crisis in American Institutions*, 9th ed. New York: HarperCollins, 1994, 23–38, at 37.

91 Miyo Geyelin, "How a Memo Written 26 Years Ago is Costing General Motors Dearly," *Wall Street Journal*, September 29, 1999. www.wsj.com/articles/SB9385366607816889. Retrieved May 26, 2019.

92 Sally Simpson, "Reimagining."

93 Patricia Morgan, "The Legislation of Drug Law: Economic Crisis and Social Control," *Journal of Drug Issues*, vol. 8, no. 1 p. 58.

94 Richard Bonnie and Charles Whitebread, *The Marijuana Conviction: A History of Marijuana Prohibition in the United States*, New York: The Lindesmith Center, 1999, p. 34.

95 Foundation for Economic Education, "The Racist Roots of Marijuana Prohibition," April 11, 2017. https://fee.org/articles/the-racist-roots-of-marijuana-prohibition/. Retrieved June 10, 2019.

96 Michael Woodiwiss, *Organized Crime and American Power*, University of Toronto Press, 2001, p. 223.

97 David Musto, *The American Disease: Origins of Narcotic Control*, New York: Oxford University Press, 1987, p. 229.

98 Ibid., p. 7.

99 David Cole, *No Equal Justice: Race and Class in the American Criminal Justice System.* New York: The New Press, 1999, p. 143.

100 National Institute on Drugs Abuse, "Opioid Overdose Crisis," January 2019. www.drugabuse.gov/drugs-abuse/opioids/opioid-overdose-crisis. Retrieved May 26, 2019.

101 Centers for Disease Control, "Opioid Overdose: Understanding the Epidemic," www.cdc.gov/drugoverdose/epidemic/index.html. Retrieved May 26, 2019.

102 Most of the criticisms of "overcriminalization" that follow were detailed by Norval Morris and Gordon Hawkins in 1970. They include in their discussion drugs, gambling, prostitution, statutory rape, adultery, homosexuality, bigamy, vagrancy, disorderly conduct, and other offenses. The laws against some of these behaviors have since been relaxed in some, most, or all jurisdictions. See Morris and Hawkins, *The Honest Politician's Guide to Crime Control.* Chicago, IL: University of Chicago Press, 1970.

103 Joseph Gusfield, *Symbolic Crusade: Status Politics and the American Temperance Movement*, 2nd ed. Chicago: University of Chicago Press, 1986.

CHAPTER 5

The police

There is a large variety of law enforcement agencies and law enforcement officials at the federal level, including the Federal Bureau of Investigation, the Drug Enforcement Administration, the Secret Service, the U.S. Marshalls Office, U.S. Customs and Immigration Enforcement, and quite a few other agencies. Then there are numerous state-level agencies of law enforcement, including the state police and state bureaus of investigation. As this is a brief volume, in this chapter we will be focusing largely on local law enforcement, mainly the kinds of law enforcement that we see in our everyday lives; the "beat cops," and the patrol officers; although, we will also be examining the deployment of police officers in crowd control and in SWAT teams.

HISTORY OF THE POLICE

Early human communities were quite small and homogeneous. Everyone knew one another; and there was relatively little variation in experiences, beliefs, values, and social status. There was little temptation to deviate from the norms. For those who were tempted—in such intimate groupings—rumor, gossip, and ostracism acted as powerful means of social control. Things changed with the Agricultural Revolution. Advances in farming techniques made it possible for some people to produce a surplus of food. This meant that everyone did not have to be engaged in food production and living on farms. Towns and cities emerged; and the division of labor became more complex as people became engaged in occupations other than food production, such as merchants, craftspeople, and people offering their services for hire. People began traveling from city to city engaging in trade or looking for work. The ability to produce surpluses, the variety of occupations, and the emergence of people without work to do—all of these meant increasing levels of inequality between the haves and the have-nots, and far less homogeneity in experiences, beliefs, and values. Further, there was more temptation to commit crime; and rumor, gossip, and ostracism were less effective means of social control as the community became less intimate. As cities and towns grew larger, there was greater opportunity to commit a crime without being identified; and offenders had the opportunity to flee to another town.

All of these processes accelerated with the Industrial Revolution, when the division of labor increased exponentially, more and more people moved from the countryside to the cities for factory work, and unemployment was an ever-present problem in the new urban metropolises. *The evolution of the police closely parallels the evolution of human civilization, with the most important factor being the development of cities.* (In fact, the word "police" is derived from the Greek *polis*, meaning "city-state.") According to Gary Marx, the importance of the police in maintaining social order, "increases with the heterogeneity and size of a society."[1]

Before the Industrial Revolution, specialized police forces, as we know them, did not exist. Depending on the part of the world, those forces tasked with crime control also had responsibilities for sanitation, putting out fires, enforcing quarantines, tax collecting, and other such public concerns. Rather than being specialized work, regular citizens were conscripted into law enforcement duties. In the frankpledge system of eleventh century England, for example, each able-bodied male over the age of 12 was required to join with nine of his neighbors to form a *tithing* and each member was responsible for the behavior of all of the other members. "By being in a tithing," writes Carl Klockars, "each man promised, in advance of any wrong-doing, that he had already assembled a nine-man police force to apprehend, incarcerate, and deliver [the offender] to court ..."[2] The frankpledge system was followed by the *parish constable* system, which required one man in a parish to serve as the parish constable. He served a one-year term; and the responsibility rotated among the men in the parish. He had the authority to conscript men and to organize them into a night watch. Neither the parish constable nor the night watchmen were paid for their services and, as a result, this was a haphazard form of law enforcement. These men either had to focus their time and energies on their other jobs to earn a living; or, to put food on the table, they could use their policing authority to exact bribes from the citizenry.[3]

Such unstructured and unspecialized systems of law enforcement puttered along until they were overwhelmed by the sudden and rapid social changes brought on by the Industrial Revolution. "Roving gangs of thugs," writes Gresham Sykes, "sporadic outbreaks of violence, and the growing threat of the desperate poor living in urban squalor all gave strength to the argument that a full-time, well-trained police force was a necessity."[4] The most important proponent of such a force was Robert Peel, the British Home Secretary (roughly equivalent to the U.S. Attorney General). In 1829, Peel introduced the Metropolitan Police Act and convinced the British Parliament of the need for a specialized full-time police force. The force would be uniformed and organized along military lines. For Peel, "The basic mission for which the police exist is to prevent crime and disorder."[5] To achieve this goal, Peel considered it critically important that the police gain the public's trust. To this end, the police should only use force as a last resort; that is, "only when the exercise of persuasion, advice and warning is found to be insufficient."[6] Measuring the success of the police by measuring arrest rates encourages overzealous policing, which, in turn, weakens the public trust. Instead, success should be measured by a reduction in crime rates.[7] The principles embodied in the Metropolitan Police Act "shaped the development of modern policing in Britain and in many other countries throughout the world."[8] The British people were, at first, apprehensive of this new police force; but the officers conducted themselves with professionalism and made the streets safer. Soon they were embraced by the public and affectionately called Bobby's Boys" and later just "bobbies" (in honor of Sir Robert Peel).

Early American communities had systems of law enforcement similar to the English, with the conscription of men into constabulary and night watch service on a rotating, term-limited basis. These systems were overwhelmed by urbanization much like their British counterparts; but in the nineteenth century they also had to deal with urban riots, which occurred with quite some frequency in the United States. In 1845, New York established a full-time force similar to London's; and other major cities in the United States soon followed suit.

Unlike their British counterparts, known for their professionalism, the American police forces were notorious for their corruption. Much of this corruption stemmed from the job insecurity that was endemic to the system of patronage that was common throughout the country. In this system (also known as the "spoils system"), officials would award civil service jobs as political favors. Thus, when a new mayor took office, he would fire the old police chief and hire a new one; and when the new police chief came in, he would fire the old police officers and hire new ones. "Police posts," writes Bruce Smith, "of both low and high degree were constantly changing hands with political fixers determining the price and conditions of each change."[9] There was no job security in such an environment and police personnel could expect to be unemployed in a short period of time. This situation provided police officers and their superiors with incentive to use their position to make as much money as quickly as they could by accepting bribes and extorting money from the people they were hired to protect.

To address this kind of corruption, the Pendleton Act was passed in 1883. This legislation made it difficult to fire federal employees without just cause. Eventually, state and local laws were passed to ensure job security for almost all civil servants. Today, police officers and other public employees enjoy more job security than do their counterparts in the private sector, as long as they conduct themselves professionally. This job security has become an attractive feature of police work. "Extraordinary job security is every civil servant's most cherished perk," writes Brendan Koerner. Job security contributed to the professionalization of the police by providing a powerful incentive for police personnel to conduct themselves professionally.[10]

POLICE POWERS AND THE POTENTIAL FOR ABUSE

In the name of ensuring public safety, the police are authorized by the state to exercise coercive—even deadly—force. Force, of course, can be necessary to subdue or gain compliance from offenders, but "too much force may cause physical, financial, or psychological harm to all those involved, while too little force may cause the situation to escalate, risking harm to the community."[11] This is an awesome amount of authority; and it will be useful here to distinguish between "force" and "violence." *Force is the use of physical coercion, which is legitimated by the state; whereas violence is not legitimated by the state.* When a police officer kills someone in the line of duty, this would be considered an exercise of force. When someone kills a police officer, this would be an application of violence. The difference between force and violence is not always so clear-cut, though, because there are numerous legal and ethical constraints on the police use of force; and the use of excessive force by the police can cross the line into violence.[12]

Furthermore, the police have the authority to make an arrest; that is, the power to deprive someone of their freedom—another awesome responsibility; and this one allows the potential for corruption. Implicit in the power to make an arrest is the power *not* to make an arrest; and a corrupt police officer may accept a bribe to look the other way during or after the commission of a crime. Carl Klockars describes the somewhat unique work of the police officer, "Unlike most work, policing can be done not only too passively but also too aggressively as well. In addition, policing provides opportunities for abuse and corruption that far exceed those in most other occupations."[13]

RECRUITMENT AND TRAINING

As police officers are vested with these enormous powers—the power to use coercive force and the power to make an arrest—it is essential that police departments be selective in their recruitment and invest in the training of their recruits. Bad recruits, poor training, and police misconduct can jeopardize citizen safety, the relationship between the police and the citizenry, and even the legitimacy of the state.

A leading figure in the professionalization of the American police was August Vollmer. Vollmer was the first chief of police in Berkeley, California in the early twentieth century. According to the city's website, Vollmer established "what we now call a 'Code of Ethics,' which included eliminating the acceptance of gratuities, rewards or favors."[14] Through his connections with the University of California, Vollmer is credited with helping to establish the academic study of police science, criminal justice, and criminalistics; and he was founder and first president of what was to become the American Society of Criminology (ASC).[15] Though the ASC currently has thousands of members worldwide and is open to everyone, the group originally decided "that membership was to be restricted to persons actively engaged as officials and teachers in college and university police training programs."[16] Indeed, Vollmer was among the first to suggest that police officers should have a college education. He was very concerned about public perceptions of the police and he believed that a college education would not only improve the officer's performance of his or her duties, but would also improve their image, arguing for, "higher education as the central element for professionalizing the police, for giving them dignity and raising their social status."[17]

Vollmer's dream of a college education for most or all officers has hardly been realized nearly one hundred years later. According to the Christie Gardiner's research for the Police Foundation, based on a nationwide survey of nearly a thousand agencies, just over 80 percent of those agencies require *only* a high school degree for new recruits.[18] However, Gardiner finds a college degree "can be highly important for promotion" to a supervisory position.[19] A slight majority of agencies provide incentives for their officers to take college-level courses, including tuition assistance and/or higher pay. Two important variables influencing whether an agency encouraged or required a college education in its employment policies were whether the force was unionized and whether the CEO had a master's degree or above. In sum, Gardiner's report found,

> Slightly more than half (51.8%) of sworn officers in the United States have at least a two-year degree, 30.2% have at least a four-year degree, and 5.4% have a graduate degree. This varies considerably by state, region, agency size, CEO education level, union presence, and department type.[20]

The percentage of police officers reported to have a four-year degree today, is roughly the same as that reported for the general population.[21] Distinguishing between "actual" and "perceived" benefits of a college education,

Gardiner found that college educated police officers tended to be better at report writing and better at the use of advanced technology than their lesser educated counterparts.[22]

Under Vollmer's leadership, the Berkeley police department employed intelligence tests in the screening of police recruits, and later employed the psychiatric screening of recruits.[23] Today, all—or virtually all—police departments put their applicants through some form of screening process, including some combination of tests for physical ability, medical condition, written and oral communication skills, problem-solving skills, personality, psychological ability to handle stress; and, of course, there are background checks for criminal behavior; and polygraph tests are quite common. Agencies vary in terms of their standards. For example, a polygraph test that reveals past use of illegal drugs could disqualify a candidate in one jurisdiction and not in another; or, one agency might require that the candidate not have used cannabis within the past two years; for another agency, the standard might be three years. (Of course, this calculus changes when a state legalizes cannabis.)

Few, if any screening techniques are without controversy. Height restrictions, for example, could exclude more applicants of certain national origins than others.[24] If a test of physical prowess does not compensate for the fact that men tend to have greater upper body strength than women, then it could be criticized for discriminating against women; if the test does compensate, then it will be criticized for lowering standards to admit women.[25] Tests of written communication skills and certain personality tests often exclude people of lower socio-economic status. Minorities are at greater risk of this form of discrimination.[26] Psychological tests are supposed to predict who will perform better at police work; but there is little empirical evidence that they serve as successful predictors of such. Psychologist Ellen Kirschman writes,

> Psychologists who screen prospective officers are the first to admit that they are more effective screening problem people out than predicting who will make a good cop and why. Screening is a snapshot of the entry-level officer, considered valid for only one year. The psychological profile you get after the wear and tear of the work itself can look very different …"[27]

Lastly, the ability of polygraph machines to detect lies has been in doubt since they first came into use. A report from the American Psychological Association states,

> The accuracy (i.e., validity) of polygraph testing has long been controversial. An underlying problem is theoretical: There is no evidence that any pattern of physiological reactions is unique to

deception. An honest person may be nervous when answering truthfully and a dishonest person may be non-anxious. Also, there are few good studies that validate the ability of polygraph procedures to detect deception. … Some confusion about polygraph test accuracy arises because they are used for different purposes, and for each context somewhat different theory and research is applicable. Thus, for example, virtually no research assesses the type of test and procedure used to screen individuals for jobs and security clearances.

No one doubts that there is a need to screen applicants for jobs in police work; and, yet, there is little agreement on suitable methods for screening applicants.[28] Increasingly, though, law enforcement executives are coming to recognize the need for diversity on the force. *Beyond the issue of fairness in hiring that is addressed by federal anti-discrimination laws, executives understand that police-community relations require that diversity on the police force reflects the diversity in the community that they are serving.* Executives must ensure that their screening methods are not screening out candidates because of their sociodemographic characteristics, in particular, those groups that are protected by anti-discrimination statutes. As effective police work depends on police–community relations, discriminatory selection practices not only run afoul of the law; but they can also be counterproductive in ensuring public safety.

With regard to diversity, law enforcement agencies are far behind the curve in the recruitment and retention of female police officers. While metropolitan police forces were first established in the United States in the mid-nineteenth century, it would be about a half century before women entered into police work in 1910, working almost exclusively "with women, children, and typewriters."[29] It would be another half century before the first two women were assigned to the same patrol car in Indianapolis in 1967.[30] Today, another half century later, women make up only about 13 percent of all police officers;[31] in 2011, 12 percent of police officers were women; and in 2001, the figure was 11.2 percent.[32] In other words, *progress has been remarkably slow, with the representation of women in policing increasing by only about one percentage point per decade.* The representation of women in police leadership positions is and has been even lower.[33]

Retention of female police officers is especially problematic. Often when they start on the job, they are regarded as "token females;" and they are frequently reminded that they are a "female police officer," and not just a "police officer." They face a number of hurdles over their careers, "such as the 'boys club,' adverse or hostile environments, explicit and subtle harassment, sexism, skewed physical fitness assessments, double standards, and a lack of support and opportunity."[34] Beyond the sexism of their male colleagues and superiors, they also must deal with the sexism of their clients. For example, one officer reports that "citizens would ask when the 'real police' would arrive when she and her female partner responded to a call."[35]

Much of the formal training of new recruits takes place at the police academy. The following description provides an overview of the kinds of instruction typical of police academy training:

> After gaining acceptance into the police academy, recruits participate in classroom and practical instruction. They learn state laws, criminal investigations, patrol procedures, firearms training, traffic control, defensive driving, self-defense, first aid and computer skills. Police academy recruits also undertake physical training and fieldwork that demonstrates their comprehension of classroom instruction. Field exercises include investigating mock criminal scenes, directing traffic, operating police vehicles, arrest techniques, using firearms, fingerprinting and interrogation methods. Police academy training usually takes 22–27 weeks to complete.[36]

Kaitlyn Lynch describes her experience during the "Combat Course" at the police academy in California, including a test that required the cadet to jump out of the passenger seat of a patrol car, fire six rounds into a target 25 yards away, reload, fire at another target 15 yards away, reload, fire six more rounds with their non-dominant hand, reload, fire six more rounds from a kneeling position, and then "run up to and fire at point-blank range two rounds of ammunition into the chests and one round in the heads of two of the three remaining targets."[37] Cadets had to complete this test in both daylight and at nighttime.

One of the dilemmas in police training involves striking a balance between training cadets to serve as "officers of the peace" and honing their skills at self-defense. As peace officers, they need to exhibit good interpersonal skills, inspire trust, cultivate good community relations, and de-escalate potential conflicts. The combat training and the culminating test, described by Lynch above, is problematic. For one thing, the pass/fail test, in Lynch's view, is selecting out "compassionate, respectful, and level-headed" cadets,[38] people who may have become very adept at peacekeeping. Another problem is that new recruits are being trained to see the world as a dangerous place, ready to erupt into violence at any moment. Someone who views the world through this lens may be inclined to be overly aggressive. No doubt, the purpose of such training is to save lives, including the lives of police officers. However, when training emphasizes overcoming resistance and minimizing risks, combat skills take priority over social skills, while the latter are more important in the daily work of policing. Lynch writes,

I watched as cadet after cadet was denied entry into the profession because of their inability to effectively navigate a scenario that mirrored more closely that of a video game than any situation we would likely encounter throughout the duration of our law enforcement careers.[39]

POLICE WORK

The daily activities involved in police work are far more mundane than one might expect from watching crime dramas at the movies, in which "more often than not, police officers are pitted against psychotic killers, serial murderers, and international terrorists."[40] "Reality-based" cop shows on television may only be a little more accurate in their representation of police work. If we think of the scenes captured on video in these shows as a "sample" of police work, we come to realize that this sample is not randomly selected and, therefore not representative. Heiner writes, "The images presented in these shows are far from randomly selected. They are selected, first, on the basis of their entertainment value."[41] Scores of hours of video are edited out in order to produce less than an hour of programming. The problem is that the media are in the business of entertaining and most police work is not very entertaining. "The average cop on television," write Kappeler and Potter, "probably sees more action in a half-hour than most officers witness in an entire career."[42] A great deal of police work is consumed by patrolling, waiting for traffic violations, writing tickets, investigating traffic accidents, writing reports, and responding to calls. Most of the calls deal with crimes that turn out not to be crimes, or with everyday complaints by citizens who do not know who else to call. Barkan and Bryjak write,

> These calls for help range from the silly and absurd to the poignant and tragic. A man stops a patrol car and asks officers if they have a needle-nosed pliers to fix the zipper on his pants. A woman brings her parakeet to the station house to be weighed because she thinks the bird is ill. An invalid falls out of bed and calls for assistance. A man wants the police to notify his sister (who does not have a phone) that their brother has died.[43]

Summarizing a variety of studies looking at the workloads of police officers, Kappeler and Potter conclude that only 10 to 20 percent of their work "matched public perceptions of police officers as crime fighters;" and based on their research, Greene and Klockars found that "the average police officer spent about one hour per week responding to reports of crimes in progress."[44]

The uniformed police officers most people see in their everyday lives are on patrol; and people assume that patrol is a necessary and effective means of crime control. Indeed, about two-thirds of police officers in the United States are assigned to patrol duties.[45] However, the effectiveness of police patrol has been challenged by numerous research studies. The most classic of these was conducted by George Kelling and his associates in Kansas City in the early 1970s.[46] With the cooperation of the police department, researchers divided the 15 police beats in the city into three sectors. In the first sector, the routine preventive patrol in marked police cars was eliminated and police only entered the area to respond to calls from residents; in the second sector, police patrols were maintained at their normal level; and in the third sector, police patrols were doubled or tripled. The researchers were surprised to find that crime rates did not change in any of the three sectors, indicating that routine police patrols had no effect on the incidence of crime. The researchers also tested whether police patrols had any effect on the public's sense of security and, again, they found no effect.[47] (Subsequent research, however, has indicated that foot patrol by uniformed officers "although it does not affect the amount of crime, it does reassure the public psychologically, reducing their fear of crime and increasing their satisfaction with police service.")[48] One important implication of the Kansas City findings was that police executives could safely pull their patrol away from certain areas while they experimented with different models of force deployment, allowing for more flexibility and creativity in their use of their officers.

While police executives and politicians point to crime rates when they call for the hiring of more police officers, research suggests that the number of officers on the beat, in the department, or in the country has little effect on crime rates. In fact, even as the number of police officers per 1,000 residents has been on the decline for the past two decades,[49] as we have seen, so have crime rates. Renowned police scholar David Bayley writes, "Police shouldn't be expected to prevent crime. They are outgunned by circumstances." In other words, if we want to prevent crime, we need to address the causes of crime; and the presence or absence of police has little to do with poverty, unemployment, gender and age distributions of the population, or any of the myriad causes of crime addressed in Chapters 2 and 3 of this volume. On the other hand, this does not mean that we should be eliminating or drastically reducing our police forces because, as Bayley notes, "although criminals do not seem to notice normal changes in the number of police, they would surely notice if there were no police."[50]

POLICE DISCRETION

As we have noted, the police are granted the powers to make an arrest and to employ physical coercion. The very word "power" implies discretion, that is, the authority to decide when to make an arrest, when to employ physical coercion, and when not to. "Discretion can be defined as the power to make a choice."[51] In all hierarchies, the people at the top have more discretion than the people at the bottom; and their decisions are more consequential. Policing is exceptional, however, in that the police officer on the street is often not very high in the chain of command; but she or he has the authority to make decisions that are enormously consequential in the lives of those they police. Richard Uviller writes,

> Wherever power is lodged, discretion flows. Wide or narrow, considered or unconscious, authoritative choices are made by police up and down the line of command. Recognized, studied, described, and criticized, field discretion exercised by police often guides the decision to charge a person with the commission of a crime."[52]

In essence, police officers act as judges and jurors in deciding whether or not real judges and jurors need to play a subsequent role in a given case.

Discretion is part of the everyday work of police, also, because their resources are limited; they simply cannot enforce all of the laws all of the time. Therefore, individual officers set their own priorities, and others are imposed upon them by their supervisors. Albert Reiss writes, "The extent to which police officers are encouraged to exercise discretion varies from department to department, from shift to shift, and among divisions within the same department, but *the exercise of discretion is routine in all police agencies.*"[53] See Figure 5.1.

Beyond setting priorities, there are a number of other variables that may influence the use of discretion. For one, the law is often written in vague terms and it may not be clear to the officer whether the behavior in question constitutes a crime. Or, it may not be clear whether the person in question committed the crime. Likewise, it may not be clear that there is or will be sufficient evidence to enable a successful prosecution. These doubts can interact with one another, along with the officer's and the department's priorities. The officer's decision to make an arrest can also depend on his or her mood and/or personality. Hence, some officers are known on the street or by their colleagues as tough cops or easy cops. While we cannot eliminate the influence of mood and personality on the officer's use of discretion, the extent to which either plays a role compromises the dispensation of even-handed justice. All of these factors concern whether or not to make an arrest; the decision, however, to use coercive force is often more complicated and made very quickly, in what are usually volatile situations.

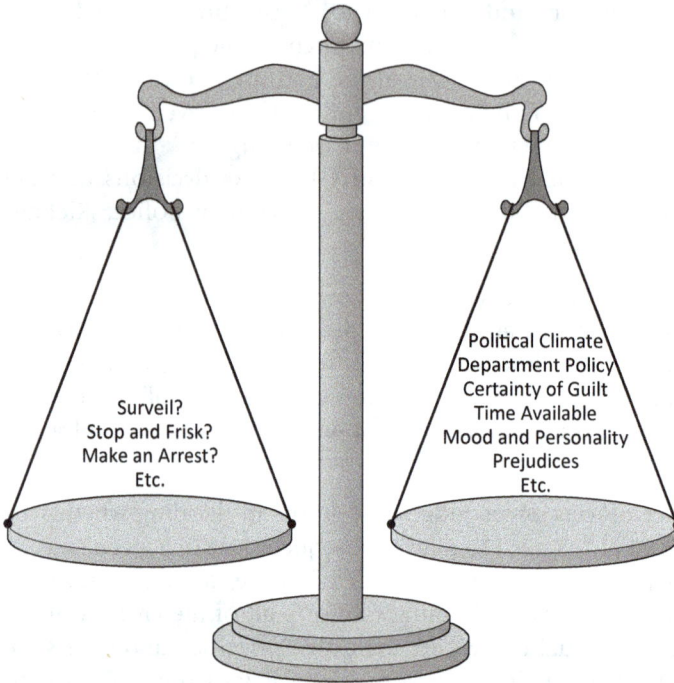

FIGURE 5.1
Factors affecting the police officer's use of discretion.

RACE

While there are numerous factors that influence an officer's use of discretion, racial and ethnic prejudices are not supposed to be among them. Before proceeding with a discussion on race and policing, there are a few points that we should note about the nature of prejudice. First, psychological studies on implicit bias reveal that almost everybody has some racial bias,[54] but that certainly does not mean that we are all equally prejudiced. Second, there is a difference between prejudice and discrimination. Prejudice refers to an attitude or belief about one group's superiority over another; whereas discrimination refers to the act of treating members of one group better or worse than members of another group. Further, and most importantly for our discussion, *prejudice is all the more problematic when it is possessed by individuals or groups with power because it can manifest itself in forms of discrimination that are far more consequential than prejudice possessed by individuals or groups without power.* The police, as we have noted, have enormous power vested in them, with the authority to deprive a person of his or her freedom and the authority to use coercive force.

Members of the white majority are often insensitive to claims of racist policing because they are far less likely to have ever experienced racial discrimination at the hands of the police than members of racial minorities.

While most people have heard of "racial profiling," it is a very difficult term to define and it is, therefore, difficult to determine when it has happened or is happening. Or, to put it another way, it is difficult to draw the line between acceptable use of race as a basis for arrest and unacceptable use. The most objectionable standard of racial profiling would be when race is the sole basis for stopping a suspect, or searching a suspect, or making an arrest. We might call this a "race-only" definition. Another standard of racial profiling includes situations when a police officer employs race as one of several reasons for stopping, searching, or arresting a suspect. This, we will call the "race-plus" definition. Most people would consider the race-only definition an unacceptable standard; and the U.S. Supreme Court has ruled it an unacceptable basis for police decision-making as well. The problem, however, is that it is often difficult or impossible to tell when the officer's decision is based on a race-only standard or a race-plus standard because she or he can always invoke reasons other than race as the basis for their decision. (For example, in one case outside of Philadelphia when four black men were stopped and detained, the police reported that the car was stopped because the car's windshield was obstructed by a string hanging from the rearview mirror.)[55] While most jurisdictions allow the race-plus standard, it, too, is problematic because when race figures into an officer's decision-making, it is more likely to be in cases involving black would-be suspects than in cases involving white would-be suspects.

In the 1990s, many American cities instituted stop and frisk policies where the police would routinely stop people on the street, ask their names, perhaps ask for identification, and pat them down. Daniel Bergner writes,

> In cities across the country, stop-and-frisk strategies have gained great currency. They aim to get guns off the street, to glean information and solve crime sprees, and, perhaps above all, to act as a deterrent, by letting criminals and would-be lawbreakers know that they might find themselves getting a pat-down at any given moment.[56]

Civil rights activists and civil libertarians vigorously opposed stop and frisk policies, arguing that they were a violation of people's fourth amendment rights against unwarranted search and seizure, and that they were more likely to be used against minorities, depriving them of their fourteenth amendment right of equal treatment under the law. Police officials defended these tactics, arguing that they were largely responsible for the ongoing drop in crime rates and that they were not being used in a dis-criminatory manner. If blacks were being stopped and frisked at a higher rate than whites, they argued, it was because blacks were more likely to be living in neighborhoods with high crime rates where such methods were being deployed. Defending stop and frisk policies, Michael Bloomberg the former mayor of New York, is quoted as saying,

> Ninety-five percent of your murders—murderers and murder victims—fit one M.O. You can just take the description, Xerox it and pass it out to all the cops. They are male minorities, 16 to 25. That's true in New York. That's true in virtually every city. And that's where the real crime is. You've got to get the guns out of the hands of the people that are getting killed.[57]

Between 2004 and 2012, 83 percent of those who were subject to a stop and frisk in New York City were blacks and Hispanics.[58] In 2014, the Federal District Court in Manhattan ruled that the use of stop and frisk in minority communities constituted a "policy of indirect racial profiling;" and the judge ordered the NYPD to reform its practices.[59] Since then, the policy has fallen into disrepute in much of the country.

There are several points worthy of note concerning this history of stop and frisk policies. First, like so many other racist policies in American history, stop and frisk enjoyed a great deal of popular support before it fell into disrepute. The defenders of Jim Crow laws, the convict leasing system, and other racist policies of the past did not consider those policies (or themselves) as racist. Today, people have no doubt that they were racist. If people could appreciate this historical fact, it may cause them to become more critical of current criminal justice policies, such as the War on Drugs and the implementation of the death penalty (see Chapter 7). Another point to be made is that while police officials attributed the drop in crime rates to stop and frisk policies, crime rates continued dropping even after the use of stop and frisk fell precipitously (for reasons discussed in Chapter 4). In evaluating the effectiveness of stop and frisk, we should also con-sider the costs of such policies in terms of police–minority relations, when young black and Hispanic males could not leave their residence without fear of being accosted, stopped, and frisked by the police. Whatever hostili-ties there were towards the police in minority communities, these were surely exacerbated by stop and frisk policies.

Although police data indicate a drop in the use of stop and frisk, there are "lower level encounters" still going on. The NYPD, for example, now distinguishes between Levels 1, 2, 3 and 4 encounters. The level depends on the basis for suspicion, from weakest to strongest. Level 1 allows for only non-accusatory questions to be asked, and allows for no searches; Level 2 allows for accusatory questions to be asked, but only allows for a search with consent; Level 3 is the equivalent of the "old" stop and frisk, and allows for a search without consent; Level 4 involves an actual arrest.[60] Presumably, at Levels 1 and 2, the would-be suspect is allowed to walk away; but assuredly, most would-be suspects—especially minorities— would not feel they are free to do so. As one black man involved in such an encounter explains, "You never feel free to leave when you have someone asking you questions with a badge and a gun."[61]

Not surprisingly, there is concern that discrimination occurs at all levels of encounters. Darian Agostini, a youth organizer in NYC, says these encounters are part of "the everyday experience of black and brown young people in New York City. We know that's not going on in other parts of the city that are either whiter or more affluent."[62] The official data, however, will not allow us to determine if the lower level encounters are applied on a discriminatory basis because, while they may be the most frequent of encounters, they are the least likely to be recorded.

Lastly, we should note that stereotypes and prejudices cut both ways. Just as a police officer may act on prejudices he may have about young black men, a young black man may act on prejudices he may have about the police. Either party's expectation of hostile behavior on the part of the other could well result in a self-fulfilling prophecy, with both parties participating in an escalation of hostilities. Police training often does focus, and should focus more, on de-escalating such situations. Unfortunately, *many black and brown parents in today's society are finding it necessary to train their own children in de-escalation tactics by giving their children what has been called in the popular culture as "the talk."* The talk informs their children of the potentially lethal dangers of police encounters, and emphasizes the need to be on their very best behavior in the presence of a police officer. The talk gained currency in the black middle class with the publication of Ta-Nehisi Coates, "Letter to My Son" in *The Atlantic*. The following is a passage from Coates's darkly inspirational essay.

> I write you in your 15th year. I am writing you because this was the year you saw Eric Garner choked to death for selling cigarettes; because you know now that Renisha McBride was shot for seeking help, that John Crawford was shot down for browsing in a department store. And you have seen men in uniform drive by and murder Tamir Rice, a 12-year-old child whom they were oath-bound to protect. And you know now, if you did not before, that the police departments of your country have been endowed with the authority to destroy your body. It does not matter if the destruction is the result of an unfortunate overreaction. It does not matter if it originates in a misunderstanding. It does not matter if the destruction springs from a foolish policy. Sell cigarettes without the proper

authority and your body can be destroyed. Turn into a dark stairwell and your body can be destroyed. The destroyers will rarely be held accountable. Mostly they will receive pensions.[63]

Officer-involved killings

In 2014, a white police officer in Ferguson, Missouri shot and killed Michael Brown, a black teenager. The police were responding to a complaint that Brown had reached across the counter at a convenience store, pushed the clerk, and grabbed a pack of cigarillos. Brown was unarmed and he was shot at least six times shortly after the police arrived. Early media reports suggested that pushing the clerk, petty theft, and failure to comply with the police officer were all that Brown had done; and there was no other reason for the deadly response from the police. Subsequent investigations, though, supported the police officer's claim that Brown reached inside the patrol car and acted aggressively towards him.[64] Details of the case are still unclear; but this incident was a watershed moment in the recent history of police–minority relations.

The media were saturated with accounts of the incident; and it sparked a national conversation about the police use of force against the minority community—in particular, about the disregard the police show for the lives of black people—fueling the Black Lives Matter movement, triggering protests, and culminating in a federal investigation that revealed that Ferguson's mostly white police department did indeed routinely discriminate against its mostly black population.[65] Even though Brown's innocence and the police officer's culpability, in this case, may or may not have been exaggerated by the media, numerous other incidents of police-involved killings have received national attention in the aftermath (such as those mentioned in the Ta-Nehesi Coates passage above).

The *Washington Post* also began compiling statistics on police shootings after the Brown case. According to the *Post's* data, Figure 5.2 shows a breakdown of police involved killings by race. As these data concern "rates" they are adjusted by racial composition in the general population; and they reveal that blacks are more than two and a half times more likely than whites to be killed by the police, while Hispanics are almost twice as likely. The *Washington Post's* data show similar, if not greater racial disparities when the victims of police shootings are unarmed. The *Post* reports,

> Of all of the unarmed people shot and killed by police in 2015, 40 percent of them were black men, even though black men make up just 6 percent of the nation's population. And, when considering shootings confined within a single race, a black person shot and killed by police is more likely to have been unarmed than a white person.[66]

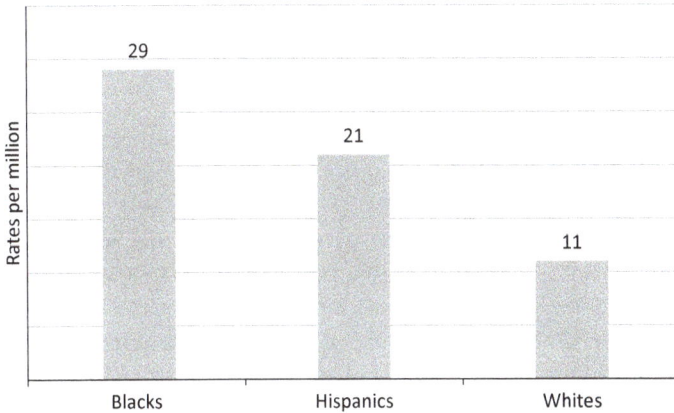

FIGURE 5.2
Rates of police-involved killings by race.

Source: *Washington Post*, "985 People Have Been Shot and Killed in the Past Year," Updated February 11, 2020. www.washingtonpost.com/graphics/investigations/police-shootings-database/.

Racial disparities grow larger as the victims of police shootings grow younger. According to an analysis of FBI data collected before the Brown incident, between 2010 and 2012, black teens (age 15 to 19) were killed at a rate 21 times greater than white teens.[67]

Before the Civil Rights Movement in the mid-twentieth century, when the police killed a black suspect, the officer was rarely held accountable. Today, police officials and civil libertarians, conservatives and liberals, whites and blacks argue over whether officers involved in such killings are held sufficiently accountable. Usually it boils down to the officer's word and perhaps the word of a discreditable witness. Usually the departments will accept the officer's account and the district attorneys will rarely seek an indictment; and when they do so, it is only after a public furore over the case. As we will see in the next chapter, grand juries return an indictment in over 99 percent of the cases presented to them; but they almost never do so in officer-involved killings.

Again, critics argue that the dismissal of such cases is due to racism. However, we should note that the laws in most states are written in such a way as to give the police wide latitude in the use of force. For example, in Missouri, where Michael Brown was shot dead, the law reads,

> In effecting an arrest or in preventing an escape from custody, a law enforcement officer is justified in using deadly force ... when the officer reasonably believes that such use of deadly force is immediately necessary to effect the arrest or prevent an escape

from custody and also reasonably believes that the person to be arrested … is attempting to escape by use of a deadly weapon or dangerous instrument.[68]

The phrase "reasonably believes" in this statute make an indictment and the prosecution of such cases quite difficult and explains why officers are rarely held accountable for killing suspects.

On the other hand, with the advent of the smartphone and social media, the police are held to account by the public in ways they could not have been before. Videos of the police abusing their power are circulated widely on the internet. One such video was of Eric Garner, put in a choke-hold by the police and gasping "I can't breathe, I can't breathe" before he died. His crime: selling cigarettes illegally. The existence of the video meant that the case should not have depended on the officer's account of the incident; but still, the grand jury did not return an indictment. Protests erupted around the country; the officer was suspended and eventually fired.

More recently, in May 2020, another such video went viral. This one showed a Minneapolis police officer subduing a black suspect, George Floyd, with Floyd cuffed and lying prone on the street, and the officer with his knee on Floyd's neck. Floyd can be heard repeatedly saying, "I can't breathe." Officer Derek Chauvin is seen with his knee still on Floyd's neck for several minutes beyond the point where Floyd appears to go unconscious. (In another video from a different angle, more officers appear to be kneeling on Floyd.[69]) Passersby are seen urgently imploring the officers to get off Floyd, indicating that he looked to be in medical distress. An ambulance arrived, Floyd was transported to the hospital and pronounced dead. Floyd's alleged crime: passing a counterfeit $20 bill. The original video went viral and sparked demonstrations—many of them organized by Black Lives Matter—in over a hundred cities in the United States and around the world. Protesters, politicians, and civic leaders called for reforms in police procedures, addressing the unequal treatment of black suspects. Unusual for the time, and likely because of the existence of the video and the political unrest that it triggered, all four police officers were arrested. Chauvin was charged with second degree murder and the other three officers with aiding and abetting. As this book goes into production, it remains to be seen if substantive reforms will follow.

The disparity in police shootings of black men is highly politicized; and the police are sensitive to charges of racism. However, reformers are not charging that all police officers are racist. Indeed, as Georgetown University law professor Paul Butler writes, "Most police officers are decent working-class men and women with no more racial hang-ups than teachers, doctors, or anyone else."[70] However, as we have noted, racial biases matter more when they are held by people in power; and officer-involved killings are an extreme example.

In June 2020, President Donald Trump threatened to order the military to quell the civil unrest provoked by the killing of George Floyd. Before that, in the aftermath of the killing of Michael Brown, there had been a series of public protests, and the Ferguson police deployed military tactics and military armaments to handle crowd control. ABC News reported the scene at the Ferguson unrest, "The latest images of unrest in Ferguson, Missouri, evoke scenes from a battlefield: heavily-armed officers in camouflage, carrying rifles in armored vehicles, firing at civilians."[71] (They had been firing rubber bullets.) Such images sparked public debates about the militarization of the police. These debates, though, had already been going on among criminologists because the militarization of the police had begun much earlier.

THE MILITARIZATION OF THE POLICE

Up until the middle of the twentieth century, jurisprudents and lawmakers had drawn a sharp distinction between police forces and military forces. Police forces ensured our domestic tranquility and conducted their operations within the United States; and military forces provided for our national defense and did so outside of U.S. territory. The idea of a military controlling U.S. citizens reeked of the kind of government control that America's revolutionary forefathers had rebelled against. Indeed, when we think of countries in which the line between police and military forces is blurred, we think of the military being used to prop up authoritarian regimes. The American distaste for military involvement in domestic matters was enshrined into law with the Posse Comitatis Act of 1878, which restricted the federal government's ability to call in military forces to enforce domestic policies.[72]

By the "militarization of the police," we mean the process whereby the police take on the tactics, technology, ideas and culture of the military. To a certain extent, this is not new. As we noted earlier, Robert Peel's vision for the police in London was to be a force organized along military lines; and the early American metropolitan police were similarly organized and were soon issued uniforms and standardized weapons, much like the military. While militarization of the police may have proceeded incrementally, the pace began to pick up substantially in the 1960s. Two facets of law enforcement were particularly influenced by militarization: crowd control and the deployment of police paramilitary units, popularly called SWAT (Special Weapons and Tactics) teams. We will discuss crowd control first.

Crowd control

As mentioned earlier in this chapter, the formation of the urban police in nineteenth century America was, in part, a response to urban riots that were relatively common in major American cities. Riots usually involve some significant sector of society protesting domestic polices and and/or seeking a redress of grievances from the state. Throughout history and throughout the world, riots usually start out as public protests and often they do not turn violent until law enforcement authorities turn violent. Over the past 60 years, most of the riots in the United States have involved African Americans demanding racial justice; and many of these riots did not turn violent until the police overreacted. Sociologist John Lofland summarized the gist of numerous influential reports on the causes of civil disorder coming out of the 1960s,

> The investigations of the '60s—the Kerner (Commission) report and others—showed that in black ghettos … police were the primary stimulants of rioting. It was just indisputable that it was the bungling overaggressiveness of police on any number of scenes that were the precipitants of the riots.[73]

More recently, Paul Butler observes the same phenomenon:

> Most of the times that African Americans have set aside traditional civil rights strategies like bringing court cases and marching peacefully and instead have rioted in the streets, destroyed property, and attacked symbols of the state have been because of something the police have done. Watts in 1965, Newark in 1967, Miami in 1980, Los Angeles in 1992, Ferguson in 2015, Baltimore in 2016, Charlotte in 2016—each of these cities went up in flames sparked by the police killing a black man.[74]

These American race riots were especially common from the mid-1960s to early-1970s, during the time Dana Parsons of the *Los Angeles Times* called the "Riot of the Week period."[75] In large part, in response to the urban unrest, the California Specialized Training Institute (CSTI) was established. Among other things, the CSTI began training the National Guard in crowd control techniques, many of them borrowed from the military. "From its beginning," writes Matt Ehling, "CSTI worked to merge military techniques into domestic law enforcement."[76] Trainees were introduced to the use of CS gas and similar non-lethal chemical weapons, which had been used in Vietnam to flush combatants out of the fields.[77] Later, police detailed to crowd control would use other "non-lethal" (or less lethal) weapons developed for or by the military, including rubber bullets, concussion grenades, and sound cannons.

The pace of the militarization of the police accelerated with the War on Drugs (see Chapter 7) and the passage of the National Defense Authorization Act in the 1990s. A section of this legislation allowed the transfer of surplus military technology to domestic local police agencies, and has since come to be known as the "1033 program." Donald Bruce and his colleagues describe this program and its magnitude, "The U.S. Department of Defense 1033 program transfers decommissioned military goods to local police departments. This is one of the largest grant-in-kind initiatives in the country's history, accounting for over $5.2 billion in transferred goods and vehicles since 1997."[78]

Not surprisingly, the use of military technology in local law enforcement is often seen as an overly aggressive, if not an outright hostile, action. Police in Watertown, CT. received a mine-resistant, ambush protected (MRAP) vehicle, although there is no record of a mine ever going off in the town; and the town of Bloomington, GA, received four grenade launchers.[79] The police department in Concord, NH, requested an armored vehicle and justified their request by the presence of members of the Free State movement in the area. Free Staters are a libertarian group that encourages its members to move to the small "Live Free or Die" state, where they can have a greater influence over electoral politics. They have shown no signs of violent tendencies, and members were understandably offended by their mention in the police request.[80] This incident struck many people familiar with New Hampshire politics as humorous; however, exaggerated police responses are all the more problematic when minorities are being treated as enemy combatants.

SWAT

In August 1966, Charles Whitman took an elevator to the top of the University of Texas Tower in Austin, killed the receptionist, barricaded the door, went to the observation deck and, with a high-powered rifle, began to open fire on the people below. By the time the police finally managed to reach the observation deck and shoot Whitman dead, he had shot and killed 17 people and wounded 30 more. According to police historians, it was this event that gave rise to the development and deployment of Special Weapons and Tactics (SWAT) teams.[81] These teams are comparable to the specialized elite forces in the military services, such as the Navy SEALS and the Army Rangers. Originally, SWAT teams were conceived of as a means to deal with hostage situations and/or cases where an armed suspect has barricaded himself inside a building. In these cases, according to former Minneapolis police chief, Anthony Bouza, the mission is to contain the situation so that fewer civilians are at risk, and negotiations can proceed; then, only as a last resort, the SWAT team is trained and equipped to use overwhelming and deadly force.[82]

Peter Kraska and Victor Kappeler call SWAT teams "paramilitary police units" (PPUs) and write,

As opposed to the traditional police, paramilitary units can be distinguished in the following ways. PPUs are equipped with an array of militaristic equipment and technology. ... The weapon most popular among these units is the Heckler and Koch MP5 submachine gun. ... Other weapons include tactical semi-automatic shotguns, M16s, sniper rifles, and automatic shotguns referred to as "street sweepers."

PPUs have an array of "less-than-lethal" technology for conducting "dynamic entries" (e.g. serving a search warrant). These include percussion grenades (explosive devices designed to disorient residents), stinger grenades (similar devices containing rubber pellets) CS and OC gas grenades (tear gas) and shotgun launched bean-bag systems (nylon bags of lead shot). "Dynamic entries" require apparatuses for opening doors, including battering rams, hydraulic door jams, and C4 explosives.[83]

SWAT teams are very well suited for active shooter, hostage and barricade situations; and, on rare occasions, no other police tactics or forces can substitute for SWAT's effectiveness. *The concern, however, about the militarization of the police arises from the overreliance on SWAT deployments. As the War on Drugs escalated (see Chapter 7), SWAT teams came to be used primarily in drug raids.* According to an American Civil Liberties Union (ACLU) report, of 800 SWAT deployments in 2011 and 2012, only 7 percent were "for hostage, barricade, or active shooter scenarios;" the vast majority of the rest were to serve search warrants, mostly in drug cases; and "61 percent of all the people impacted by SWAT raids in drug cases were minorities."[84]

Typically, with so-called "no-knock" warrants in hand, the SWAT team approaches the home of the suspect drug dealer in the middle of the night, hoping to catch him asleep; they breach the door, enter rapidly, and scan the room with night vision goggles. If they come across a resident with a gun in hand, they are trained to shoot to kill. Stan Goff, a former Army Ranger who became a SWAT trainer, states, "If there's a weapon in the hands during a dynamic entry—it does not matter what that weapon is doing—that person dies. ... Two rounds center of mass and keep on going."[85] In other words, the same tactics and overwhelming force that you may have seen in the movies depicting military forces liberating hostages from well-armed terrorists—these are now being used to apprehend sleeping suspected drug dealers. The difference between an active shooter/hostage/barricade situation and a drug raid is that, in the former, the SWAT team arrives on the scene where violence has already taken place; in a drug raid, the SWAT team instigates the violence.

There have been a number of occasions where the SWAT teams have gone to the wrong address and killed innocent civilians. Naturally, sensing an intruder in the house, many residents—guilty and innocent ones—will immediately reach for a gun and get killed by the police. Larry Pratt, former Executive Director of Gun Owners of America, reports, "There was a man in Denver—but it's happening in many jurisdictions—wrong address; but the guy gets killed because he reaches for a gun, thinking his home is under attack—and he's dead. Sorry. That's the problem when you play war in a civilian environment."[86]

Defenders of SWAT-led drug raids argue that the technology and tactics that they use are necessary to protect the police from well-armed criminals. For example, a report from the U.S. Department of Justice argues, "As more and more military technology finds its way into criminal hands, law officers today confront threats that have more and more military aspects. For example, narcotics traffickers and smugglers use bullet-proof vests, electro-optic devices that enable them to see at night, and semiautomatic and even automatic weapons."[87] Surely, it would be quite unusual to find this kind of military technology in the hands of the typical drug dealer; and the justification for a warrant often simply states that the police have reason to believe that the suspect "is likely to be armed." The same can be said of about half of all U.S. households. The ACLU report referred to above states "Given that almost half of American households have guns, use of a SWAT team could almost always be justified if this were the sole factor."[88]

In sum, the overuse of military technology and tactics in crowd control and in drug raids, —besides putting civilians at risk—undermines the image of "the even hand of justice" that the police need to project to secure their credibility and ensure good community relations, especially when these technologies and tactics disproportionately treat minorities as hostiles. Radley Balko, who has written extensively about the militarization of the police, says, "When you arm police like soldiers and outfit them with military weapons and train them on military tactics and tell them they're fighting a war, whether it's a war on crime or drugs or looters and rioters, they're going to start seeing themselves as soldiers, and seeing the people they serve less as citizens with rights and more as potential threats."[89]

CONCLUSION

Modern industrialized societies do indeed need the police to ensure order. However, we must be mindful of the awesome powers vested in the police; and everything must to done to ensure that that power is used competently and even-handedly. Such insurance requires careful selection and training of recruits, and that the police be held accountable when they abuse their power. Just as Beccaria and Bentham (see Chapter 2) insisted that too much punishment is counterproductive; it can also be said that too much law enforcement is counterproductive, especially when some groups suffer more from over-enforcement than others.

NOTES

1 Gary Marx, "Police and Democracy," online and elongated version of an article from *The Encyclopedia of Democracy*, S. Lipset, ed., Routledge, 1995. https://web.mit.edu/gtmarx/www/poldem.html. Retrieved January 15, 2020.
2 Carl Klockars, *The Idea of Police*, Law and Criminal Justice Series, James Inciardi, editor. Beverly Hills: Sage, 1985, p. 23.
3 Ibid.
4 Gresham Sykes, *Criminology*, New York: Harcourt, Brace, Jovanovich, 1978, p. 368.
5 "Sir Robert Peel's Nine Principles of Policing," New York Times, April 15, 2014. www.nytimes.com/2014/04/16/nyregion/sir-robert-peels-nine-principles-of-policing.html. Retrieved January 15, 2020. As the article states, there is some controversy as to whether Peel actually stated this and the following principles, or if they were made by one (or both) of the first police commissioners.
6 Ibid.
7 Ibid.
8 T. Whetstone, W.F. Walsh, et al., "Police," *Encyclopedia Britannica*, September 12, 2019. www.britannica.com/topic/police/The-development-of-professional-policing-in-England. Retrieved January 15, 2020.
9 Quoted in Sykes, *Criminology*, p. 370.
10 Brendan Koerner, "What are Civil Service Protections?, Slate, July 29, 2002. https://slate.com/news-and-politics/2002/07/what-are-civil-service-protections.html. Retrieved January 14, 2020.
11 K. Hine, L. Porter, N. Westera, G. Alpert, A. Allen, "What Were They Thinking: Factors Influencing Police Recruits Decisions about Force," *Policing and Society*, 2019, vol. 29, no. 6, p. 673.
12 When an officer is dismissed or prosecuted for a particular act of physical force, the state is essentially announcing that this act was not authorized and, hence, it crossed the line into violence.
13 Klockars, *The Idea of Police*, p. 37.
14 City of Berkeley, Our History. www.cityofberkeley.info/police/history/history.html. Retrieved January 23, 2020.
15 The Vollmer Institute. https://vollmerinstitute.com/who-we-are/. Retrieved January 23, 2020.
16 Edward A. Petty, "Historical Perspectives on the American Society of Criminology." Unpublished history written in 1959. Available on the ASC website. www.asc41.com/History.html. Retrieved January 23, 2020.
17 Sherman, Lawrence W. and the National Advisory Commission on Higher Education for Police Officers 1978. *The Quality of Police Education*. San Francisco, CA: Jossey-Bass Publishers, p. 31.
18 Christie Gardiner, "Policing Around the Nation: Education, Philosophy, and Practice," in collaboration with Center for Public Policy at California State University, and the Police Foundation, September 2017. www.policefoundation.org/wp-content/uploads/2017/10/PF-Report-Policing-Around-the-Nation_10-2017_Final.pdf. Retrieved January 25, 2020.
19 Ibid. p. 3.
20 Ibid., p. 4.
21 The report states that 30.2 percent of police officers have a 4 year degree. The report was published in September 2017. I am assuming the data were collected in 2016.

Extrapolating from U.S. Census data for that year, 29.6 percent of the general population had a four year degree. U.S. Census. "Years of School Completed by People 25 Years and Older, by Age and Sex, Selected Years 1940–2018." www.census.gov/data/tables/time-series/demo/educational-attainment/cps-historical-time-series.html. Retrieved January 25, 2020.

22 Gardiner, Policing Around the Nation," p. 3.

23 City of Berkeley.

24 U.S. Equal Employment Opportunity Commission, "Employment Rights of Immigrants under Federal Anti-Discrimination Laws," www1.eeoc.gov//eeoc/publications/brochure-immigrant_workers_rights.cfm?renderforprint=1. Retrieved January 24, 2020.

25 Val Van Brocklin, "Physical Fitness Double Standards for Male and Female Cops?" PoliceOne.com, December 18, 2013. www.policeone.com/evergreen/articles/physical-fitness-double-standards-for-male-and-female-cops-T5v9FXnfrfs55jEH/. Retrieved January 24, 2020.

26 Clyde Winters, "Socio-Economic Status, Test Bias, and the Selection of Police," *Police Journal*, vol. 15, no. 2, April 1992, pp. 125–135.

27 Ellen Kirschman, "Pre-Employment Psychological Screening for Cops," *Psychology Today*, September 5, 2017. www.psychologytoday.com/us/blog/cop-doc/201709/pre-employment-psychological-screening-cops. Retrieved September 24, 2020.

28 American Psychological Association, "The Truth About Lie Detectors (aka Polygraph Tests)." www.apa.org/research/action/polygraph. Retrieved January 34, 2020.

29 S.E. Martin, "On the Move: Status of Women in Policing," The Police Foundation, 1990. www.policefoundation.org/publication/on-the-move-the-status-of-women-in-policing/?gclid=Cj0KCQiAqNPyBRCjARIsAKA-WFzG98lalsr6_GAXO-Nzvj09aNfB_NgeKCy2Ku3wAL8ZAk3IA96SXMgaApG3EALw_wcB. Retrieved February 25, 2020.

30 National Law Enforcement Museum, "Robinson and Blankenship: The First Female Patrol Partners," March 8, 2018. https://lawenforcementmuseum.org/2018/03/08/celebrating-womens-history-month/. Retrieved February 25, 2020.

31 U.S. Department of Justice, "Women in Policing: Breaking Barriers and Blazing a Path, 2019," *National Institute of Justice Special Report*, www.ncjrs.gov/pdffiles1/nij/252963.pdf. Retrieved February 25, 2020.

32 Kevin Johnson, "Women Move into Law Enforcement's Highest Ranks," *USA Today*, August 13, 2013. www.usatoday.com/story/news/nation/2013/08/13/women-law-enforcement-police-dea-secret-service/2635407/. Retrieved February 25, 2020.

33 USDOJ, "Women in Policing."

34 Ibid., p. 2.

35 Ibid.

36 "Police Officer: An Overview of Police Academy Training," Study.com, September 13, 2019. https://study.com/articles/Police_Officer_An_Overview_of_Police_Academy_Training.html. Retrieved January 28, 2020.

37 Caitlin Lynch, "You Have the Right to Remain Violent: Police Academy Curricula and the Facilitation of Police Overreach," *Social Justice*, vol. 45, no. 2/3, 2019, p. 75.

38 Ibid.

39 Ibid. p. 76.

40 Victor Kappeler and Cory Potter, *The Mythology of Crime and Criminal Justice*, 4th ed., Long Grove, IL: Waveland Press, 2005, p. 236.

41 Robert Heiner, *Social Problems: An Introduction to Critical Constructionism*, 5th ed., New York: Oxford University Press, 2014, p. 143.

42 Ibid. p. 237.

43 Steven Barkan and George Bryjak, *Myths and Realities of Crime and Justice*, Sudbury, MA: Jones and Batlett, 2009, p. 186.

44 Kappeler and Potter, *The Mythology of Crime and Criminal Justice*, p. 238. J. Greene and Carl Klockars, "What Police Do," *Thinking about Police: Contemporary Readings*, 2nd ed., C. Klockars and S. Mastrofski, New York: McGraw-Hill, 1991, p. 283.

45 Jordi Blanes, Vidal Mastrobuoni, and Giovanni Mastrobuoni, "Police Patrols and Crime," Research Briefs in Economic Policy, No. 112, Cato Institute, May 9, 2018. https://duckduckgo.com/?q=cato+organization&t=ffnt&atb=v205-3&ia=news. Retrieved February 1, 2020.

46 George Kelling, Tony Pate, Duane Dieckman, and Charles E. Brown, "The Kansas City Preventive Patrol Experiment: A Summary Report," Washington, DC: The Police Foundation, 1974. www.policefoundation.org/publication/the-kansas-city-preventive-patrol-experiment/. Retrieved, February 1, 2020.

47 Ibid.

48 David Bayley, *Police for the Future*. NY: Oxford University Press, 1994, p. 6.

49 Simone Weischelbaum and Wendi Thomas, "More Cops: Is it the Answer to Fighting Crime," *USA Today*, February 12, 2019. www.usatoday.com/story/news/investigations/2019/02/13/marshall-project-more-cops-dont-mean-less-crime-experts-say/2818056002/. Retrieved February 1, 2020.

50 Bayley, *Police for the Future*, p. 4.

51 Joanna Vitek "Police Discretion and the Use of Force: A Study of the Use of Force among Law Enforcement Officers in Brevard County," 2002, p. 3 www.theiacp.org/sites/default/files/all/p-r/Police_Discretion_and_Use_of_Force.pdf. Retrieved February 7, 2020.

52 Richard Uviller, "The Unworthy Victim: Police Discretion in the Credibility Call," *Law and Contemporary Problems*, vol. 47, Autumn 1984, p. 15.

53 Albert Reiss, "Police Organization in the Twentieth Century," *Modern Policing*, M. Tonry and N. Morris, eds., University of Chicago Press, 1992, p. 74. Emphasis added.

54 See Mahzarin Benaji and Anthony Greenwald, *Blindspot: The Hidden Biases of Good People*, New York: Bantam Books, 2016. Readers are encouraged to take the implicit bias test at https://implicit.harvard.edu/implicit/takeatest.html.

55 Renee McDonald Hutchins, "Racial Profiling: The Law, the Policy, and the Practice," *Policing the Black Man*, A. Davis, ed., New York: Pantheon, 2017, pp. 95–134.

56 Daniel Bergner, "Is Stop and Frisk Worth It?" *Atlantic*, vol. 313, no. 3, April 2014, p. 57.

57 Quint Forgey, "Bloomberg in How Water over Stop and Frisk Audio Clip," *Politico*, February 11, 2020. www.politico.com/news/2020/02/11/michael-bloomberg-stop-and-frisk-clip-113902. Retrieved February 12, 2020.

58 Bergner, "Stop and Frisk," p. 56.

59 Benjamin Weiser, "Shira Sheindlin, Judge behind Stop and Frisk Ruling, Will Step Down," *New York Times*, March 23, 2016. www.nytimes.com/2016/03/24/nyregion/shira-scheindlin-judge-behind-stop-and-frisk-ruling-will-step-down.html. Retrieved February 13, 2020.

60 Katarina Zimmer and Elise Hansen, "'Stop and Frisk' is Over, But Low-Level NYPD Encounters Now Raise Concerns," *City Limits*, June 21, 2018. https://citylimits.org/2018/06/21/stop-and-frisk-is-over-but-low-level-nypd-encounters-now-raise-concerns/. Retrieved February 12, 2020.

61 Ibid.

62 Ibid.

63 Ta-Nehesi Coates, "Letter to My Son," *The Atlantic*, July 4, 2015, www.theatlantic.com/politics/archive/2015/07/tanehisi-coates-between-the-world-and-me/397619/. Retrieved February 13, 2020.

64 Louis Jacobson, "The Death of Michael Brown: Legal Facts and Democratic Messaging," *Politifact*, August 14, 2019. www.politifact.com/article/2019/aug/14/death-michael-brown-legal-facts-democratic/. Retrieved February 13, 2020.

65 U.S. Department of Justice, "Investigation of the Ferguson Police department," March 4, 2015. www.justice.gov/sites/default/files/opa/press-releases/attachments/2015/03/04/ferguson_police_department_report.pdf. Retrieved February 13, 2020.

66 Wesley Lowery, "Aren't More White People Killed by the Police than Black People? Yes, But No," Washington Post, July 11, 2016. www.washingtonpost.com/news/post-nation/wp/2016/07/11/arent-more-white-people-than-black-people-killed-by-police-yes-but-no/. Retrieved February 13, 2020.

67 Ryan Gabrielson, Eric Sagara, and Ryann Grochowski, "Deadly Force, In Back and White," *ProPublica*, October 10, 2014. www.propublica.org/article/deadly-force-in-black-and-white. Retrieved February 13, 2020.

68 Jacobson, "The Death of Michael Brown."

69 Paul Murphy, "New Video Appears to Show Three Police Officers Kneeling on George Floyd," CNN, June 3, 2020. www.cnn.com/2020/05/29/us/george-floyd-new-video-officers-kneel-trnd/index.html. Retrieved June 6, 2020.

70 Paul Butler, *Chokehold*, New York: The New Press, 2017, p. 2.

71 Colleen Curry and Luis Martinez, "Ferguson Police's Show of Force Highlights Militarization of America's Cops," *ABC News*, August 14, 2014. https://abcnews.go.com/US/ferguson-police-small-army-thousands-police-departments/story?id=24977299. Retrieved February 18, 2020.

72 When Donald Trump threatened to call in the military to deal with the civil unrest sparked by the killing of George Floyd by the Minneapolis police (discussed earlier in this chapter), he would have had to invoke the Insurrection Act of 1807, which would supersede restrictions on the use of the military for civilian law enforcement embodied in the Posse Comitatis Act. Many pundits, legal scholars, and military officials questioned whether events warranted such a drastic action; and Mark Esper, the Secretary of Defense, advised against it. As this book goes into production, the Insurrection Act had not been invoked.

73 Quoted in Dana Parsons, "Police Learn '60s Riot Experience has Relevance to the '80s," *Los Angeles Times*, September 24, 1986, www.latimes.com/archives/la-xpm-1986-09-24-vw-8927-story.html. Retrieved February 16, 2020.

74 Paul Butler, *Chokehold*, p. 2.

75 Dana Parsons, "Police Learn."

76 Matt Ehling, "Police Response to Occupy Protests has a Long (and Coordinated) History," writingforgodot, December 7, 2011. https://readersupportednews.org/pm-section/444-occupy/8775-police-response-to-occupy-protests-has-a-long-and-coordinated-history. Retrieved February 16, 2020.

77 Stuart Schrader, *Badges without Borders: How Global Counterinsurgency Transformed American Policing*, Oakland: University of California Press, 2019.

78 D. Bruce, C. Carruthers, M. Harris, M. Murray, and J. Park, "Do In-Kind Grants Stick? The Department of Defense 1033 Program and Local Government Spending," *Journal of Urban Economics*, vol. 112, July 2019, p. 111.

79 Taylor Wofford, "How America's Police Became an Army; The 1033 Program," *Newsweek*, August 13, 2014. www.newsweek.com/how-americas-police-became-army-1033-program-264537. Retrieved February 18, 2020.

80 Gavin Aronson, "N.H. City wants a 'Tank' to Use Against Occupiers and Libertarians," *Mother Jones*, August 6, 2013. www.motherjones.com/politics/2013/08/occupy-free-state-project-dhs-police-concord/. Retrieved February 18, 2020.

81 Michael Rosenwald, "The Loaded Legacy of the UT Tower Shooting," *Washington Post*, July 31, 2016. www.washingtonpost.com/sf/local/2016/07/31/the-loaded-legacy-of-the-ut-tower-shooting/?hpid=hp_rhp-top-table-main_uttower-0840pm:homepage/story&itid=lk_interstitial_manual_10&tid=a_inl&tid=lk_interstitial_manual_10&utm_term=.432154cff289. Retrieved February 21, 2020.

82 Interview from documentary film, Urban *Warrior*, Matt Ehling, director, 2002. Available form Monarch Films.

83 Peter Kraska and Victor Kappeler, "Militarizing American Police: The Rise and Normalization of Paramilitary Units," *Social Problems*, vol. 44, no. 1, February 1997, p. 3.

84 American Civil Liberties Union, "War Comes Home: The Excessive Militarization of American Policing," New York, June 2014, p. 5. www.aclu.org/sites/default/files/assets/jus14-warcomeshome-report-web-rel1.pdf. Retrieved February 23, 2020.

85 Interview from documentary film, Urban *Warrior*.

86 Ibid.

87 U.S. Department of Justice, "Department of Justice and Department of Defense Joint Technology Program, Second Anniversary Report," Research Report, February 1997. www.ncjrs.gov/pdffiles/164268.pdf. Retrieved February 18, 2020.

88 ACLU, "War Comes Home," p. 32.

89 Quoted in Curry and Martinez, "Ferguson Police's Show of Force."

CHAPTER 6

The courts

SOME LEGAL BASICS

We can distinguish between substantive laws and procedural laws. Substantive laws essentially define what we consider crimes; that is, what people may not do. These laws specify the *elements* that must be present to constitute a crime. These elements vary from state to state; but, for example, in many states, to be charged with felony driving while intoxicated, a person must (1) have been operating a motor vehicle, (2) on a public roadway, (3) while intoxicated, and (4) have had previous DWI convictions. *Procedural laws are those laws that govern the way that the courts must process a case.* Generally, substantive laws limit the behavior of people, while procedural laws limit the behavior of government in the handling of criminal and civil cases. Both types of law are in a constant state of flux as legislatures make new laws, or drop or revise old laws; and as the courts are continually interpreting these laws.

The Bill of Rights

The procedural laws that govern the behavior of all courts in all states are embodied in the first ten amendments to the United States Constitution; these are known as the Bill of Rights. At first, the Bill of Rights only applied to the federal courts; but the passage of the Fourteenth Amendment bound the state courts to the same procedural requirements. Below we will discuss those amendments that are most often invoked in, or relevant to, contemporary cases going through the criminal courts.

First Amendment. Congress shall make no law respecting an establishment of religion, or prohibiting the free exercise thereof; or abridging the freedom of speech, or of the press, or the right of the

people peaceably to assemble, and to petition the Government for
a redress of grievances.

The first clause in this amendment is known as the "establishment clause"
which prohibits the establishment of an official religion and relates to the
freedom to practice the religion of our choice. This is rarely invoked in
criminal cases unless a particular religion involves practices that may be
outlawed. For example, the federal government has exempted the Native
American Church from the application of laws prohibiting the use of the
hallucinogenic drug peyote; but other people have claimed that the same
exemption should be made for their spiritual practices as well. Free speech
and freedom of the press are also embodied in the First Amendment.
Freedom of the press can potentially compromise a defendant's right to a
fair trial when a case has so much negative media coverage that it is difficult to select an impartial jury. In such cases, defense attorneys may request
a change of venue; and, if granted, the trial will be held in a jurisdiction
other than the one where the alleged crime occurred. Lastly, people frequently argue that the right to peaceably assemble is compromised when
the authorities require demonstrators to obtain permission, specifying the
time and place in which they may assemble. In that demonstrations almost
always involve sensitive political issues (such as recent protests concerning
police use of deadly force), the authorities that make decisions about
allowable times and places risk accusations of political bias.

> *Second Amendment:* A well regulated Militia, being necessary to the
> security of a free State, the right of the people to keep and bear
> Arms, shall not be infringed.

While the Bill of Rights has generated controversies since its inception, at
this moment in time, no amendment generates as much controversy as the
Second Amendment. This is the amendment that deals with gun control,
or the lack thereof. Much of the controversy hinges on interpretations of
the intent of the founding fathers when they crafted this provision. The Bill
of Rights was written in 1789, shortly after the American Revolutionary
War, when the founding fathers were still sensitive to the threat of tyranny.
If so many of the American colonists had not had guns in their possession,
the revolution could well have been lost. Gun control advocates argue that
the wording of the amendment is obsolete in a country with a democracy
with a well-established republican form of government. If the government
did turn toward tyranny, it would have the most powerful military on
earth at its disposal, against which guns and rifles would be no match.
Many opponents of gun control, however, are especially sensitive to government overreach and do not think that a turn to tyranny is out of the
question. Many of these opponents also invoke the right to keep firearms

for hunting and target practices, forms of recreation not mentioned in the Constitution. Opponents frequently invoke the "slippery slope" argument, arguing the any gun control measure will inevitably lead to other more restrictive measures. (The issue of firearm possession is discussed further in Chapter 4.)

> *Fourth Amendment:* The right of the people to be secure in their persons, houses, papers, and effects, against unreasonable searches and seizures, shall not be violated, and no Warrants shall issue, but upon probable cause, supported by Oath or affirmation, and particularly describing the place to be searched, and the persons or things to be seized.

This amendment has to do with search and seizure laws, requiring the authorities to have a solid reason for entering our homes and seizing our effects. When we think of former and current authoritarian regimes in the world, we often think of the police raiding the homes of political adversaries and violently rummaging for contraband. The Fourth Amendment was designed to protect the people from such abuses of power. *Ancillary to the Fourth Amendment is the exclusionary rule, which prohibits evidence that is illegally obtained from being used in court proceedings.* The exclusionary rule does not appear in the Constitution; but it evolved over time as a means of enforcing the Fourth Amendment and protecting us all from illegal searches and seizures. It is controversial because people often imagine murderers getting off on "a technicality." However, convictions are very rarely set aside because of illegally obtained evidence; and those cases that are set aside are usually drug cases.[1] Fewer cases are set aside as a result of the exclusionary rule because the U.S. Supreme Court (USSC) has relaxed the application of the rule over the past few decades. One pivotal decision was that if the police acted "in good faith," the introduction of illegally obtained evidence is not, in and of itself, grounds for reversal. Another pivotal decision was that if the evidence that was illegally obtained and introduced into the trial was "immaterial" to the verdict, then a conviction should not be overturned. In other words, if the rest of the evidence was sufficient to obtain a conviction, then the introduction of illegally obtained evidence is not grounds for reversal.

> *Fifth Amendment:* No person shall be held to answer for a capital, or otherwise infamous crime, unless on a presentment or indictment of a Grand Jury, except in cases arising in the land or naval forces, or in the Militia, when in actual service in time of War or public danger, nor shall any person be subject for the same offence to be twice put in jeopardy of life or limb; nor shall be compelled in any criminal case to be a witness against himself; nor be

deprived of life, liberty, or property, without due process of law; nor shall private property be taken for public use without just compensation.

The Fifth Amendment is packed full of provisions, including the grand jury, double jeopardy, self-incrimination, and due process. Perhaps most controversial of these is the right against self-incrimination (i.e., "nor shall be compelled in any criminal case to be a witness against himself"). This is meant to prevent the extraction of information or confessions by way of coercion (e.g., torture, duress, or trickery). In 1966, in the case of Miranda v. Arizona, in a 5 to 4 decision, the USSC ruled that suspects must be advised of their rights before interrogation. This resulted in the Miranda warning that we have all heard so often on television and in the movies: "You have the right to remain silent. Anything you say can, and will, be used against you in court of law. You have the right to an attorney. If you cannot afford one, one will be appointed to you." As with other evidence obtained outside of legal parameters, incriminating statements made by suspects who are in custody, who are interrogated, and who are not advised of their rights are subject to the exclusionary rule. As you can imagine, when the Miranda ruling first went into effect, law enforcement officials complained bitterly, claiming that it hamstrung their investigations. However, in retrospect, it did curtail law enforcement's abuse of power and many agree that the Miranda ruling contributed significantly to the professionalization of the police.[2]

Regarding the double jeopardy clause in the Fifth Amendment, to clear up a popular misunderstanding, if an appeals court overturns a guilty verdict, that does not mean the defendant is found not guilty; and a prosecutor can pursue a new trial without running afoul of the double jeopardy protection.

> *Sixth Amendment:* In all criminal prosecutions, the accused shall enjoy the right to a speedy and public trial, by an impartial jury of the State and district wherein the crime shall have been committed; which district shall have been previously ascertained by law, and to be informed of the nature and cause of the accusation; to be confronted with the witnesses against him; to have compulsory process for obtaining witnesses in his favor; and to have the assistance of counsel for his defense.

This amendment contains the right of the defendant to confront witnesses against her and to present witnesses in her own defense. The right to counsel is specified in the Sixth Amendment. This right is not controversial; but the right to counsel to be appointed by the court when the defendant cannot afford a lawyer has undergone a substantial evolution over the years. There was no such right until 1932, when the USSC ruled that indigent defendants have the right to a court-appointed attorney when they are facing the death penalty; in 1963, the USSC ruled that indigent defendants have a right to a court appointed lawyer in all felony cases in both state and federal courts; and in 1972 the Court ruled that indigent defendants have the right to a court-appointed attorney—even in misdemeanor cases—when the defendant is facing jail time. In the 1980s and 1990s, many states started requiring defendants to pay the state back for the services of their court-appointed lawyers—in some states—even when the defendant is found not guilty. This is a cruel irony, when it was the state that falsely charged the defendant in the first place.

> *Eighth Amendment:* Excessive bail shall not be required, nor excessive fines imposed, nor cruel and unusual punishments inflicted.

This amendment is brief and quite vague. Benjamin Wittes of the Hoover Institution calls the Eighth Amendment a "jurisprudential train wreck."[3] It mentions bail, but it is not considered to guarantee the right to bail, nor does it define what might constitute "excessive" bail (or fines). It is generally agreed that the purpose of bail is not punishment, but to ensure that the defendant shows up for trial. (We will discuss bail at more length in this chapter and in Chapter 7.) The mention of excessive fines refers not just to fines imposed by the court, but also to assets and property that can be seized by the court. Also contained in this amendment is the prohibition on cruel and unusual punishment, another vague term. This phrase has frustrated legal experts for well over a century. (Perhaps most baffling is the juxtaposition of "cruel" and "unusual." That is, if a punishment is cruel, why does it matter if it is "unusual"?) The USSC has failed to provide a consistent standard for the interpretation of this provision. As such, it is difficult, if not impossible, to explain why the Court has deemed one punishment cruel and unusual and another not.

Packer's Two Models of Criminal Process

In his often-cited work, Herbert Packer delineated two models that govern the workings of the criminal justice system: the crime control model and the due process model. Each of these models represents competing sets of values.[4]

The crime control model is primarily concerned with the maximal reduction of crime. A crime is an act that infringes on the freedom of others and, if crime is not controlled, all of our freedoms are at stake. Accordingly, criminal justice authorities should be trusted to do their jobs and there should be few constraints on their efforts because these hinder their ability to control crime. A good criminal justice process is an efficient one, one that produces swift and certain results. The criminal justice system should

operate like an assembly line, quickly weeding out suspects who are innocent and sending the rest through a process that swiftly metes out justice to
those who are guilty. The process should be as informal as possible
because formalities slow down the system. The crime control models leans
toward a presumption of guilt.

*The due process model is primarily concerned with the abuse of power by the
state.* The powers to deprive someone of their freedom and possibly
execute them are awesome powers that need to be controlled. The fact-
finding mission of the police and district attorneys is biased by a presumption of guilt because their job is to solve crimes, make arrests, and secure
convictions. Without formal constraints, authorities are inclined to coerce
confessions, influence witness testimonies, or distort criminal proceedings,
either for political reasons or because they are convinced of the suspect's
guilt. Fact-finding should be an adversarial process, with the interests of
the suspect defended by an attorney. Packer writes, "If the crime control
model resembles an assembly line, the due process model looks very much
like an obstacle course,"[5] with each stage in the process designed to ensure
that those who are innocent proceed no further. The due process model
leans toward a presumption of innocence.

These two models are best seen as extremes on a continuum because
there are few if any purists in either camp. Everyone recognizes a need for
both crime control and for due process. However, wherever one lies on
this continuum determines one's position on a great many controversial
issues in criminal justice. Generally, on the American political spectrum,
conservatives lean toward the crime control side of the continuum; and
liberals lean toward the due process side. For example, conservatives tend
to be more dismissive of the Miranda rule and the exclusionary rule, seeing
them as formal constraints on criminal justice authorities that hinder their
ability to control crime. Liberals see them as more beneficial, curtailing the
abuse of power by criminal justice authorities, and diminishing the possibility that innocent people will be deprived or their freedom—or their lives.
As another example, in the previous chapter, with regard to cases in which
a police officer kills a black suspect, we mentioned that "police officials
and civil libertarians, conservatives and liberals, whites and blacks" argue
over whether the police are held sufficiently accountable. These pairings,
very roughly, reflect how the crime control advocates and due process
advocates are positioned against one another.

Torts and crimes

The essential difference between torts and crimes lies in who is considered
the victim of an illegal action. *In a tort, an individual or private entity is considered the victim;* and the individual who considers herself or himself to be
the victim initiates civil proceedings by suing the alleged offender. These

cases are decided in a civil court by a judge or jury based upon a preponderance of the evidence, that is, on whether the evidence balances in favor of the plaintiff. If the evidence favors the plaintiff, then the defendant usually has to pay financial damages to the plaintiff.

In a crime, the state is considered the victim; and the prosecutor representing the state initiates legal proceedings. Thus, we hear cases titled "the People versus," or "the Commonwealth versus," etc. The notion of the state as victim dates back to early English law, which considered crimes to be offenses "against the king's peace." An orderly and peaceful society requires that people not go around robbing, raping, and killing other people with impunity. Hence, robbery, rape, and homicide are, first and foremost, crimes against society (or the "state," which is responsible for maintaining an orderly society). In criminal proceedings, the defendant has the right to a trial by jury; although, he or she may waive that right and have the case heard only by a judge. Decisions are based on innocence or guilt, where a conviction is based on the "beyond a reasonable doubt" standard. Penalties may include fines, imprisonment or execution. The differences between torts and crime are depicted in Table 6.1.

The distinction between torts and crimes can be confusing because many offenses can be tried in both civil and criminal courts. The classic example of this was the case of O.J. Simpson. Simpson, a former football star who appeared often in the movies and on television, was charged in the murders of his ex-wife, Nicole Brown Simpson and her friend, Ron Goldman, in the *People of the State of California v. Orenthal James Simpson*. In 1995, at the end of a months-long, media-saturating trial, a jury found him not guilty. Subsequently, the families of Nicole Brown Simpson and Ron Goldman sued O.J. Simpson in civil courts for wrongful death. The jury found him "responsible" for the murders and ordered him to pay compensatory and punitive damages. As criminal cases apply the beyond a reasonable doubt standard, while civil cases apply the preponderance of

TABLE 6.1 Torts versus crimes

Torts (civil cases) lawsuit	Crimes (criminal cases) criminal prosecution
Who is considered the victim and who initiates proceedings?	
Individual or private entity	The state, the people, the commonwealth, etc.
Decision is based on what standard?	
Preponderance of the evidence	Beyond reasonable doubt
What are the possible penalties?	
Financial damages, corrective action	Fines, imprisonment, death

the evidence standard, the evidence may not be sufficient to secure a conviction in a criminal case, while it is enough to win a civil case.

Infractions, misdemeanors, felonies, and treason

Infractions are the least serious of offenses. Typical infractions include most traffic violations, jaywalking, littering, and fishing without a license. When they encounter someone committing an infraction, police often look the other way, or give the offender a verbal warning. When the authorities do respond in an official manner, the punishment is usually a fine, and offenders usually waive their right to a hearing.

The difference between misdemeanors and felonies lies not in the act itself, but in the law, which varies from state to state. *Misdemeanors are less serious crimes that are punishable by a fine and/or less than a year's imprisonment. Felonies are more serious crimes with a maximum sentence of a year or more.* For examples, a first offense of shoplifting is typically a misdemeanor; and murder is always a felony.

Treason is the only crime defined by the U.S. Constitution. The Constitution has this to say about treason:

> Treason against the United States, shall consist *only* in levying War against them, or in adhering to their Enemies, giving them Aid and Comfort. No Person shall be convicted of Treason unless on the Testimony of two Witnesses to the same overt Act, or on Confession in open Court. [Italics added]
>
> The Congress shall have Power to declare the Punishment of Treason, but no Attainder of Treason shall work Corruption of Blood, or Forfeiture except during the Life of the Person attainted.

Jurisprudents find it interesting that the document contains so much detail about the crime of treason, while it mentions no other crime. The wording in this provision was designed to limit the use of the charge of treason because the English kings would abuse the charge, using it as a weapon against their political enemies and reserving the slowest and most horrible forms of execution for this offense. David Shestokas writes, "In English law, for a long time before the Revolution, just thinking about the king's death (known as "compassing") was treason. The charge was used freely against political adversaries and the danger of an arrest for treason due to mere criticism of the government could chill most opposition."[6] (The "corruption of blood" and the "life of the person" phrases in the excerpt above were included to prevent the state from punishing the heirs of the traitor, as the old English law had done.)

THE STRUCTURE OF THE AMERICAN COURT SYSTEM

The federal court system is made up of 94 U.S. District Courts, 13 U.S. Courts of Appeal and the U.S. Supreme Court. Judges in all of these courts are nominated by the President and confirmed by the Senate. Generally, the federal courts hear cases that include the constitutionality of a law, U.S. laws and treaties, disputes between states, and maritime law. The U.S. District Courts hear cases that deal with federal crimes.

The structure of state court systems is determined by each state's constitution and may differ from state to state; but the state systems generally mirror the structure of the federal system as depicted in Figure 6.1. Most criminal and civil cases are heard in the state trial courts.

In both the federal and state courts, parties that are dissatisfied with the trial court's decision can appeal their case to the higher court; and the higher court usually has the authority to decide whether or not to hear the case. The federal court system has the U.S. Court of International Trade and the U.S. Bankruptcy Court. Both the federal and the state court systems have special courts, or "courts of limited jurisdiction." Some states, for example, have family courts that deal with divorces, adoptions, child custody and child support; some states have probate courts that deal with wills and estates; and some cities have gun courts to deal with gun-related

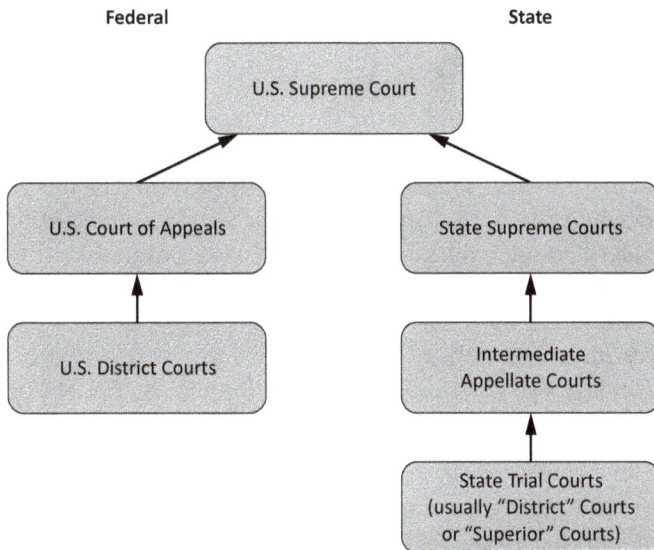

FIGURE 6.1
The structure of the U.S. court system.

crimes. The availability of such special courts vary from jurisdiction to jurisdiction.

Special Courts

Juvenile court

Juvenile courts are hardly "special" anymore because all states have them. *In 1899, Chicago established the first juvenile court in the United States; and "juvenile justice"—as a distinct form of justice—was born.* Before this, kids as young as seven were handled by the regular (adult) court system. The founding of the juvenile court was part of a larger social movement that organized on behalf of children's welfare. During the latter half of the nineteenth century the "Child Savers" movement helped to bring about a number of social and legal reforms, including child labor laws, kinder-gartens, compulsory school attendance, and the juvenile court.[7] Kids were understood to be in a special period of development; and how they turned out as adults was strongly influenced by how they were treated during this special period. The philosophy behind both the juvenile courts and the early juvenile reformatories was *parens patriae*, which held that if the child's parent(s) was unwilling or unable to perform his or her parental duties, the state would step in and protect the child. *The purposes of the juvenile justice system, versus the adult system, were protection and treatment, not pun-ishment.* Since protection was a primary purpose of the juvenile justice system, the juvenile could be held accountable for behaviors not pro-hibited by criminal statutes. These are called "status offenses;" that is, offenses for which juveniles can be held accountable by virtue of their minority status. These include offenses such as truancy, incorrigibility, and drinking under age.

Since the role of the state was to protect and treat the juvenile, he or she was not seen as needing the same constitutional protections provided to alleged adult offenders. As such, juveniles were dealt with more informally than adults. The police and court officials were less constrained by the Bill of Rights, and therefore had more discretion when dealing with juveniles. That discretion was meant to work in the juvenile's favor; but discretion lent itself to the arbitrary disposition of cases. According to the Center for Juvenile and Criminal Justice,

> By the 1950s and 1960s public concern grew about the effective-ness of the juvenile justice system, because of the disparities in treatment that resulted from the absolute discretion of juvenile court judges. Similarly situated youths could receive vastly different sentences based on the mood, temperament, or personal philosophy of individual judges.[8]

With the emergence of the civil rights movement in the 1950s and 1960s, criminologists and activists came to recognize that discretion in the juvenile justice system manifested itself not so much arbitrarily, but prejudicially, with poor kids, racial minorities, and children of immigrants being treated more harshly than middle class and wealthy white kids.[9] Reflecting the paternalistic nature of *parens patriae*, since the beginning of the juvenile court, girls were victims of discrimination as they were being held to stricter behavioral standards. Girls were often charged with "wayward" behavior and far more likely to be institutionalized for such offenses than boys.[10]

In 1964, 15 year-old Gerald Gault, who was on probation at the time, was committed to a state reformatory for the period of his minority—roughly six years—for making a lewd phone call. (If an adult had been convicted of the same crime, he would have received a maximum penalty of a $50 fine or two months in jail.) There was no advance notice of charges, no Miranda warning, no trial, no jury, no attorney, no transcript, and no live testimony from the alleged victim. Gerald was alleged to have admitted to the crime, but later refuted that he had done so. As there were no transcripts, there is no way to determine whether or not he did indeed admit guilt. The Arizona Supreme Court upheld the juvenile court ruling, holding that procedural safeguards afforded to adult defendants would interfere with the "necessary flexibility for individualized treatment."[11] In 1967, the United States Supreme Court overruled the Arizona courts. Questioning whether treatment was any different from punishment, the USSC held that Gault's procedural rights had been violated. Justice Abe Fortas wrote in the Court's majority opinion, "Under our Constitution, the condition of being a boy does not justify a kangaroo court."[12] Subsequent to the Gault decision, juveniles are granted some of the legal protections granted to adults, including the right to legal representation, the right to be given notice of charges, the right against self-incrimination, and the right to cross-examine witnesses.

From the inception of the juvenile court, an important goal of the juvenile justice system is to keep juveniles out of the criminal justice system, allowing them to avoid the corrupting influence of adult criminals and, just as importantly, allowing them to avoid the stigma associated with involvement in the criminal justice system. Even in the early days of juvenile justice, reformers had some sense of the self-fulfilling nature of criminal labels (see "Labeling theory" in Chapter 4). Depending on the state, the terminology used in juvenile courts is different from that in the adult courts, at least in part to minimize the stigmatizing nature of court proceedings. For examples, instead of being found "guilty," the charges are found to be "true;" the adjudicated child is a "delinquent" rather than a "criminal;" and the juvenile may be "committed" to an institution rather than be "sentenced" to prison.

Part of the effort to keep kids out of the system can include any number of juvenile *diversion programs*, intended to divert kids from penetrating further into "the system." For example, the juvenile justice system makes extensive use of probation as a means of keeping kids out of juvenile institutions. Probation and other forms of diversion are also available in the adult criminal justice system; but they are even more fundamental to the juvenile justice system with its emphasis on protection and treatment. With the informality and lack of constitutional safeguards of the juvenile justice system, it is also easier to compel juveniles into one diversion program or another. It may even be done at the level of police intake, without a court hearing. The Rochester, New Hampshire, Police Department posts information about its juvenile diversion program on its website, providing the following details,

> Court Diversion is a community-based alternative to the formal court process that integrates restorative justice practices, promotes positive youth development, and reduces juvenile crime and recidivism. Diversion programs recognize that you made a mistake. The program gives you the opportunity to take responsibility for and learn from your mistakes without ending up with a juvenile court record.
>
> This option is offered to first-time offenders with a misdemeanor level charge under the age of 18, within the Rochester Police Department's jurisdiction. You must be willing to take full responsibility for the offense and do not contest the facts of the police report.[13]

The Rochester diversion program can include "behavioral health assessments," "referral to community-based services", and "3 to 6 months of monitoring and support."[14]

Again, the intent of such diversion programs is to protect children from further penetration into the system; and it can be quite effective at that. However, there are two criticisms of such policies. First, authorities usually have a good deal of discretion in deciding whom to allow into their diversion programs. Where there is discretion, there is room for discrimination. For example, in a racially diverse jurisdiction, it may be that poor minorities are more likely to be placed into a diversion program, while wealthy white kids are let off with just a warning. Or, worse yet, wealthy white kids are offered a diversion program while more severe punishments await poor minority kids.

The second criticism of diversion has to do with allegations that these programs lead to "net widening." Keep in mind that kids are often put into these programs without a hearing or an adjudication of guilt. While the goal of diversion is to minimize the juvenile's penetration into the system, as the interventions seem more benign, and as there is no due process, these conditions allow criminal justice authorities to bring kids into the system that they would not have brought in otherwise. The charges may not have been serious enough to warrant the expenditure of police and court resources; or the evidence against the juvenile may have been too weak to secure a conviction. Thus, critics of the net-widening effect of juvenile diversion suggest that while most kids who have an encounter with the police do not penetrate deeply into the juvenile justice system, were it not for diversion, a great many of them might not have penetrated the system at all. Diversion enables more kids to be caught up in the system, allowing the state to extend its net of social control to further reaches of the juvenile population.

While it has long been a goal of the juvenile justice system to protect juveniles from adult proceedings, most state statutes allow or require that juveniles who commit serious crimes to be transferred into the adult criminal justice system. This phenomenon will be discussed in Chapter 7.

Drug court

There are over 3,000 drug courts in the United States.[15] Drug court guidelines and operations vary from state to state; but they usually operate within the adult criminal justice system and they rarely deal with violent criminals. They deal instead with addicts who are charged with drug possession or "drug-driven" crimes (namely, property crimes committed for the purpose of acquiring money to buy more drugs.) The drug court option is usually made available to the offender either as an alternative to criminal court (i.e., diversion), or as an alternative to a jail sentence.[16] Charges are dismissed, or sentences are suspended once the offender completes a rigorous drug treatment program in the community, supervised by the drug court. Offenders are given frequent drug tests and report frequently (perhaps once a week) to the drug court team—likely consisting of the judge, prosecutor, defense attorney and treatment coordinator—so that his or her progress may be assessed. Graduated sanctions and rewards may be applied accordingly.

While drug courts are becoming increasingly prevalent, the research on their effectiveness is inconsistent.[17] Some critics charge that, like other forms of diversion, drug courts contribute to the widening net of state control. One study, for example, found that "a large number of drug court participants were arrested for the possession of one drug only (often marijuana) and that more than half of participants came to the attention of the criminal justice system through a traffic stop rather than through repeated encounters with the criminal justice system."[18]

Mental health court

As we will see in Chapter 7, people with mental illness are disproportionately represented in American correctional populations; the experience of jail and prison can exacerbate their mental illness;[19] and jails and prisons are ill equipped to treat mental illness. The fact that so many people in jails and prisons suffer from mental illness has become a very serious problem in the United States. One means of addressing this problem has been the development of mental health courts (MHCs). There are over 400 MHCs in the United States.[20] Their operations vary, but typically, an offender with a diagnosed mental illness is given the option of completing a court-supervised treatment program rather than having his or her case heard in the criminal court; or, the adjudicated offender is offered MHC treatment as an alternative to incarceration. Like the drug courts, the treatment programs are usually administered by teams, including the judge, prosecutor, defense attorney, a mental health professional, and/or a caseworker. MHCs across the country vary in terms of eligibility: some are offered only to misdemeanants, some to felons, some to both; some are limited only to nonviolent offenders, some are not. As the programs are varied, it should not be surprising that research results are varied in terms of MHCs' effectiveness relative to traditional criminal justice responses.[21]

Immigration court

The Executive Office of Immigration Review is an office within the U.S. Department of Justice and it is responsible for the administration of the 58 immigration courts in the United States. These courts conduct removal proceedings to determine whether a non-citizen should be removed from the United States. They also decide on applications for asylum. People may be granted asylum if they can convince the court that they would be persecuted in their home country because of their "race, religion, nationality, membership in a particular social group, [or] political opinion."[22]

While by constitutional design the executive, legislative, and judicial branches of government are supposed to act as a check on one another, immigration courts are unusual in that they fall within the purview of the executive branch. This gives the President and the Attorney General more power over immigration courts than over other courts. With the election of Donald Trump in 2016, the workings of immigration courts have become highly politicized; and there have been numerous efforts in recent years to increase the number of removal proceedings, to expedite these proceedings, and to limit eligibility for the granting of asylum. Some of these efforts have been foiled by the federal judiciary, and some have not.

Human trafficking court

Human trafficking involves "The recruitment, harboring, transportation, provision, or obtaining of a person for labor or services, through the use of force, fraud, or coercion for the purpose of subjection to involuntary servitude, peonage, debt bondage, or slavery."[23] As there has been increased recognition of the pervasiveness of human trafficking, a number of states have established special courts to deal with the problem. These are usually cases calling for delicate treatment because the defendant is often also the victim. For a case to reach the human trafficking court, it must be flagged first as a case of human trafficking, which can be problematic. Victims of human trafficking do not share a profile; they often do not consider themselves victims; and those that do, may be afraid to report it. Flagging may take time-consuming and costly investigative work. A number of states automatically flag prostitution cases; but truancy, shoplifting, drug-related crimes, panhandling, and lack of legal residency may also be indicators of trafficking.[24]

When the case does reach the human trafficking court, judges often collaborate with prosecutors and defense attorneys to ensure the proper disposition of the case. Ideally, the courtroom players have received special training in issues involved with human trafficking, in particular with the trauma many victim-defendants have undergone. An example of such a disposition might be that the victim-defendant attend counseling sessions in lieu of a jail term. Victim-defendants are also often required to appear in court periodically to assess their progress. Some critics and stakeholders, however, consider these victim-defendants as purely victims and argue, therefore, that they should not be required to adhere to any such protocols.

Tribal court

Native American tribes are sovereign and run their affairs—including civil and criminal justice—independently of state and federal governments. Each Native American tribe has its own traditions, its own laws and, therefore, its own way of administering justice. Reservations have their own police, their own courts, and their own jails.

The laws establishing tribal jurisdiction are quite complicated. Some states, for example, are subject to Public Law 280 (Alaska, California, Minnesota, Nebraska, Oregon, and Wisconsin), which allows state law to supersede tribal law in some instances; and some states are not subject to PL 280. If a crime committed by a Native American on Native American land appears on the list in the Major Crimes Act, it can be prosecuted by the federal government.[25] Furthermore, the Indian Civil Rights Act of 1968 extends much of the Bill of Rights to tribal residents.[26] This legislation also limits the punishment that can be levied by tribal courts to a maximum of one year in jail and a fine of $5,000. Numerous other federal laws constraining tribal courts could fill one or more volumes of legal text.

As reservation residents are disproportionately represented among those living in poverty, and the needs of the reservations are given low priority by state and federal government, reservation infrastructures, including their criminal justice systems, tend to be underfunded.

ELECTION OF COURT OFFICIALS

The district attorney (titles vary by state) is the chief prosecutor in a given jurisdiction, usually a county. She supervises the other prosecuting attorneys in that jurisdiction and is in charge of deciding which cases will be brought to court and what crimes defendants will be charged with. In all but three states and the District of Columbia, the district attorney is an elected official.[27] The United States is the only country in the world where local prosecutors are elected.[28] Following the Revolutionary War, most chief prosecutors were appointed either by governors, legislators, or judges; but, in 1832, Mississippi made this an elected office and, within 30 years, most states had followed suit.[29] When prosecutors were appointed, patronage systems often emerged and appointments were handed out as political favors, with the appointers expecting favors in return. Making the prosecutor an elected official was intended to mitigate patronage and make prosecutors answerable to the people.

Similarly, the United States is one of only three countries in the world in which judges are elected.[30] More than three-quarters of all state court judges are elected officials.[31] In contrast, in France aspiring judges must pass a 4-day entrance exam to be admitted to Ecole Nationale de la Magistrature, an elite 27-month long training program for judges.[32] While, in theory, the election of judges and chief prosecutors in the United States makes these officials "answerable to the people," it also introduces a political element to the administration of justice that European jurisprudents find quite astonishing. Referring to the French system of training judges, Cornell law professor Mitchel Lasser states,

> You have people who actually know what the hell they're doing. They've spent years in school taking practical and theoretical courses on how to be a judge. These are professionals ... The rest of the world is stunned and amazed at what we do [in the U.S.], and vaguely aghast. They think the idea that judges with absolutely no judge-specific educational training are running political campaigns is both insane and characteristically American.[33]

Critics argue that the American electoral system turns the administration of justice into a popularity contest, with judges and prosecutors more concerned with what actions will garner the most votes than with justice and fairness. When candidates think ahead to their campaign, they often consider their conviction rates and this will bias the way they perform their duties. When we hear about prosecutors suppressing evidence that favors the defendant, or judges ruling in favor of prosecutors' motions, but not those of defense attorneys—these may be tactics designed to secure higher conviction rates and win elections.

People running for these offices will also find it useful in their campaigns to pander to voters' prejudices. Even when candidates do not pander, voter prejudices may affect election outcomes. In 2014, in a study that identified more than 2,400 elected prosecutors, 95 percent of them were white, and 83 percent were men. Women of color represented only one percent of elected prosecutors.[34] Referring to these numbers, Zak Cheney-Rice notes,

> This is not particularly surprising, given the lack of diversity in electoral politics overall. But it does erase any belief that the officials running our criminal justice system actually reflect the people [of color] they're throwing in jail by the hundreds of thousands.[35]

Lastly, competitive campaigns can be costly, with various interest groups and wealthy donors contributing to a given candidate. This sets the stage for corruption, or the appearance of corruption, creating problems similar to those associated with the old patronage system. Once elected, the judge or prosecutor owes a favor to his or her wealthy patron. Their debt could influence their decisions when their wealthy donor is charged (or could be charged) with a crime, or if the donor has a civil suit being heard in the judge's court. Worse yet, the media and the public are often unable to find out the identity of campaign donors. The Brennan Center for Justice found that of the money raised from interest groups for state supreme court elections in the 2015–2016 election cycle, 54 percent of it was from unknown sources (known as "dark money"); another 28 percent of the contributions came from sources that were difficult to trace because they passed through one or more intermediaries ("gray money").[36] Concerned about the increasing amounts of money entering into judicial elections, the Brennan Center warns, "As powerful interests increasingly see the courts as an effective vehicle for furthering their political, ideological, or financial agendas, [the] promise of both the appearance and reality of evenhanded justice is at risk."[37]

ADVERSARIAL VERSUS INQUISITORIAL SYSTEMS

In the United States, the trial courts operate within an adversarial system of fact-finding whereas many other parts of the world use an inquisitorial system. In inquisitorial systems, pretrial hearings are critical and the judge plays a much more active role, freely questioning suspects, witnesses, and attorneys. The role of the judge is not so much to determine innocence or guilt, but to find the truth. If he or she determines that the preponderance of the evidence is compelling, then the judge decides to move the case on to trial. The trial itself plays a less critical role in the process. Since a judge has already determined in the pretrial hearing that the case against the defendant is compelling, the trial starts out with a presumption of guilt.

In the United States, for serious felonies (and sometimes not-so-serious felonies), instead of a judge conducting a pretrial hearing, a grand jury does so. Prosecutors present their evidence to a grand jury; the grand jury may call witnesses and request documents; the jurors deliberate; and, if they determine that there is probable cause, the defendant is indicted. The grand jury was designed to serve as a check on the power of prosecutors; and, presumably, it operates independently of the prosecutor. However, since only the prosecution presents its case, grand juries almost always vote to indict. According to a 2014 report in the *Washington Post*, federal grand juries return an indictment in 99.99 percent of cases presented to them.[38] Sol Wachtler, the former chief judge of New York's Court of Appeals, is famously quoted for saying that prosecutors could get a grand jury to "indict a ham sandwich."[39] Given the predictable nature of the grand jury hearing, there is less basis for a presumption of guilt in American adversarial trials than in countries in continental Europe, which have an inquisitorial system of justice, with its elaborate pretrial investigation.

In the adversarial system, prosecuting and defending attorneys compete with one another to present the most compelling version of the truth. There is an intricate system of rules that constrain this competition and the judge serves to enforce those rules and act as a referee. The truth is not so much in dispute as the opposing attorneys. In fact, in their effort to present the most compelling version of the story, neither side is required to disclose certain facts unless specifically asked for them by the opposition. Thus, while, in theory, the duty of the prosecutor is to seek truth and justice, both parties are allowed to obscure the truth in the adversarial system.

Both the inquisitorial and adversarial systems have their advantages and their disadvantages. Probably most people favor the system with which they are most familiar. Most Americans would likely be concerned about the power wielded by the judges in the inquisitorial process. The judge's prejudices could have an enormous influence on the outcome of the case.

Most people from countries in continental Europe, on the other hand, would likely be concerned that the outcome of cases in American courts depends more upon the performance of the attorneys than it does upon the facts. They might also be concerned that in the competition between prosecution and defense, as we will see, the system is tilted in favor of the prosecution, especially when the defendant is poor.

PUBLIC DEFENDERS

As we have discussed above, the Sixth Amendment provides the right to counsel and the USSC has ruled that counsel would be provided by the court when defendants are indigent. It is generally assumed that justice should be blind to the defendant's race and social class. Thus, in theory at least, representation by a public defender should be as good as representation by a private attorney. For that matter, representation by an attorney who bills at $100 per hour should be just as good as that provided by an attorney who bills at $1,000 per hour. Most of us, however, do not make such assumptions.

The well-recognized problem for public defense systems has to do with resources and caseloads. Most public defenders are not given the resources they need to deal equitably with their caseloads. Even the USSC has recognized this problem, implicitly recognizing the system is unfair, but failing to offer a solution.[40] There are three basic models for funding and implementing public defense systems briefly described by Jessa DeSimone:[41]

> (1) the public defender model, in which salaried attorneys provide representation on indigent cases; (2) the assigned counsel model, in which the court assigns indigent cases to private attorneys who are compensated on a case-by-case basis; and (3) the contract model, in which there is a private bar contract with an attorney or group of attorneys that will provide representation in some or all of the indigent defense cases.

A good defense requires hours, days, weeks, or months of investigation into the facts and the evidence. The majority of public defenses come out of specially dedicated public defenders offices (Model 1 above).[42] These offices are particularly prone to being swamped with huge caseloads (with perhaps hundreds of cases per attorney)[43] where it becomes impossible to conduct the thorough investigation needed for each case. According to one study in the state of Louisiana, a "reasonably effective" defense for high-level felonies should require 70 hours of the defense attorney's attention; and mid-level felonies should get 41 hours of attention.[44] Public defenders have to engage in a sort of triage, quickly determining which cases deserve more time than others. In the Models 2 and 3 above, public defender fees are determined by the state or the local jurisdiction; and these fees are likely to be limited or substantially less than what these attorneys charge their private clients. In which case, indigent defendants could well not receive the priority given to their private clients.

For all three models, the problem of public defender systems is one of inadequate funding; and it is not unusual to hear references to the crisis in public defense "by everyone from academics, practitioners, journalists, and advocacy organizations, to the ABA."[45] James Silkenat, former president of the American Bar Association, states that "lawyers in public defender programs are being asked to carry outlandish, excessive workloads that prevent them from adequately representing their clients and making a mockery of the constitutional right to counsel."[46] David Carroll of the Sixth Amendment Center in Boston argues, "There is no greater tyranny than a well-resourced prosecution and law enforcement when individuals don't have a proper defense."[47]

While there has been little or no research specifically examining how race influences the ways public defenders prioritize their cases, there is substantial research on how unconscious racial biases "are ubiquitous and can influence judgments, especially when information deficits exist. Worse," write law professors Song Richardson and Phillip Goff, "these biases are particularly influential in circumstances where time is limited, individuals are cognitively taxed, and decisionmaking is highly discretionary—exactly the context in which PDs find themselves."[48] Given emerging research on the pervasiveness of implicit racial bias, more research is required to understand the extent to which such bias influences public defenders in prioritizing their cases.

If indigent defendants are incompetently represented and then found guilty, they have little legal recourse. Courts apply the *Strickland* rule to determine whether such cases should be overturned. By this rule, the appellants must prove that the verdict would have been different if they had had a competent attorney—a very high standard. DeSimone reports, "courts have not used *Strickland* even when public defenders were unaware of current law, were intoxicated at the trial, or slept through the trial."[49]

JURY SELECTION

The Sixth Amendment entitles defendants to an impartial jury (contrary to popular belief, "a jury of one's peers" does not appear in the U.S. Constitution). In the social sciences, in order to ensure that our sample is unbiased, or impartial, we try to employ random selection. A randomly selected sample is not one without biased members; but we often presume that it contains members with random biases that cancel each other out. While random sampling is difficult (see Chapter 1), what we most want to avoid is a sampling method in which people with certain biases are systematically included or excluded from our sample. The same goes for jury selection.

Jury selection has been called "the most important part of any criminal trial."[50] Typically, to assemble a jury, the court sends a letter to randomly selected names from some comprehensive list of community members such as voter registration rolls or a list of people with a driver's license provided by the department of motor vehicles. Recipients are instructed when and where to appear for the jury selection process, or the *voir dire* (French for "to see to speak" or "to speak the truth"). The judge and/or the prosecuting and defense attorneys ask candidates screening questions. Judges can exclude a potential juror if there is reason to believe that he or she may be biased; this is a dismissal "for cause." The randomness of the selection process can be compromised by the comprehensiveness of the original list, by who actually shows up for the voir dire as instructed, and by the judge's biases—all three of which may be problematic in the empaneling of any given jury. Poor people are less likely to appear on voter registration lists, less likely to have a driver's license, and, because getting to the voir dire can require travel over some distances, less able to make the trip. Furthermore, the judge's prejudices or his or her leanings in a particular case can influence their decisions on which jurors to dismiss for cause.

In addition to exclusions based on cause, the prosecuting and defense attorneys are each allowed a certain number of "peremptory strikes" that require no explanation. This is the more controversial aspect of the jury selection process. Joshua Revesz writes in the *Yale Law Journal*, "Legal scholars, by and large, revile peremptory challenges. Allowing parties to unilaterally strike prospective jurors without explanation has been attacked as undemocratic, as prone to manipulation, as a potential First Amendment violation, and—most often of all—as racist."[51] *In 1986, in the case of Batson v. Kentucky, the USSC ruled that striking jurors because of their race was unconstitutional.* Later court cases extended the *Batson rule* to prohibit the exclusion of women and Latinos and Hispanics.[52] Before *Batson*, many prosecutors routinely struck black jurors in cases where the defendant was black. After *Batson*, if called upon, prosecutors merely have to explain why the exclusion of a black juror was not based on race. Racially biased peremptory strikes may have declined, but they were and are still rife.[53] In the few years following Batson, a number of convictions were reversed due to racist jury selection; but, some prosecutor's offices adapted to the new rule, training their attorneys "to mask their exclusion of minorities from juries."[54] As USSC Justice Thurgood Marshall noted, "any prosecutor can easily assert facially neutral reasons for striking a juror, and trial courts are ill equipped to second-guess those reasons."

Empowered by peremptory strikes and recognizing the importance of a jury's makeup, many attorneys turn toward consultants to assist them in jury selection. *Scientific jury selection (SJS) emerged in the early 1970s* in the case of the "Harrisburg Seven" when anti-Vietnam war activists were charged with conspiracy to kidnap the National Security Advisor, Henry Kissinger.[55] The defense team hired a sociologist who developed a community survey and, based on its results, provided the defense with profiles of desirable and undesirable jury candidates. The trial resulted in a hung jury and SJS was recognized to be a potential benefit to either side in both criminal and civil trials. By the mid-1990s, SJS had become a $400 million industry, employing people trained in sociology, in marketing research, and especially in psychology.[56] SJS consultants employ social scientific methods, including surveys, focus groups, trial simulations; and, according to Jane Hu, "The creepiest consultants complete full 'pre-trial investigations' on potential jurors, which include background checks, interviews with acquaintances, and drive-by observations of jurors' homes."[57] Today, trial consultants also advise attorneys on matters concerning change of venue and on the conduct of the trial itself. SJS consultants advised in such cases as "O.J. Simpson, the Menendez brothers, Martha Stewart, Bernie Ebbers, the first Rodney King trial, the William Kennedy Smith rape trial, and the $1 million McDonald's verdict."[58] Employing SJS consultants can be costly and, therefore, the prosecution may turn to them only in high profile cases; and the defense may only use them when they are defending wealthy clients. In such cases, SJS has become a routine expense and can cost several hundred thousand dollars.[59]

Critics of SJS charge that it defeats the goal of having an impartial jury. Remember that to achieve this goal, we want to avoid systematic bias in jury selection; and SJS directly contravenes that objective. Critics also charge that, given the costs of SJS, its use further widens the gap between the quality of "justice" that is dispensed to wealthy and poor defendants. Finally, we should note that, according to some critics, such ethical criticisms of scientific jury selection are irrelevant because SJS does not indeed lend any advantage to either legal team.[60] Summarizing the research, Randolph Jonakait, writes,

> Social science studies have consistently found that *the overwhelming determinant of verdicts is the evidence presented to the jury.* Much research has been done trying to find correlations between the race, gender, age, economic status, political views, and other characteristics of jurors and their verdicts. Although every finding is not precisely the same, one conclusion is consistently reached—verdicts cannot be predicted accurately simply by knowing the makeup of the jury.[61]

Yet, Jonakait acknowledges that "5 to 15 percent of the variations [in verdicts] can be connected to demographic and personality variables."[62] While opposing attorneys have only limited ability to shape a jury, and while SJS has only limited ability to identify the relevant demographic and personality variables, that 5 to 15 percent variation could easily be the difference between a guilty verdict and a hung jury. It is no wonder that those who can afford it would engage the services of SJS consultants. Thus, to lessen the advantage of wealth, some have suggested that the court engages SJS services for indigent defendants (or that SJS consultants be required to perform pro bono work for indigent defendants); or, for myriad reasons, many jurisprudents have argued that legislatures should abolish peremptory challenges altogether.[63]

PLEA BARGAINING

Most criminal cases in the United States never get to the point of jury selection. Americans should know that 95 percent of convictions in the United States are the result of a guilty plea.[64] The formalities of the courtroom trial that are so often depicted on television and in the movies are very much the exception, not the rule. Including attorney preparation and jury selection, a trial can take days, weeks, or months (and occasionally years). Instead, in the overwhelming majority of cases, decisions that can have radically life-altering consequences for the accused can be made in as little as a few minutes. Milton Heuman describes the process in one jurisdiction,

> Typically … a line forms outside the prosecutor's office the morning before court is convened. Defense attorneys shuffle into the prosecutor's office and, in a matter of two or three minutes, dispose of the one or many cases "set down" that day. Generally, only a few words have to be exchanged before agreement is reached. The defense attorney mutters something about the defendant, the prosecutor reads the police report, and concurrence on "what to do" generally, but not always, emerges.[65]

This happens where the U.S. Constitution—the most binding of all legal documents—guarantees the accused the right to a trial by jury.

To put this into perspective, we need to keep in mind that a mere 10 percent decrease in the proportion of convictions resulting from a guilty plea would translate to nearly a 200 percent increase in the number of cases going to trial. Given the already-burgeoning caseloads of the courts, prosecutors, and public defenders, a doubling or tripling of cases going to trial would overwhelm the system. In theory, plea bargaining serves the interests of all parties by allowing judges a manageable court docket, prosecutors reasonable time to spend on the cases that do go to trial, and defendants a lighter sentence. However, all justifications for plea bargaining require that the defendant enters into the agreement/confession voluntarily. Otherwise, innocent people will be punished.

Critics of the U.S. court system's heavy reliance on plea bargaining argue that the process leaves too much room for coercion. The essence of this critique revolves around the question, How much pressure should the prosecutor be allowed to put on the defendant to make him or her plead guilty? Surely, we would all agree that if the prosecutor told the defendant, "If you don't plead guilty, we will kill you," that would constitute an unacceptable degree of coercion; and even innocent people would plead guilty. However, more realistically, prosecutors could tell a defendant, "If you do not plead guilty to second degree murder and accept a ten year prison sentence, we will try you in court; and, if you are found guilty, you may get the death penalty." The difference between these two scenarios is one of degree and has to do with the certainty of punishment. Critics argue that both scenarios are coercive; those that defend the status quo would argue that the second scenario is not.

Another critique holds that plea bargaining encourages prosecutors to "overcharge" defendants. That is, if prosecutors did not have the option to plea bargain, they would only charge the defendant with crimes for which there is enough evidence to persuade a judge or jury in a courtroom. However, with plea bargaining in mind, they are inclined to charge the defendant with more crimes—or a more serious crime—than the evidence supports in order to scare him or her into pleading guilty to a lesser crime.

Overcharging is part of a larger criticism having to do with the so-called "trial penalty." If the difference between the sentence that is offered to someone if they plead guilty and the sentence that they are threatened with should she or he be found guilty during a trial is too great, then it may be a rational decision for the defendant to plead guilty to a crime that he or she did not commit. For example, imagine if the defendant is told that if he pleads guilty to larceny, he will receive a one-year sentence; but, if the case goes to court, he is told, the prosecutor will seek punishment under the three-strikes law and he will get 20 years to life in prison. In such a situation, a person who is innocent of the charge may plead guilty to avoid such a severe sanction. The trial penalty, or the difference between the plea sentence and the trial sentence, is at least 19 years and amounts to penalizing the defendant for exercising his constitutional right to a trial.

According to data from the Innocence Project, a well-known organization which works to exonerate wrongfully convicted defendants, just over 10 percent of convicts who were exonerated by DNA evidence had pled guilty to their crimes; and according to the National Registry of Exonerations, 18 percent of all those who have been exonerated of their crimes had pled guilty. Using these figures, between 10 and 18 percent of those convicted of crimes based upon a guilty plea are innocent. Given that 95 percent of convictions are based on guilty pleas, this would mean that, of the 1.7 million people serving time in state and federal prisons in 2016, between 161,000 and 290,000 were innocent of the charges to which they had pled guilty.[66] Of the 166 people who were exonerated and released from prison in 2016, 74 (45 percent) had been serving sentences for which they had pled guilty.[67] These numbers indicate that innocent people serving time in prison is not such a rare circumstance; and they are an indicator of the pressure that prosecutors and/or judges can put on defendants in the process of plea bargaining. The greater that pressure, the more likely innocent people will confess to crimes they did not commit.

Unlike private attorneys, public defenders who represent poor defendants are often not paid by the billable hour; and they are often motivated to encourage their clients to accept a plea so that they can move on to their next case. Thus, prosecutors can bring to bear the most pressure on people who cannot afford private attorneys and poor people are the most susceptible. Worse yet, poor defendants who plead guilty to drug crimes (unlike other felonies) may not be aware that their conviction could render them ineligible for welfare benefits, federally subsidized housing, or financial aid for college.

Not surprisingly, since research has found race to be a factor at all levels of the criminal justice process—from arrest to conviction to incarceration—it also comes into play in the plea bargaining process. A recent study by Carlos Berdejó of Loyola Law School confirms this is especially the case for misdemeanor and lower-level felony charges (the majority of criminal cases) in which the accused has no prior convictions. Charges are more likely to be dropped, or reduced from the initial charge, for white defendants than for black defendants. Berdejó concludes that, as these are lower level charges and the defendant has no priors, prosecutors assume white defendants will pose no more danger to the community; but for black defendants, racist assumptions are being made about the "defendant's latent criminality and likelihood to recidivate."[68]

"PROSECUTORS GONE WILD"

Essentially, all of these criticisms of plea bargaining add up to suggest that the prosecutor has too much power in the process of adjudication. Judges used to have more power; but minimum sentencing laws passed in the 1980s and 1990s at both the state and federal levels (see Chapter 7), stripped judges of much of their discretion and handed it over to prosecutors, giving them harsher sentences with which to threaten defendants and leverage guilty pleas. Guilty pleas reduce their caseloads and enhance their conviction rates, making incumbent prosecutors more appealing for the next election cycle. In order to gain convictions—whether by plea or by trial— prosecutors have been known to use underhanded tactics, perhaps the worst of which is hiding exculpatory evidence. When prosecutors use such tactics, they are rarely caught; and when they are caught, they themselves are usually immune from prosecution.

Until recently, conservatives in the United States have favored tougher crime control policies than liberals. But many conservative organizations have come to realize how costly tough-on-crime measures have been for federal, state, and local budgets. Today, liberals and conservatives are finding common ground with regard to criminal justice reform. In 2015, the Conservative Political Action Conference (CPAC)—one of the largest and most influential annual conservative gatherings in the country— hosted a panel called "Prosecutors Gone Wild." This panel was so popular that CPAC did it again two years later and over a thousand people attended.[69] Sidney Powell, one of the 2015 panel members writes in the *National Review*, a leading conservative magazine, that an "epidemic" of prosecutorial misconduct, "is devastating the lives of innocent people and breaking families; it is devouring our tax dollars; and it has destroyed the public's faith in our justice system." Powell continues,

> At a time when the federal deficit is out of control, all resources are scarce, the very seams of our prisons are bursting from over-crowding, and we lead the world in incarceration, it is outrageous that we continue to incarcerate innocent people and harass and destroy the lives of others through prolonged, baseless prosecutions. … The truth about victims of prosecutorial misconduct is that, but for the grace of God, there go any one of us …
>
> Fortunately, most prosecutors strive to do their difficult jobs with honor, fairness, and integrity. They internalize and exemplify the Supreme Court's mandate that the United States Attorney seek justice—not convictions. Unfortunately, however, as the reversals, exonerations, and belated disclosures have begun to show, far too many prosecutors pursue their own personal agendas instead of justice.[70]

Because both conservatives and liberals see an advantage to reducing the number of people being incarcerated, progress has been made in recent years to limiting the power of prosecutors. *In 2018, the First Step Act was passed with bipartisan support in Congress. Among other things, this legislation reduced minimum sentences for certain federal crimes.* Many states have been moving in this direction as well. These reductions in minimum sentences lessen the likelihood of overcharging and reduce prosecutors' leverage in the bargaining process. In addition, many progressive candidates have been running for office around the country in recent years with platforms advocating reductions in sentences, alternatives to incarceration, and reducing the incarceration rate in the United States.[71]

For additional reforms, we might look at the plea bargaining process in other countries as well. There are other countries that employ plea bargaining, but none are as reliant on the process as the United States.[72] In France, for example, plea bargaining cannot be engaged when the maximum sentence for the crime is greater than five years; and the sentence offered by the prosecutor has to be less than one year. In 2005, only 4 percent of decisions in criminal cases in France were settled by a guilty plea.[73] Likewise, in Germany, plea bargaining can only be used for lesser crimes; and even when the defendant pleads guilty, the case must go to trial.[74] As there is a guilty plea, less evidence is required for a conviction at trial; the trials are quicker, and serve as a form of quality control on the bargains struck by prosecutors. By limiting the use of plea bargains to lesser crimes, the French and German systems are limiting the potential disadvantage that comes with choosing to take your case to trial, thereby limiting the pressure that can be applied by the prosecutor and limiting the prosecutor's power in any given case. It is also noteworthy that prosecutors are not elected in these countries, so there is little or no political capital to be gained by prosecutors for high conviction rates.

CONCLUSION

As we conclude our tour of the American court system, it is difficult not to be struck by the disjuncture between the ideal of justice and the reality of its dispensation. Yet, paradoxically, this disjuncture, while striking on one level, comes as no surprise on another level. Almost everybody would agree that the quality of justice that is meted out should not depend upon the social class, race, or ethnicity of the defendant, yet we know that it often does; and yet this disjuncture scores low on most people's list of priorities—especially for members of the white middle and upper classes.

Much of the problem is related to resource allocation. As we have noted, for example, the unequal dispensation of justice is often engendered by the process of plea bargaining; we also noted that just a slight reduction in cases that are plea bargained would cause an enormous increase in the number of cases that would go to trial, in a court system that is already overburdened. Thus, opponents of reform argue that we simply do not have the resources to radically change the system's heavy reliance on plea bargaining. However, as we shall see in Chapter 7, the United States has the highest incarceration rate in the world; a major reason for this is the length of sentences dispensed by our courts; and the poor and minorities are disproportionately represented in the prison inmate population. The criminal justice system is indeed a "system," which means that changes in one part of the system lead to changes in other parts. If the length of sentences were reduced and brought into line with most other industrialized countries, the money saved on incarcerating hundreds of thousands of Americans could be diverted to the courts, allowing for the reduction in the courts' overreliance on plea bargaining, and the dispensation of justice could be brought closer into alignment with our ideals of justice.

NOTES

1 Samuel Walker, *Sense and Nonsense about Crime, Drugs, and Communities*, 7th edition, Belmont, CA: Wadsworth, 2011.
2 Milner, Neal. "Comparative Analysis of Patterns of Compliance with Supreme Court Decisions: 'Miranda' and the Police in Four Communities." *Law & Society Review*, vol. 5, no. 1, 1970, pp. 119–134. Liqun Cao and Bu Huang, "Determinants of Citizen Complaints Against Police Abuse of Power," *Journal of Criminal Justice.* May/Jun2000, vol. 28, no. 3, 203–213.
3 Benjamin Wittes, "What is Cruel and Unusual?" Policy review, Hoover Institution, December 1, 2005. www.hoover.org/research/what-cruel-and-unusual. Retrieved June 20, 2019.
4 Herbert Packer, "Two Models of the Criminal Process," *University of Pennsylvania Law Review*, vol. 113, no. 1, November 1964, pp. 1–68.
5 Ibid., p. 13.
6 David Shestokas, "Treason: The Only Crime Defined by the U.S. Constitution." www.shestokas.com/constitution-educational-series/treason-the-only-crime-defined-in-the-us-constitution/. Retrieved June 23, 2019.
7 Roger McNally, "Nearly a Century Later – The Child Savers – Child Advocates and the Juvenile Justice System," *Juvenile and Family Court Journal*, August 1982, vol. 33, no. 3, pp. 47–52.
8 Center on Juvenile and Criminal Justice, "Juvenile Justice History," www.cjcj.org/education1/juvenile-justice-history.html. Retrieved July 14, 2019.
9 Irving Piliavin and Scott Briar, "Police Encounters with Juveniles," *The American Journal of Sociology*, vol. 70, September 1964, pp. 206–214. See also National Research Council and Institute of Medicine, *Juvenile Crime Juvenile Justice*, Joan McCord, Cathy Widom, and Nancy Crowell, eds., Washington, DC: National Academy Press, 2001.
10 National Research Council and Institute of Medicine, *Juvenile Crime Juvenile Justice*.
11 In re Gault Opinion. http://njdc.info/wp-content/uploads/2013/11/In-re-Gault-slip-opinion.pdf. Retrieved July 27, 2017.
12 Ibid.
13 Rochester Police Department *Official Website* (italics in original), Juvenile Services, "So What is Juvenile Court Diversion?" https://rochesterpd.org/divisions/juvenile-services/. Retrieved July 13, 2019.
14 Ibid.
15 National Institute of Justice "Drug Courts," Office of Justice Programs. www.nij.gov/topics/courts/drug-courts/Pages/welcome.aspx. Retrieved August 31, 2017.
16 National Institute of Justice, "Practice Profile: Adult Drug Courts" (modified May 1, 2018). www.crimesolutions.gov/PracticeDetails.aspx?ID=7. Retrieved July 16, 2019.

17 For a review of finding, see Timothy DeGiusti, "Innovative Justice: Federal reentry Drug Courts—How Should We Measure Success?" *Federal Probation*, vol. 82, no. 3, December 2018, pp. 11–20.

18 O. Hayden Griffin, Vanessa Griffin, Heith Copes and John Dantzler (2018) "Today Was Not a Good Day: Offender Accounts of the Incidents that Led to Their Admission to Drug Court," *Criminal Justice Studies*, vol. 31, no. 4, September 2018, pp. 388–401.

19 Kelly Canada, Stacey Barrenger, and Bradley Ray, "Bridging Mental Health and Criminal Justice System: A Systematic Review of the Impact of Mental Health Courts on Individuals and Communities," *Psychology, Public Policy, and Law*, vol. 25, no. 2, May 2019, pp. 73–91.

20 Ibid.

21 Ibid.

22 U.S. Citizenship and Immigration Services, "Asylum," www.uscis.gov/humanitarian/refugees-asylum/asylum. Retrieved July 26, 2019.

23 U.S. Department of Justice, "Human Trafficking Task Force e-Guide: Understanding Human Trafficking," Office of Justice Programs, Office for Victims of Crime. www.ovcttac.gov/taskforceguide/eguide/1-understanding-human-trafficking/. Retrieved April 18, 2020.

24 U.S. Department of Justice, "Human Trafficking Task Force e-Guide: Human Trafficking Courts." www.ovcttac.gov/taskforceguide/eguide/6-the-role-of-courts/64-innovative-court-responses/human-trafficking-courts/. Retrieved April 18, 2020.

25 See Cornell Law School, Legal Information Institute, Indians, Section 1153, Offenses Committed within Indian Country, www.law.cornell.edu/uscode/text/18/1153. Retrieved July 26, 2019.

26 For a list of the rights extended to tribal members/residents, see www.courts.ca.gov/documents/Indian-Civil-Rights-Act-of-1968.pdf. Retrieved September 26, 2019.

27 George Coppolo, "States that Elect their Chief Prosecutors," OLR Research Report, 2003-R-0231, February 24, 2003. www.cga.ct.gov/2003/rpt/2003-R-0231.htm. Retrieved July2, 2019.

28 Michael Ellis, "The Origins of the Elected Prosecutor," *The Yale Law Journal*, vol. 121, 2012, pp. 1528–1569. Emily Bazelon, *Charged: The New Movement to Transform American Prosecution and End Mass Incarceration*, New York: Random House, 2019.

29 Ellis, "The origins of the Elected Prosecutor."

30 In Switzerland canton judges are elected, and in Japan, Supreme Court judges are appointed, but face elections to retain their appointments. Adam Liptak, "U.S. Voting for Judges Perplexes other Nations," *New York Times*, May 25, 2008. www.nytimes.com/2008/05/25/world/americas/25iht-judge.4.13194819.html. Retrieved July 2, 2019.

31 Ibid.

32 Ibid.

33 Ibid.

34 Amita Kelly, "Does it Matter that 95 Percent of Elected Prosecutors are White?" National Public Radio, July 8, 2015. www.npr.org/sections/itsallpolitics/2015/07/08/420913118/does-it-matter-that-95-of-elected-prosecutors-are-white. Retrieved July 2, 2019.

35 Zak Cheney-Rice, "You Can Probably Guess how White the U.S.'s Elected Prosecutors Are," *Mic*, July 8, 2015. www.mic.com/articles/121919/79-percent-of-criminal-prosecutors-are-white-and-male. Retrieved July 3, 2019.

36 Alicia Bannon, Cathleen Lisk, and Peter Hardin, *Who Pays for Judicial Races?*, The Brennan Center for Justice at New York University School of Law, The Politics of Judicial Elections 2016–16. www.brennancenter.org/sites/default/files/publications/Politics_of_Judicial_Elections_Final.pdf. Retrieved July 15, 2019. For a discussion of gray money, see Chisun Lee and Douglas Keith, "How Semi-Secret Spending Took over Politics," *The Atlantic*, June 28, 2016. www.theatlantic.com/politics/archive/2016/06/the-rise-of-gray-money-in-politics/489002/. Retrieved June 16, 2019.

37 Ibid.

38 Ibid.

39 There is some question as to whether Wachtler was the first to use this phrase. See Ben Zimmer, "'Indict a Ham Sandwich' Remains on the Menu for Judges, Prosecutors," *Wall Street Journal*, June 1, 2018. www.wsj.com/articles/indict-a-ham-sandwich-remains-on-the-menu-for-judges-prosecutors-1527863063. Retrieved July 25, 2019.

40 Citing Jones v. Barnes (1983), Harvard law professor, Charles Ogletree, "An Essay on the New Public Defender for the 21st Century," *Law and Contemporary Problems*, vol. 58, no. 1, Winter 1995, pp. 81–93.

41 Jessa DeSimone, "Bucking Conventional Wisdom: The Montana Public Defender Act," *Journal of Criminal Law and Criminology*, vol. 96, no. 4, Summer 2006, pp. 1482.

42 Song Richardson and Phillip Goff, "Implicit Racial Biases in Public Defender Triage," *Yale Law Journal*, vol. 122, no, 8, June 2013, pp. 2626–2649.

43 Richard Oppel, Jr. and Jugal Patel, "One Lawyer, 194 Cases, and No Time," New York Times, January 31, 2019, www.nytimes.com/interactive/2019/01/31/us/public-defender-case-loads.html. Retrieved July 21, 2019.

44 Postlethwaite and Netterville, APAC and the American Bar Association, *The Louisiana Project: A Study of the Louisiana Defender System and Attorney Workload Standards, 2017.* www.americanbar.org/content/dam/aba/administrative/legal_aid_indigent_defendants/ls_sclaid_louisiana_project_report.pdf. Retrieved July 21, 2019.

45 Ibid., 1484.

46 American Bar Association, "Public Defender Caseload Tracking Shows How Systems are Overburdened, Panelists Say," September 17, 2014. www.americanbar.org/news/abanews/aba-news-archives/2014/02/public_defender_case/. Retrieved July 21, 2019.

47 Phil McCausland, "Public Defenders Nationwide Say They're Overworked and Underfunded," NBC News, December 11, 2017. www.nbcnews.com/news/us-news/public-defenders-nationwide-say-they-re-overworked-underfunded-n828111. Retrieved July 21, 2019.

48 Richardson and Goff, "Implicit Racial Bias," p. 2628 (emphasis added).

49 Ibid., p. 1483.

50 Herald Fahringer, "In the Valley of the Blind: A Primer on Jury Selection in a Criminal Case," *Law and Contemporary Problems*, vol. 43, no. 4, Autumn 1980, p. 116.

51 Joshua Revesz, "Ideological Imbalance and the Peremptory Challenge," *Yale Law Journal*, vol. 125, no. 8, June 2016, p. 2535.

52 National Legal Research Group, "Exercising Peremptory Challenges in Light of J.E.B." www.nlrg.com/our-services/jury-research-division/jury-research-publications/-exercising-peremptory-challenges-in-light-of-jeb. Retrieved July 23, 2019.

53 Quoted in Bryan Stevenson, "Illegal Discrimination in Jury Selection: A Continuing Legacy," *Human Rights*, vol. 37, no. 4, p. 5.

54 Ibid.

55 Bryan Myers and Michael Arena, "Trial Consultation: A New Direction in Applied Psychology," *Professional Psychology: Research and Practice*," vol. 32, no. 4, 2001, pp. 386–391.

56 Ibid.

57 Jane Hu, "The Unscientific Science of Jury Selection," *Pacific Standard*, November 18, 2014. https://psmag.com/news/jody-arias-quackery-behind-scientific-jury-selection-94423. Retrieved July 23, 2019.

58 Richard Seltzer, "Scientific Jury Selection: Does it Work?" *Journal of Applied Social Psychology*, 2006, vol. 36, no. 10, p. 2417.

59 Myers and Arena, "Trial Consultation."

60 Seltzer, "Scientific Jury Selection" and Hu, "The Unscientific Science."

61 Randolph Jonakait, *The American Jury System*, New Haven: Yale University Press, 2003, p. 159 (emphasis in the original).

62 Ibid.

63 Revesz, "ideological Imbalance," and Hu, "The Unscientific Science."

64 Sherod Thaxton, "Leveraging Death," *Journal of Criminal Law and Criminology*, vol. 103, no. 2, 2013, pp. 475–552. Tina Fryling, "The Ethics of Prosecutors," *Society, Ethics, and the Law: A Reader*, D. Mackey and K. Elvey, eds., Burlington, MA: Jones and Bartlett, 2021, pp. 180–187.

65 Quoted in Marc Morjé Howard, *Unusually Cruel: Prisons Punishment, and the Real American Exceptionalism*, New York: Oxford University Press, 2017, p. 31.

66 These figures are not likely to include those who plead guilty to misdemeanors, as these organizations that work on exonerating innocent defendants do not have the time or resources to spend on those given short prison sentences. Hence we only included inmates serving time in prisons, not jails (see Chapter 6). Thus, our numbers are likely to be underestimated because innocent misdemeanants who cannot afford bail often plead guilty so they can get out of jail for "time served." (On the one hand, our estimates could be overestimated because these agencies do focus on inmates with lengthier sentences, so the base of 1.7 million inmates would be smaller.)

67 National Registry of Exonerations, "Exoneration in 2016," March 7, 2017. www.law.umich.edu/special/exoneration/Documents/Exonerations_in_2016.pdf. Retrieved July 10, 2019.

68 Carlos Berdejó, "Criminalizing Race: Racial Disparities in Plea Bargaining," *Boston College Law Review*, vol. 58, no. 4, April 26, 2018, p. 1188.

69 See Emily Bazelon, *Charged*.

70 Sidney Powell, "Time to Tame Prosecutors Gone Wild," *National Review*, February 23, 2015. www.nationalreview.com/2015/02/time-tame-prosecutors-gone-wild-sidney-powell/. Retrieved July 11, 2019.

71 Bazelon, *Charged: The New Movement to Transform American Prosecution and End Mass Incarceration*.

72 Ibid.

73 Ibid.

74 Ibid.

CHAPTER 7

Corrections

WHY PUNISH?

We can imagine that from the earliest days of our human ancestors, when one member of the tribe broke the rules, he or she was met with some form of negative reaction—dispensed by one, some, or all members of the group—that we would call punishment. The forms that punishment takes have varied over time and across cultures. The reasons for punishment are just as varied. It may be to set an example to potential wrongdoers; it may be to appease the gods or spirits; it may be to intimidate real or potential enemies of a society's ruling class. It is not always clear to lay observers—or to criminologists—why we punish, because there are competing explanations for punishment, all of which make intuitive sense, but none of which have much data to back them up. The fact that these explanations are alternatively called "theories," "philosophies," and "justifications" suggests their tenuous validity and may reflect more of what we want from our penal system than what we get. In the West, when we think of punishments meted out to criminals, we typically think of incarceration. Following are the four explanations for imprisonment most commonly discussed by criminologists, policymakers, and the public.

Incapacitation

Incapacitation refers to the process of segregating dangerous people from the rest of the population. It certainly makes intuitive sense that when we put a dangerous person in prison, he or she is far less likely to do harm to people outside of prison. The truth to this assertion depends upon a number of variables. For one thing, we should consider how dangerous that person would be if he or she were not incarcerated. For less serious and/or for non-violent offenses, it may well be that the costs of imprisonment far outweigh the risks associated with reoffending.

We should also consider what happens to inmates while they are incarcerated. Since their inception, critics of incarceration have called prisons "schools for crime," and, in fact, recidivism rates—the rates at which ex-inmates are rearrested—have always been high. One of the more comprehensive studies by the Bureau of Justice Statistics estimates that two-thirds of released prisoners are rearrested within three years, and three-quarters are rearrested within five years.[1] Thus, when inmates are released, there is a good chance they will be even more dangerous than they were before incarceration. (Although, it is worth noting that, contrary to popular belief, property criminals are more likely to be rearrested than violent criminals.)[2]

If incapacitation were a reliable effect, then we would expect that the more criminals a society puts behind bars, the less crime will occur among the populace at large; that is, the higher a country's incarceration rate, the lower its crime rate would be. Indeed, as we shall see, the United States has the highest incarceration rate in the world, and, since the early 1990s, for the most part, we have been seeing crime rates go down. However, even with the highest incarceration rate in the world, the United States still has very high rates of crime—especially lethal violence—compared with other industrialized countries. A report from the National Research Council addresses the complexity of the relationship between incarceration rates and crime rates in light of recent trends:

> There is, of course, a plausibility to the belief that putting many more convicted felons behind bars would reduce crime. Yet even a cursory examination of the data on crime and imprisonment rates makes clear the complexity of measuring the crime prevention effect of incarceration. Violent crime rates have been declining steadily over the past two decades, which suggests a crime prevention effect of rising incarceration rates. For the two decades of rising incarceration rates, however, there was no clear trend in the violent crime rate—it rose, then fell, and then rose again.[3]

Thus, while it is difficult to refute the assertion that a person behind bars is less likely to do harm to people outside of the prison, the argument in favor of incapacitation is inconclusive, especially given the costs of incarceration and the fact that most people behind bars will eventually be released.

Deterrence

Those who argue for the deterrent effect of incarceration hold that imprisonment serves to deter would-be criminals from committing crime. The loss of freedom and the other noxious elements of the prison experience set an example to the general population of what will happen to them if they commit a crime. Proponents of deterrence adhere to the assumption common among classical criminologists (see Chapter 2) that crime is rational behavior, and would-be offenders mentally weigh the benefits of crime versus its costs; and if the benefits outweigh the costs, crime will result. If the costs of crime are not certain, swift, and severe enough, more people will engage in criminal behavior. Thus, crime should be met with severe consequences and the public should be made aware of these consequences. Otherwise, there will be dramatic increases in crime and the social order will be jeopardized.

Again, the argument in favor of deterrence makes a great deal of intuitive sense, but it is very difficult to test its validity. We could compare crime rates in a society before and after it implemented more severe sentencing guidelines; or, we could compare crime rates in a society that dispenses lengthy prison sentences to one that does not. There, are in fact, many European countries with much lower incarceration rates, that dispense much shorter sentences, where prison conditions are much more benign, *and* which have much lower crime rates than the United States. These penal policies, vis-à-vis the United States, cast doubt on the deterrent effect of incarceration.

However, there are so many factors that contribute to a society's crime rates that criminologists have not developed the methods that would allow them to say that the differences in crime rates—between countries or between time frames—are due to incarceration policies, and not due to the presence or absence of other criminogenic factors. So, like incapacitation, the logic of deterrence is intuitively compelling, but the data in favor of deterrence are inconclusive.

Thus far, we have been discussing *general deterrence*, or whether incarceration has an effect on deterring members of the general population. Criminologists also speak of *specific deterrence*, or whether the prison experience will deter the inmate from crime once he or she is released. In terms of consequences, specific deterrence is difficult to differentiate from rehabilitation.

Rehabilitation

During various periods in the history of the American prison system, there have been high hopes that the prison experience would improve the inmates' character and that they would eventually leave the prison as better, law-abiding citizens. This history is tellingly revealed in the choice of words that have been used to refer to prisons and their operations: "houses of correction," "department of corrections," "correctional officer" (implying that the purpose of prison is to *correct* an inmate's character), "penitentiary" (referring to the prison as a place for offenders to do their *penance* and come out a better person for it), and "reform school" (a term used for earlier penal institutions for juveniles, suggesting they were places where kids would be *formed* into someone better than they were before entering the facility).

In the early days of prisons, it was felt that the prison experience itself would accomplish the goal of rehabilitation, but soon after and still today, most or all prisons in the United States have various programs to facilitate the inmate's rehabilitation. Such "programming" includes drug treatment, group therapy, and remedial education and high school and college classes.

Since most prisoners are eventually released, rehabilitation would seem to be a laudable goal. However, the high rates of recidivism call its effectiveness into question. It may well be that the exigencies of the prison experience and rehabilitation are incompatible forces. Or, as Norval Morris and David Rothman put it, "It is hard to train for freedom in a cage."[4] On the other hand, recidivism rates might be even higher than they are now were it not for programming currently being offered in today's prisons. Either way, like incapacitation and deterrence, the case for rehabilitation is sketchy. Though the evidence does favor some types of prison programming over others, high recidivism rates cast a shadow over rehabilitation as a goal for imprisonment.

Retribution

Retribution is sometimes defined as "revenge," but might be better described as the satisfaction that people feel when they think justice has been served. People's sense of fairness requires that the criminal justice system ensures that bad things happen to bad people. Because its goal involves public "feelings" and not crime reduction, retribution is the only one of the four justifications for prison that does not depend on an empirical examination of crime rates to verify its effectiveness. As such, it is not as easily dismissed as the other three justifications.

It has been suggested, and many people assume that the concept of "fairness" should include some element of proportionality, that the punishment should fit the crime. Thus, almost 4,000 years ago, when the ancient Mesopotamian King, Hammurabi, developed a code of law involving the concept of *lex talionis*, which required "an eye for an eye," this is lauded as one of the most important developments in the history of criminal justice.

However, retribution refers to *public* sentiments; it involves emotional responses to crime; and since public calculations of proportionality are usually either absent or slipshod, the public frequently favors harsher punishments than may be called for, given the crime. The fact that large segments of the public consistently feel that criminals are getting off too easily—no matter how harshly criminals are being treated,[5] and no matter whether any of the other three justifications for punishment have been proven—suggests that retribution does indeed play a critical role in the purpose of punishment/incarceration.

Retribution, however, may actually be counterproductive to crime reduction in that it encourages fear and hatred of criminal offenders. These emotions foster more sentences and longer sentences in harsher prison environments, producing inmates who are more "hardened." Fear and hatred also foster continued stigma and ostracism once the inmate is released, making it more difficult for the ex-offender to obtain decent employment and be reintegrated into the community. Thus, retribution may be the single greatest explanation for high rates of recidivism, and, if retribution played a less critical role than it does, then perhaps rehabilitation would work more effectively, and incapacitation would be more cost-effective.

THE HISTORY OF PRISONS

In the long history of humanity, the idea of concentrating convicted felons in a building divided into cells is a fairly new one, only emerging in the last few centuries. Before the emergence of prisons, there were systems of banishment, fines and restitution; there were various forms of corporal punishment, with flogging figuring most prominently; there were numerous shaming techniques, including stocks and pillories, marked clothing, branding, and amputations; and there were myriad and imaginative ways of putting alleged and convicted criminals to death. In various periods and places, felons could be sentenced to slavery. In the seventeenth and eighteenth centuries, when European countries were colonizing the world with their vast navies and merchant fleets, the ships were often powered by convicts, chained to their rowing stations. Another method of punishment used by the British was to send convicts to toil in their American colonies. (It was only because of the Revolutionary War in America that the British started to send their criminals to the Australian colonies.[6]) The British also used prison "hulks." These were usually retired naval vessels retrofitted to serve as floating prisons. As these were severely overcrowded and very unsanitary, inmates often quickly succumbed to disease.

Perhaps the closest predecessors to the modern day prison were the British workhouses and almshouses. However, it was in America that prisons, as we know them, were conceived and developed. Colonial Americans had no illusions about eradicating crime. Crime is to be expected in a sinful and corrupting world.[7] Communities took care of their own wrongdoers, usually with harsh corporal punishments and sometimes executions. Then, in the late eighteenth century, Quakers in the state of Pennsylvania began mobilizing for a new, more humane form of punishment, believing that the old ways were too harsh and that they actually encouraged more criminality. In 1790, a 16-cell facility was built within the Walnut Street Jail in Philadelphia. Prisoners in the "Penitentiary House" were held in solitary confinement, not even allowed to catch sight of one another, and not allowed visitors (except for the occasional clergyman). They worked on individual crafts within their cells, and they were allowed only one book, the Bible, so that they may ponder the evil of their ways. Jessica Mitford writes,

> The basic feature of the penitentiary was total isolation of the offender from his fellow miscreants, to the end that he would be sheltered from their contaminating influence and, serving out his sentence in solitude with only the Bible for company, would in the course of time be brought to penitence for his sins and thus to eternal salvation.[8]

In 1821, the Pennsylvania legislature approved funds for the construction of Eastern State Penitentiary, which opened in 1829 in Cherry Hill, outside of Philadelphia. Guided by much the same philosophy as the Walnut Street Jail, its goal was "to change the behavior of inmates through confinement in solitude with labor."[9] At the time, this was the most costly construction project ever completed in the United States and Eastern State was one of the largest buildings in the world. Officials were careful to minimize any human contact. "Masks [were] fabricated to keep the inmates from communicating during rare trips outside their cells. Cells [were] equipped with feed doors and individual exercise yards to prevent contact between inmates, and minimize contact between inmates and guards."[10]

An alternative to the Pennsylvania prison model was built in Auburn, New York in 1819. This prison utilized the "congregate hard labor" system. Prisoners were dressed in striped outfits, they were kept in the individual cells at night, silence was enforced; they walked in lock step, congregated during the day to work with silence still enforced; they picked up their frugal meals from the kitchen on their way back to their silent cells at

IMAGES 7.1 AND 7.2
Eastern State Penitentiary is no longer operating, but it is still open for tours and is a popular destination on Halloween night.

night. Elam Lynds was the prison's first warden. He was famous for carrying around his cat-o-nine-tails, a particularly insidious form of whip; and he is quoted as saying, "In order to reform a criminal, you must first break his spirit."[11] (From Auburn, Lynds moved on to supervise the construction, and become the first warden, of the infamous Sing Sing prison 40 miles north of New York City.)

While both the Pennsylvania system and the Auburn system were founded on Christian principles and were considered more humane than alternative punishments of the time, the debilitating effects of solitary confinement in Pennsylvania were becoming evident, with madness befalling many an inmate. Early critics of incarceration pointed out that before the advent of prisons, punishment had taken place in the public arena where there was, at least, some form of public oversight; whereas now it was taking place behind the gates of the prison, where there was no oversight, and where untold abuses could be occurring. Indeed, prison officials have long been notorious for covering up extra-judicial punishments as well as prisoner-on-prisoner violence. It is said that the history of the prison reform movement began with the history of prisons.

Nevertheless, the novelty and enormity of Eastern State drew visitors from around the country as well as parts of Europe. The congregate hard labor system at Auburn had its prisoners engaged in productive work, which appealed to policymakers, politicians, and the public as well. As with Eastern State, people were traveling to Auburn from all over the country to observe this new form of punishment, and they took what they learned back to their own states to replicate what they had seen. Just as importantly, intellectuals and reformers from Europe came to observe and took their observations back with them. Within decades the American idea of prison took root in many parts of the world; and today, we take it for granted that incarceration is a natural response to crime.

THE STRUCTURE OF THE AMERICAN PRISON SYSTEM

There are three basic types of institutions in which people are incarcerated: jails, state prisons, and federal prisons. Following is a brief discussion of each types of institution.

Federal prisons

The Federal Bureau of Prisons was established as an agency within the Department of Justice in 1930. It manages the operations of 122 facilities across the United States. The Director, who is appointed by the President, runs it. Six regional directors report to the Director; and the wardens of the federal prisons report to the regional directors. At the time this book is going to press, the federal prison system houses almost 200,000 inmates who have been charged or convicted of federal crimes.

About 10 percent of all people behind bars in the United States are housed within the federal prison system.[12] Federal crimes include those involving the crossing of state or international borders, mail fraud, counterfeiting, kidnapping, and organized crime. These are specialized crimes and, until the 1980s, federal prisons housed a relatively specialized class of criminals; the federal prison system has traditionally housed a higher proportion of white-collar criminals and a lower proportion of violent offenders than the state prisons. Then, with the War on Drugs, the federal prison system saw the proportion of its inmates convicted of drug offenses dramatically increasing from the 1980s through the first decade of the new millennia. Consequently, today the federal system houses a higher proportion of drug offenders than state prisons.

As the War on Drugs has peaked in recent years, a number of other trends are affecting the federal prison inmate profile. With the profusion of the internet, the federal system has, and will continue to see, more people convicted of internet-related offenses, including fraud, child pornography, hacking, the distribution of malware, and various other cybercrimes. In addition, with recent crackdowns on immigration, the federal system has, and will continue to see, more inmates being held for deportation hearings or convicted of immigration violations.

Offenders in the federal system tend to be slightly older than those in the state systems. This may have to do with the fact that violent offenders tend to be more youthful offenders who are more likely to end up in state facilities. It may also have to do with the fact that drug offenders, who make up a larger proportion of the federal inmates, are more likely to face mandatory minimums and remain in custody until they are older.

Federal prisons are classified into five different security levels (minimum, low, medium, high, and "administrative"). According to the Bureau of Prisons website, "Security levels are based on such features as the presence of external patrols, towers, security barriers, or detection devices; the type of housing within the institution; internal security features; and the staff-to-inmate ratio."[13] The minimum security prisons are also known as Federal Prison Camps and they are often derisively called "Club Fed" (nicknamed for their exaggerated resemblance to the all-inclusive resort chain, Club Med). Victor Conte, who was convicted of charges extending from a doping scandal involving Olympic athletes, describes his introduction to one such prison camp:

> [They] drove me around to the minimum security camp that they call Club Fed. And they don't call it Club Fed for no reason. No fences. I would say maybe every couple of hundred feet around

the compound, they had a stake in the ground with a white sign and black letters that simply said, "Out of Bounds." First morning when I got up and I walked out and they had a big billboard in the center of the compound and it said "Sports Complex." Football, baseball basketball, soccer, handball, volleyball, bocce ball. What do I say? Everybody was having a lot of fun.[14]

"Administrative" institutions in the federal prison system are those "with special missions, such as the detention of pretrial offenders; the treatment of inmates with serious or chronic medical problems; or the containment of extremely dangerous, violent, or escape-prone inmates."[15] This latter category includes the Administrative-Maximum Security Penitentiary, a "super-max" prison in Colorado (sometimes called the "Alcatraz of the Rockies") which has held such notorious offenders as Timothy McVeigh, the Oklahoma City bomber, and Zacarias Moussaoui, the so-called "20th hijacker" in the 9/11 attacks. With its inmates kept in 24-hour solitary confinement and not allowed visitors, conditions there "are considered so harsh that in recent years, defense lawyers have increasingly used the specter of the prison fortress to persuade jurors to vote against the death penalty and instead send their clients to supermax. They argue, in effect, that time there would be worse than capital punishment."[16]

State prisons

Just over half of all people behind bars in the United States are housed in over 1,500 prisons funded and operated by state governments. State prisons are for those offenders convicted of felonies—as defined by the various state legal codes—and sentenced to more than a year in prison. Most of their violations correspond to the FBI's "index crimes" (see Chapter 1 for further discussion); these include homicide, rape, aggravated assault, robbery, burglary, larceny, auto theft, and arson. There is also a sizeable number of drug offenders in the state prisons, however, as noted above, proportionately fewer than in the federal prisons. As the largest category of offenders in state prisons have been sentenced for violent crimes, state prisons have a reputation for violence between prisoners and between guards and prisoners.

Like the federal system, most or all states classify their prisons by security level (low, medium, and maximum, for example). As each state operates its own prison system, there is a large range of architectural styles and structural amenities, especially given that some nineteenth century prisons are still in operation and that there are hundreds of new facilities that were built during the prison construction boom between 1990 and 2005. As each state is subject to the vagaries of the budgetary process, prisons also vary in terms of the adequacy of staffing and the availability of programming for the inmates.

Many prisons across the United States are housing more inmates than they were designed to handle and are facing problems and court challenges dealing with overcrowding. Prison overcrowding presents a number of challenges in terms of the constitutional prohibition on cruel and unusual punishment, in terms of providing proper medical care, in terms of heightening the risks of inmate suicide and prison violence (including prison riots), and in terms of providing the programs and services prisoners need to ensure the best chances for their rehabilitation and reintegration into the community.

California prisons are among a number of state prison systems that have been notorious for overcrowding, and in 2011 the U.S. Supreme Court upheld a lower court decision and ruled that the state had to reduce its prison population by 30,000 inmates. The ruling caused a good deal of turmoil within California's political and criminal justice systems, causing a lot of inmates to be shifted from the prison system to the jail system, as well as the release of thousands of inmates from prison to parole. "Within 15 months," writes Tom Jackman, "more than 27,500 inmates had been 'realigned' from state prisons to county jails or to parole in what was called 'an act of mass forgiveness unprecedented in U.S. history.'"[17] Despite public fears, the release of so many prisoners due to overcrowding did not lead to increased crime rates in California.[18]

Jails

Jails are used to hold people awaiting trial *and* to imprison people who have been sentenced to less than a year of incarceration. There are over 3,000 jails in the United States; most are operated by municipal and county governments and administered by local law enforcement agencies. Roughly, one-third of the people behind bars are incarcerated in local jails. While there are over 700,000 people in jail at any given moment, some 11 million people spend time in jail in any given year.[19] People detained in jail can stay there for hours, days, weeks, or months, with the average length of stay being 23 days.[20]

Many criminologists argue that, of all correctional institutions, jails are the most in need of reform; but, given how extensively they are used throughout the country, they receive relatively little attention from policymakers, the media and the public. According to one popular textbook on corrections by Todd Clear and his colleagues,

> Students interested in improving corrections during their future careers could find no area in more obvious need of reform than U.S. jails. Among the institutions and programs of the corrections system, jails are the most neglected by scholars and officials and least known to the public. Uniformly jam-packed and frequently

brutalizing, jails almost never enhance life. Many criminal justice researchers agree that of all correctional agencies, jails are the oldest, most numerous, most criticized, and most stubbornly resistant to reform.[21]

Much of the urgency for reform relates to the fact that most people—three out of five—incarcerated in jails are awaiting trial and have not been convicted of any crime; and the proportion of jail inmates who have not been convicted has been growing in recent years.[22]

The American ideals of freedom and justice are severely compromised by the reality of American jails. In a society that prides itself on the freedom it allows its citizens, there is no more serious an infringement by government than the deprivation of freedom; and *presumably*, all or most Americans believe that a person should be considered innocent until proven guilty. American jails stand as a glaring contradiction to these ideals. If most jail inmates represented a clear and present danger to the community, the compromises to these American ideals may be necessary, but most jail inmates are not accused of violent crime; "nearly 75 percent of the population of both sentenced offenders and pretrial detainees are in jail for nonviolent traffic, property, drug, or public order offenses."[23]

The contradiction between the ideal and the reality of jail is further exacerbated by the bail system in the United States. Most people awaiting trial are given the opportunity to be released on bond. This results in a system where the unconvicted—"presumed innocent"—jail populations are made up mostly of poor people, and disproportionately people of color. This has consequences that extend beyond the poor inmate's time in jail. A person who has to stay in jail because he or she cannot afford bail is quite possibly going to lose their job; and his or her family is going to lose the income that comes with that job. People held in pretrial detention are more likely to be convicted of their charges and given longer sentences "because defendants already in jail receive and accept less favorable plea agreements and do not have the leverage to press for better ones."[24] Miriam Aroni Krinsky and Christian Gossett summarize elements of the critique of the bail system in the United States,

> What money bail can do is cause people to be incarcerated unnec-
> essarily. This can seriously destabilize people's lives—and in turn,
> their families and communities—by causing them to lose their
> jobs, homes or children. A money-based bail system can even
> cause presumptively innocent people to plead guilty, simply so
> they can get out of jail with time served. In some cases, inmates
> have served more time awaiting trial than they would have for the
> crimes they are accused of committing.[25]

Critics of money bail argue that it "criminalizes poverty," and in recent years, a number of states have moved to reduce the use of money bail. These reforms have "ranged from minor tweaks for only the lowest-level crimes to blanket eliminations of cash bail."[26] These reforms have stirred a good deal of controversy, as some people fear that dangerous criminals are being put back on the streets. We need to keep in mind, though, that the purpose of bail is to ensure that the defendant show up for his or her trial. As bail reforms have been made so recently, there is insufficient data to determine their effects on the rates at which defendants show up for trial, or on crime rates.

Not only are poor people and minorities disproportionately represented in jail populations, but studies have shown that people with mental disorders make up a substantial portion of jail inmates. Jails have been called a "treatment of last resort" and "de facto mental hospitals." But, unfortunately, few jails are setup to provide mental health treatment and the jail environment—with its "constant noise, bright lights, an ever-changing population, and an atmosphere of threat and violence"—is hardly conducive to improved mental health.[27]

Many in the American public are unaware of the injustices taking place in the jail system; of those who are aware, many are probably willing to accept these injustices, thinking they are temporary inconveniences on the path to justice. However, for many people—especially the poor—a stay in jail is not so temporary, and the effects of a jail stay can be long-lasting.

THE PRISON BOOM

Mass incarceration, the War on Drugs, and race

The United States incarcerates a higher percentage of its population than any other nation on Earth (see Figure 7.1 for international comparisons). This is a fact of which all criminology students should be aware, and so should all Americans, given the popular belief that the United States stands out in the world in terms of the freedom it affords its citizens. While the United States has always had an incarceration rate that is higher than most Western industrialized countries, the rate had remained fairly steady—and only a small fraction of what it is now—until the late 1970s (see Figure 7.2). Earlier that decade, Richard Nixon ran a successful presidential campaign built on a law and order platform and, once in office, he declared a "war on drugs." Drugs, he contended, were behind the crime rates, which were rising at the time. With this declaration of "war," more resources were allocated to law enforcement, arrests went up, incarceration rates increased. The stage was set for what we today call the "era of mass incarceration."

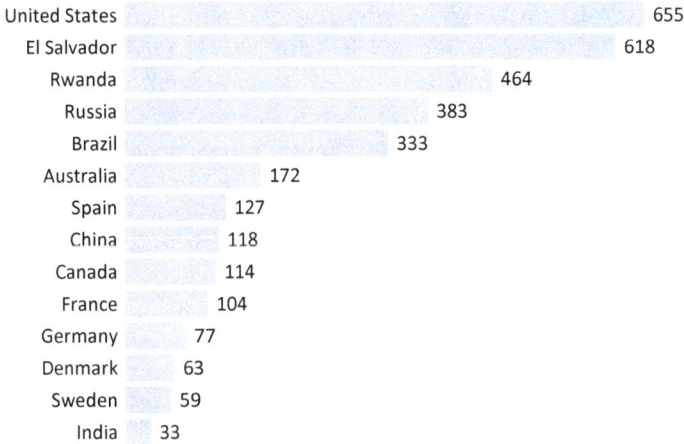

Country	Rate
United States	655
El Salvador	618
Rwanda	464
Russia	383
Brazil	333
Australia	172
Spain	127
China	118
Canada	114
France	104
Germany	77
Denmark	63
Sweden	59
India	33

FIGURE 7.1
International rates of incarceration per 100,000.

Source: Fact Sheet: Trends in U.S. Corrections, The Sentencing Project. (www.sentencingproject.org/wp-content/uploads/2016/01/Trends-in-US-Corrections.pdf). Reprinted with permission by The Sentencing Project, Washington, DC.

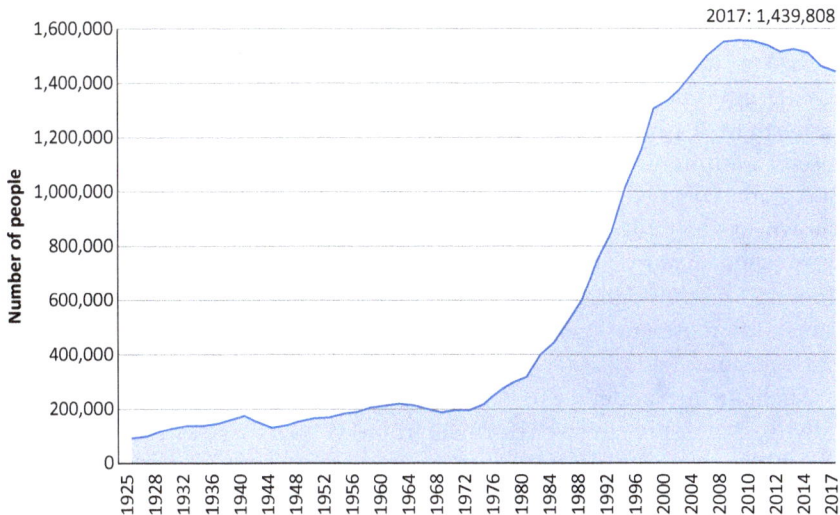

FIGURE 7.2
U.S. state and federal prison population, 1925–2017 (does not include jail populations).

Source: Fact Sheet: Trends in U.S. Corrections, The Sentencing Project. (www.sentencingproject.org/wp-content/uploads/2016/01/Trends-in-US-Corrections.pdf). Reprinted with permission by The Sentencing Project, Washington, DC.

In the 1980s, the War on Drugs was dramatically expanded under the Reagan administration. Congress pitched in with several pieces of legislation establishing zero tolerance policies and federal mandatory minimum sentences; and the legislative bodies in most states followed suit. "As of 2012, there were 171 mandatory minimum sentencing statutes at the federal and state levels, about 80% of which were for drug law violations."[28] More than any other factor, the lengthy—some would say draconian—sentences for drug offenses in the 1980s and 1990s explained the explosive growth in U.S. incarceration rates. Longer sentences meant that prisoners were not being released at previous rates, and prisoners were piling up throughout the American prison system. Corresponding to the boom in inmate populations, there was a boom in prison construction, the likes of which the world has never seen. Between 1990 and 2005, 544 new prisons were opened in the United States. That is an average of one new prison opening every 10 days, for 15 years.[29]

Much of the initial fervor behind the crackdown was spurred on by media reports of the "crack epidemic." Crack is a smokable form of cocaine, made by processing the substance with baking soda to form "rock."[30] Chemically, it is almost identical to powder cocaine; but, when smoked, a single hit—enough to get high—is cheaper than powder cocaine. It, therefore, was more accessible to poor, urban, minority populations. Crack came to represent the drug of choice for poor blacks, while powder cocaine was more common among more affluent whites.

Hence, the War on Drugs targeted poor urban minorities. The 1986 Anti-Drug Abuse Act established that first-time offenders in possession of more than 5 grams of crack cocaine—for example, 5.01 grams—would receive a minimum sentence of five years incarceration; it took more than 500 grams of powder cocaine to receive the same sentence. This came to be known as the "100-to-1 rule." Similar disparities for crack and powder were established by various state legislatures.[31] With such sentencing guidelines and discriminatory drug law enforcement practices,[32] poor minorities came to represent vastly disproportionate segments of the prison population.

Michelle Alexander's 2010 book, *The New Jim Crow*, has become a rallying cry for progressive reformers in the United States. In it, she argues that blacks have always been *legally* oppressed in the United States. With the end of the Civil War, when slavery became illegal, separate-but-equal Jim Crow were enacted in the South. When Jim Crow laws were ruled illegal by the U.S. Supreme Court, white legislatures came up with the War on Drugs as a legal means of oppressing the black population. Indeed, racist motivations may well have inspired Nixon's kickoff of the War on Drugs. John Ehrlichman, one of his top advisors, is quoted as saying in a 1994 interview,

> The Nixon campaign in 1968, and the Nixon White House after that, had two enemies: the antiwar left and black people. You understand what I'm saying? We knew we couldn't make it illegal to be either against the [Vietnam] war or black, but by getting the public to associate the hippies with marijuana and blacks with heroin, and then criminalizing both heavily, we could disrupt those communities. We could arrest their leaders, raid their homes, break up their meetings, and vilify them night after night on the evening news. Did we know we were lying about the drugs? Of course we did.[33]

Subsequent policies related to the War on Drugs may not have been so racist in intent, but critics charge they were certainly racist in effect.

In the last decade, partly in recognition of these effects, and partly to reduce the skyrocketing costs of mass incarceration, there has been a "softening" of the War on Drugs. The 100-to-1 rule for crack sentencing was reduced to an 18-to-1 ratio at the federal level. Many states have taken similar measures to reduce disparities, as well as the length of drug sentencing in general. Furthermore, during his last term in office, Barack Obama engaged in a campaign to commute the sentences of some drug offenders. By the end of the term, he had issued nearly 1,400 commutations, the vast majority of which went to non-violent drug offenders. All of these offenders had been vetted, had served at least 10 years, and had exhibited good behavior while incarcerated. With 2.3 million people living behind bars in the United States, though this was the largest number of presidential commutations in U.S. history, their effect was largely symbolic.

More recently, Congress passed the First Step Act in 2018. This shortened mandatory minimum sentences for drug violations, changed the three-strikes law from a maximum life sentence to a 25-year sentence, and gave judges more discretion in handling non-violent drug offenses. All of these changes were made at the federal level, so the First Step Act's impact on U.S. prison populations has been modest. However, the Act established a model which several states have followed since its passage.

Sentencing reforms and the softening of the War on Drugs coincided, more or less, with the recent heroin epidemic. Besides the higher number of fatalities associated with prevalence of heroin, the heroin and crack phenomena differed in that heroin use was prevalent among working and middle class whites as opposed to lower class blacks. As attention shifted from black drug abusers to white drug abusers, the resulting policies shifted from a criminal justice approach (i.e., punishment) to a more public health approach (i.e., treatment). Or, as Lance Wheeler, an NAACP chapter president, says, "Heroin now, you can get help … Crack cocaine,

you got put in jail."[34] The policy shift has been duly noted by black community leaders and by critics of the War on Drugs who have argued that
the shift toward the public health approach is an indicator that policymakers have greater sympathy toward white drug addicts than they had
toward black addicts and that the lengthy sentences of the recent past were
indeed motivated by racism.

The prison-industrial complex

In 1960, President Dwight Eisenhower, a former five-star general, warned the
nation of the "military-industrial complex." He was concerned that the connections between the U.S. military and private industry were compromising
the military's duty to serve the nation's interests. Today, people who refer to
the "prison-industrial complex" have similar concerns about U.S. prisons
serving private interests more than public interests. Over the last few decades,
there have been a number of interests, other than the public interest, that
were served by the recent incarceration boom.[35] For example, prison guards
make up one of the more powerful unions in California. The union grew in
membership from 4,000 to over 23,000 in one decade,[36] and it contributed
more than $100,000 to the committee that pushed through California's puni-
tive "three-strikes" legislation.[37] Norwegian criminologist and prison critic
Nils Christie comments, "It is quite a fantastic situation when those who
administer the pain-delivery in our society have such a great say. It's as if the
hangman's association got together to work for more hanging."[38]

Prison guards are not the only ones to benefit from the incarceration
boom of the recent past. Of course, there has also been a great deal of
money made in prison construction. Many rural areas with depressed economies and high unemployment rates have also benefitted. "Prisons have
replaced factories as the economic center-piece of many small towns."[39] In
past decades, communities would fight to avoid prison construction in
their area. They feared that a criminal population nearby was too great a
risk. Today, it is a very different story. For example, Steven Donziger
reports that 50 small towns in Texas lobbied for a new prison in their
areas. Some even offered incentives, such as country club memberships for
the wardens or longhorn cattle for the prison grounds. "A small town in
Illinois put together a rap song and bought television time as part of a
public relations blitz" to convince legislators to locate a prison in its vicinity.[40] CNBC reports, "Traditionally, 'Not in My Backyard' was the resound-
ing response small towns gave to developers proposing a new prison for
their town. But today, in some areas that are hard-pressed for jobs,
welcome mats are being rolled out to prison companies."[41] Rural jurisdictions also benefit by the fact that prison populations boost a locality's
census population while federal and state funding for social programs are
often based on census counts.

Furthermore, both governmental institutions and private corporations reap enormous cost savings from prison labor. Convicts are making such things as clothing, circuit boards, safety goggles, wiring for military aircraft, body armor, road signs, and a host of other products; they are also making phone calls for telemarketing firms and taking phone calls for airline reservations.

Compounding the problem, many prisons today are being run by private corporations whose only goal is generating a profit. "The goal of the industry is to keep prisons full. A successful company locks up as many people as possible for as long as possible," says Dr. Jerome Miller of the National Center on Institutions and Alternatives.[42] Electronics corporations have also enjoyed the boom in prison construction. They make a generous profit wiring prisons and developing monitoring systems for prisoners inside the prison and for probationers outside. Food service, medical service, and transportation service companies are among others that profit from the incarceration boom. In 2014, the *New York Times* reported,

> Within that perimeter lies the Clallam Bay Corrections Center, a state prison—and an attractive business opportunity. One private company, JPay, has a grip on Internet and financial services. Another, Global Tel-Link, controls the phones.
>
> These companies are part of a new breed of businesses flourishing inside American jails and prisons. Many of these players are being bankrolled by one of the most powerful forces in American finance: private equity. Private investment firms have invested many billions of dollars in the prison industry, betting—correctly—that it is a growth business.[43]

Recent efforts to relax mandatory sentencing guidelines could threaten corporate profits, but, instead, recent anti-immigrant legislation is likely to take up the slack. In 2000, the federal government stepped up its policy of detaining undocumented aliens mostly in facilities run by private corporations. At that time, according to journalist Matt Taibbi, the share price of Corrections Corporation of America "hovered around a dollar." By 2013, CCA's share price had soared to over $34.[44] A number of states have passed legislation making it easier to arrest undocumented aliens. The governor of Arizona, Jan Brewer, led the way in 2010 with SB 1070. Two of her top advisers were former lobbyists for the prison industry. Thirty co-sponsors of the bill in Arizona's statehouse had received donations from the prison industry in the months leading up to the vote on the bill. "The law," reports Laura Sullivan of National Public Radio, "could send hundreds of thousands of illegal immigrants to prison in a way never done before. And it could mean hundreds of millions of dollars in profits to private prison companies responsible for housing them."[45] More recently, the anti-immigration fervor led by Donald Trump has led to a surge of immigrants being detained in U.S. prisons; and the majority of those are being held in private prisons.[46]

All told, there is a large variety of interest groups, whose interests do not necessarily correspond with the public interest, that have formed powerful political constituencies with the goal of continuing or restarting the incarceration boom. For these groups, whether or not incarceration is an effective method of crime control is a distant concern. While we have seen incarceration rates peak between 2008 and 2010, there is reason to be skeptical that we will see further dramatic decreases in prison populations. If the American public ever were to come to the conclusion that U.S. incarceration policies were counterproductive or that having so many people behind bars—mostly poor minorities—is incompatible with American democratic values, it would be very difficult to reverse course. Jeremy Travis, senior fellow at the Urban Institute, writes, "[T]he prison network is now deeply intertwined with American life, deeply integrated into the physical and economic infrastructure of a large number of American counties."[47,1]

LIFE INSIDE

The inmate subculture

Partly as a result of society's desire for retribution, partly from the intent to effect deterrence, and partly from a reluctance to spend money for improvements, prison life can be harsh. Besides the deprivations that come with incarceration, it is said that the worst part of living in prison is the fact that you have to live with other prisoners. The inmate subculture—especially in maximum security institutions—is well known to be hostile, violent and dangerous, with prisoners often rewarding behaviors that are condemned outside of the prison. There are two competing explanations for how the inmate subculture acquired these qualities.

In 1958, Gresham Sykes introduced the *adaptation model*, which argues that the inmate subculture is, in large part, a result of prisoners' adaptation to the "pains of imprisonment."[48] First among these pains of imprisonment is the *deprivation of liberty*. Imprisonment represents a deliberate moral rejection by the community of the offender. It is a statement from the free community that the offender is not worthy of living among them. It is an attack on the offender's selfhood; in defense, the offender must learn to "reject his rejecters," to convince himself that they are not

---

1   This material, beginning with "In the 1960s, President Dwight D. Eisenhower" and ending here, was previously published in *Social Problems: An Introduction to Critical Constructionism*, fifth edition, by Robert Heiner, pp. 164–186 (edited). Copyright © 2016 by Oxford University Press. Reproduced with permission of the Licensor through PLSclear.

worthy of judging him. The second pain of imprisonment is the *deprivation of material goods*. The prisoner is severely limited in terms of the objects that he can have in his possession. This represents an assault on the prisoner's selfhood, especially in American society, where people identify themselves so much in terms of what they own. The third pain of imprisonment is the *deprivation of heterosexual relationships*. This is a further threat to the self in that we identify ourselves so much in terms of our sex and sexuality. The next pain of imprisonment is the *deprivation of autonomy*. The prisoner is subjected to a multitude of often trivial, seemingly capricious, rules of the prison regime. If the prisoner asks why he is not allowed to do this and such, a guard is likely to respond, "Because that's the rule," or "Because I said so." This is much the way their parents would have responded, thus reducing the prisoner to the status of a child, and threatening his selfhood. The last pain of imprisonment is the *deprivation of security*. The maximum security prison holds a lot of violent characters. Besides the physical threat that they present, this is also a threat to the prisoner's selfhood because he knows that no matter where he is in the pecking order, he may have to prove himself on any day at any time. To sum up Sykes' adaptation model of the inmate subculture, imprisonment represents an all-out assault on the prisoner's selfhood, and the ways in which prisoners have to respond or "adapt" to this assault contribute to the violent nature of the inmate subculture and are not conducive to the prisoner's rehabilitation.

A more commonsensical explanation of the inmate subculture suggests that it is the way it is because the criminal justice system serves to round-up society's most violent and unsavory characters and concentrate them in one place that we call a prison. It is no wonder, then, that the inmate subculture is as violent and unsavory as it is. This is a version of the *importation model* of the inmate subculture, which holds that the qualities of the inmate subculture depend upon the pre-existing qualities of the criminals that have been imported into the prison. In the 1960s, sociologists advanced a refinement of the importation model of the inmate subculture, which explained why different inmates adapted differently to the inmate subculture, depending upon the subcultures in which they belonged before their entrance into the prison.[49] Thus, for example, thieves and gang members belong to different subcultures. Members of each of these subcultures can expect to do time in prison. But, on the streets, the thief is advised by his peers that if he ends up in prison, he should just bide his time and stay out of trouble, while the gang member is advised that his time should be occupied with gaining status, influence and control among the other inmates. To the extent that these individuals heed the advice given to them, each will develop different modes of coping with the prison experience.

So, does an individual's response to the prison experience depend more upon the prison environment (the adaptation model), or does it depend upon the qualities and experiences that he brought with him into the prison (the importation model)? These two models do not have to be seen as being in competition with one another. Undoubtedly, they both contribute to the understanding of the inmate subculture. Nonetheless, criminologists have debated the relative value of the adaptation versus the importation models for decades. However, as gangs became an ever-more powerful force behind prison walls in the 1980s and 1990s, the importation model took on more relevance. Law enforcement officials were well aware that the gangs on the streets and those in the prisons shared the same names and the same members, and indeed were one and the same. Thus, it was apparent that the gang subculture from the streets was being *imported* into the prison.

In fact, the War on Drugs made selling drugs more risky, thereby increasing the price of illegal drugs and enticing organized crime to enter the market. This resulted in more rival gangs competing for territory in the United States, often with connections to drug cartels in Central and South America. The drug business became very lucrative and very violent. Gang members were—and still are—cycling from the street to the prison and back to the street, with the result that a stint in prison has become a routine part of gang life. According to Charles Dangerfield, head of California's Gang Task Force, "The young guys on the street look to the gang members inside as role models. ... Getting sentenced to prison is like being called up to the majors."[50]

Who's in charge?

Members of the public often do not understand why there are such frequent incidents of misbehavior within the prison walls. "Why don't the guards," they wonder, "have near-total control?" The answer lies in several factors: (1) as prisoners are held against their will, they feel no sense of duty to obey the rules, as people so often do in the "freeworld;" (2) the guards are vastly outnumbered; (3) for security reasons, the guards cannot carry firearms within the proximity of prisoners; and (4) for financial as well as legal and humanitarian reasons, they cannot keep all prisoners in solitary confinement. These factors, along with the inmate subculture (discussed above) make the prison a very volatile environment, prone to eruption at any given moment. For these reasons, according to Sykes, to keep the peace, it becomes necessary for prison authorities to cede some control to the inmates.

As there are so many rules governing inmate behavior, guards must be selective in which ones they enforce. "Thus the guard ... often discovers that his best path of action is to make 'deals' or 'trades' with the captives in his power. In effect, the guard buys compliance in certain areas at the cost of tolerating disobedience elsewhere."[51] Sykes continues, "The custodians … far from being converted into brutal tyrants, are under strong pressure to compromise with their captives, for it is a paradox that they can ensure their dominance only by allowing it to be corrupted."[52]

More recently, David Skarbek has identified prison gangs as the locus of control behind the walls. He argues that since prison authorities are unable to provide the level of control necessary to ensure prisoner safety, inmates join gangs to fill the security gap left by their custodians. Skarbek says,

> What we find when we study prisons, in really just about every setting, is that that formal governance is insufficient. It's insufficient to meet the demands for governance that inmates have. And there's a couple of different reasons for that. The first is that even when officials do much, even when they are effective at trying to make inmates feel safer, many inmates still feel vulnerable. They still feel like they are in an environment that's dangerous. And so on the margin, they want to spend some time and some energy and try to make themselves a little bit more safe.[53]

"Prison gangs," says Skarbek, "end up providing governance in a brutal but effective way. They impose responsibility on everyone, and in some ways the prisons run more smoothly because of them."[54] Organized along racial and ethnic lines, gang leaders control their members, establish rules to keep the peace, and brutally enforce those rules. The result is a system of gang control that enables prisoners' access to contraband (e.g., cellphones and drugs) and that, paradoxically, supplements the official control provided by the custodians.

Women in prison

Throughout most of the history of criminology, women's prisons and female inmates were largely ignored by criminologists. Indeed the number of women incarcerated in state and federal prisons in 2015 was less than 10 percent that of men. However, over the last several decades, *growth in incarceration rates for women have far outpaced those for men.*[55] Between 1980 and 2010, the number of women in state and federal prisons increased nine-fold, versus a five-fold increase for men.[56] Just like so many other trends described in this text, rapid growth in women's incarceration rates is, in large part, explained by the War on Drugs. As a percentage of all offenses committed by each gender, women are more likely to be sentenced for drug offenses than men. Thus, women offenders have been more severely impacted by the sentencing reforms enacted during the War on Drugs. In 2014, 24 percent of female inmates in state prisons had been sentenced for drug offenses versus 15 percent of male inmates. The discriminatory impact of the War on Drugs (discussed above) may also explain in part why black women are two times more likely to be incarcerated than white women.[57]

In what might be considered the bright side for female inmates, they are likely to be incarcerated with a smaller proportion of violent offenders. Fifty-four percent of male offenders in state prison are there for violent offenses, versus 37 percent of female inmates. As female prisoners tend to be less violent than males, security is not as prominent a concern in the design of women's prisons. Female prisoners are more likely to be housed in minimum or medium security facilities, living in cottages or dormitories, and are allowed more freedom of movement within the prison. Since there are far fewer women's prisons than men's, many states have only one women's prison; women prisoners are, therefore, often serving time farther from home than their male counterparts. As so much more attention is paid to male prisoners, women's prisons are very often lacking in the resources and programming options available to inmates in men's prisons.[58]

Classic research from the 1960s found that women prisoners were likely to organize themselves into "pseudo families," with marriages, divorces, husbands, wives, children, sisters, cousins, jealousy and power struggles. More recent research indicates that while some women "do form affectional ties that have some similarity to familial relationships," the formation of such relationships are often looked down upon by other female inmates and may be on the decline.[59]

If we were to update Sykes' list of the pains of imprisonment and apply it to women's prisons, we would have to include the "deprivation of children." Quite often, female inmates were single mothers before their arrest. The following data are reported by the National Resource Center on Children and Families of the Incarcerated at Rutgers University:

- 25 percent of children live with their fathers when a mother goes to prison.
- 90 percent of children remain with their mothers when the father is incarcerated.
- 50 percent of children with an incarcerated mother live with their grandmothers.[60]

In 1997, the federal Adoption and Safe Families Act was enacted, with the goal of reducing "the number of children in foster care and releas[ing] them for adoption."[61] It provides for the termination of parental rights for parents of children who have been in foster care for 15 to 22 months. While the motives for the legislation may have been commendable, its effects can be devastating for female inmates. (It can also be used quite effectively to leverage plea bargains from defendants who may or may not be guilty.) In 2003, 29,000 children in foster care were put up for adoption because they had a parent who was incarcerated.[62] The indefinite, or indeed permanent, separation of mother and child can have a detrimental effect on the mother's likelihood of reoffending. Ernest Drucker writes,

> The decision to place the child of an incarcerated woman in foster care typically means not only that a child loses a mother to prison but also that ties to a whole family unit of grandparents, siblings, and cousins are severed. By undermining the mother's morale and hope for the future, these wrenching separations further increase the likelihood of the mother's returning to prison after release. It is no surprise, then, that studies have shown that mothers are less likely to be rearrested and jailed if they are reunited with their child upon release.

Since 2010, a small number of states have enacted legislation to help mother and fathers maintain their parental rights.[63]

Recognizing the detrimental effects of separation for women and especially their children, many states have made provisions to ease these effects, especially for mothers and their newborn babies. Somewhere between three and six percent of women entering prison or jail are pregnant at the time.[64] While most states automatically separate mothers and their newborns, some states have established prison nurseries. These are usually limited to women who have "committed low-level offenses, face relatively short sentences, and will continue as their child(ren)'s primary caregiver upon release."[65] Women can keep their babies for a limited time, ranging from one month to three years, but averaging 18 months.[66] Research shows that such facilities promote mother–child bonding and lower recidivism rates among those women who have participated.[67] For older children, some prisons provide playrooms for children's visitation. Physical contact is permitted, and these rooms are often out of sight of the harsh realities of prison.

Not surprisingly, prison nurseries are quite controversial because, to some critics, they seem to be coddling women prisoners; to other critics, being raised in a prison is bad for the children. However, such nurseries have been around for quite some time. The prison nursery at Bedford Hills in New York has been in operation since 1901. It was in the 1980s, during the crackdown on crime, that many prisons abandoned their nursery programs, and only in the last two decades did we start to see them re-emerge. Most nurseries and playrooms today only opened in the last 20 years, and they are still only provided by a minority of women's prisons. As of 2015, only eight states had prison nurseries.[68] Many other countries provide facilities where women convicts and their children can stay together. Germany, for example, has a prison where children can stay with their mothers until the children are old enough to go to school. It also has a form of work-release program where mothers can go home during the day and care for their children, and return to the prison at night. The Mutter-Kind-Heim prison in Germany provides apartments for mothers and their children. Trained "educators" take the children off the prison grounds on field trips, such as to the zoo, and return them for lunch and a nap. The facility boasts a recidivism rate of zero.[69]

Juveniles in correctional institutions

Until the nineteenth century in America, juveniles and adults were housed in the same facilities. Juveniles—whom more recently would have been called "wayward," "neglected," or "dependent"—were often placed in these facilities even though they were accused of no crimes. According to the Center on Juvenile and Criminal Justice,

> Since few other options existed, youth of all ages and genders were often indiscriminately confined with hardened adult criminals and the mentally ill in large overcrowded and decrepit penal institutions. Many of these youth were confined for noncriminal behavior simply because there were no other options. At the same time, American cities were confronting high rates of child poverty and neglect putting pressure on city leaders to fashion a solution to this emerging social issue.[70]

Through the efforts of the Society for the Prevention of Pauperism, the New York House of Refuge opened in 1825. This was the first "reformatory" built specifically for juveniles; within three years, Boston and Philadelphia followed suit, and by the 1840s there were 25 such facilities throughout the nation.[71] Though the words "refuge" and "reformatory" suggested that the residents were to be treated differently from common criminals, these were huge buildings resembling their adult counterparts, and there were staff abuses. Before the advent of juvenile facilities, there may have been some reluctance to house juveniles with hardened adult criminals, but as juvenile facilities emerged, authorities likely became less reluctant to commit juveniles to these institutions, which quickly became overcrowded.

Today, juveniles are housed in a hodgepodge of facilities, both publicly- and privately-run. Juveniles who have not been convicted of any crime (that is, kids who are victims of abuse or neglect, or who have problems with drug dependency, or who have been found "delinquent" for status offenses) may find themselves housed with "justice-involved youth" who have been sentenced by the court for the commission of crimes. Juveniles are detained in a variety of settings, including detention centers, group homes, camps and residential treatment centers. Some facilities hold ten or fewer residents; some hold 200 or more. Some facilities are more restrictive than others. About 45 percent of them lock the kids in their rooms during sleeping hours; about 25 percent have fences or walls around the perimeter. The larger facilities are more likely to be operated by the state. State facilities have more justice-involved youth, and are more likely to have the security features just described.[72]

The benevolent notion of "treatment versus punishment" explains the grouping together of this hodgepodge of kids and facilities. All of the kids are seen as in need of treatment, and all of the facilities have treatment as their primary goal. This is, at least, the ideal—but it is better realized in some facilities than in others. The larger facilities with more justice-involved youth are more prone to having the treatment goal diluted by the goals of custody and security.

In the case of more serious crimes or recalcitrant offenders, juveniles may be "certified," "waived" or "transferred" to the adult court system. States vary in in terms of the conditions required to certify a juvenile to adult court. The U.S. Department of Juvenile Justice and Delinquency Prevention reports,

> The most common waiver standards call for courts to exercise their discretion to waive jurisdiction when the interests of the juvenile or the public (six States) or the interests of both (four States) would be served thereby; when the public safety (six States) or the public interest (four States) requires it; or when the juvenile does not appear to be amenable to treatment or rehabilitation within the juvenile system (four States). Most of the remaining standards combine these concepts in some way (the District of Columbia, for example, authorizes waiver if it is "in the interest of the public welfare and protection of the public security and there are no reasonable prospects for rehabilitation") or simply allow waiver whenever the court finds "good cause" (Kansas) or whenever the accused is not a "proper subject" for juvenile treatment (Missouri and Virginia). Besides requiring the court to consider "the best interests of the youth and of society" as a number of other States do, Oregon departs from the usual practice by focusing on whether the juvenile has the capacity "to appreciate the nature and quality of [his or her] conduct."[73]

We might note that most of the criteria for waiver described in the passage above are subject to interpretation and often represent a fairly low threshold for certification to the adult court.

With the War on Drugs and the crackdown on crime in the 1980s and 1090s (discussed earlier in this chapter), states were enacting laws that lowered the age at which juveniles could be tried in adult court, or provided for automatic certification for certain crimes at certain ages, or introduced more criteria for which juveniles could be certified. "On any given day," reports Jessica Lahey in *The Atlantic*, "10,000 juveniles are housed in adult prisons and jails."[74] Most of the juveniles in prison are charged with non-violent crimes.[75] These juveniles frequently miss out on the kinds of educational and treatment opportunities that would have been available to them in a juvenile facility. Worse yet, they are frequently the targets of sexual abuse. The National Prison Rape Elimination Commission reports, "More than any other group of incarcerated persons, youth incarcerated with adults are probably at the highest risk of sexual abuse." However, as the crackdown of the 1980s and 1990s has been reconsidered, in more recent years, many states are enacting legislation to restore the jurisdiction of the juvenile courts and reduce the number of kids going through the adult courts to adult prisons.[76]

Mental illness in prison

In the 1960s and 1970s, following a series of public revelations about abuses taking place in American psychiatric hospitals, the deinstitutionalization movement got underway, with the goal of dramatically reducing the numbers of patients in these hospitals. One prong of the movement was to curtail the use of involuntary commitments; and it was recognized that the second prong, which would be vital to the success of the movement, would be to make community-based treatment easily accessible. While the goals of the movement were commendable, thousands upon thousands of people with mental disorders did not receive the support they needed and soon found themselves homeless and in trouble with the law. The situation for those with mental disorders has not changed much since the deinstitutionalization movement. Local, state, and federal governments have been unwilling or unable to come up with the community mental health resources necessary to fill the enormous need, and our streets and prisons are filled with people who are mentally ill.

According to the Bureau of Justice Statistics, more than half of all prisoners in the United States have a mental health problem. Inmates' symptoms were associated most commonly with mania, depression, and psychosis (in descending order of incidence).[77] Undoubtedly, some mental disorders were brought on by the conditions of incarceration, while others existed before incarceration and often precipitated the criminal activity.

Prisoners with mental disorders pose particular challenges for prison officials. For one thing, they are more likely to get into fights than other prisoners.[78] For another, prison officials are challenged in terms of identifying people in need of treatment and then providing the resources needed for treatment. While often the resources needed to provide treatment are severely limited, the need for treatment can be most urgent. Besides treatment potentially reducing the incidence of violence directed toward other inmates and staff, treatment can also reduce inmate suicides. Suicides in state prisons have been on the rise, increasing by 30% between 2013 and 2014 and accounting for 7% of all deaths in prison, the "largest percentage of deaths due to suicide since tracking began."[79] As this volume goes to press, the spike in suicide rates is relatively recent and yet to be explained by criminologists.

The elderly in prison

With mandatory minimums and the sharp curtailment of parole beginning in the 1980s, inmates over 50 is the fastest growing age segment in today's federal prisons. This group grew by 25 percent between 2009 and 2013.[80] The same phenomena is happening in every state. In Virginia, for example, the proportion of state inmates age 50 and over rose from 4.5 percent in 1990 to 20 percent in 2014.[81] More and more inmates are becoming frail as they enter into their 70s, 80s and even 90s. The graying of the American prison population poses serious fiscal and practical challenges to prison officials as well as policymakers.

It is much more costly to detain elderly prisoners, especially when we take into account the costs of their medical needs. Medical expenses for older inmates are between four and eight times higher than those for younger inmates.[82] In addition to medical expenses, there are the costs of attaining compliance with the Americans with Disabilities Act. Many prisons are not compliant, but by law, if there is need, they must provide wheelchair accessibility, talking books or books in Braille, and "assistance with activities of daily living such as showering, toileting, or feeding."[83] According to Trey Fuller, acting health services director in Virginia's Department of Corrections, "Over time, we'll need more and more money for that population because they will need more drugs, more specialist visits, more nursing hours, more everything."[84]

As prisoners age, their recidivism rates drop precipitously. That is, the older a prisoner, the less likely he or she will reoffend once released. Geriatric ex-convicts pose very little risk to the community. Therefore, one way of dealing with the aging prison population would be paroling elderly inmates or commuting their sentences. This would involve some cost shifting—from caring for the elderly patient in prison to caring in the community—but state and federal prisons are not allocated the resources they need to provide such care. As federal and most state laws make few provisions for early release, these laws may very well need to be modified to make it possible. Given the mounting costs of caring for aging prisoners, it is reasonable to expect legislative changes will be made to relieve the pressure on state and federal budgets—if not for humanitarian reasons.

As this book goes to press, societies the world over are besieged by the coronavirus and the disease that it causes, Covid-19, which is very contagious and particularly deadly for the elderly. Most countries are requiring their citizens to maintain social distance measures, which are impossible in most prison settings; consequently, prisons are feared to become incubators for the disease. Even if the worst predictions do not come true, the fear of being "sitting ducks" for the disease is a major stressor—added to all of the others—for those in prison in the middle of the year 2020.

AFTER RELEASE

Many states in the U.S. strip the voting rights of people who have been incarcerated. This is called "felony disenfranchisement." Only two states have no such restrictions: Maine and Vermont. All of the rest prohibit prisoners from voting; 18 more states extend the restriction to periods of probation and parole; and 12 more states extend the restriction beyond the length of the offender's sentence. There were 6.1 million disenfranchised citizens in 2016 during the last presidential election; more than a third of them are African American (whereas African Americans make up only 13 percent of the general population).[85]

While felony disenfranchisement stirs little controversy in the United States, it is a rarity in the industrialized world. In 2005, the European Court of Human Rights ruled that banning prisoners from voting was a violation of their human rights; and "in Canada, Israel, and South Africa, courts have ruled that any conviction-based restriction of voting rights is unconstitutional."[86] The juxtaposition of U.S. disenfranchisement policies with the lack thereof in so many other countries is something of a paradox because the United States so often holds itself up as a beacon of freedom and democracy throughout the world; yet it deprives the freedom of a higher proportion of its citizens through incarceration than any other country, and continues to deprive millions of ex-offenders of their right to vote even after they have "paid their dues."

As discussed earlier in this volume, prisoners in the United States are disproportionately poor people of color. As such, they represent an important political constituency; arguably, one that does not have its needs addressed by state and federal legislatures. This is a constituency that other political factions may want to suppress. In fact, felony disenfranchisement laws have a dubious history of suppression. Disenfranchisement laws became popular after the Civil War when laws requiring voters to own property were ruled unconstitutional; thus, one legal restriction that disenfranchised poor blacks was replaced with another. In fact, many of the Southern states restricted disenfranchisement to those offenses that were more likely to be committed by blacks. For example, Jean Chung of The

Sentencing Project reports, "The author of Alabama's disenfranchisement provision 'estimated the crime of wife-beating alone would disqualify sixty percent of the Negroes,' resulting in a policy that would disenfranchise a man for beating his wife, but not for killing her."[87]

In recent years there have been successful efforts in many states to reform disenfranchisement laws, with several states repealing or waiving a waiting period for the restoration of voting rights; and other states repealing lifetime bans on voting. Cumulatively, over the generations, there have been tens of millions of U.S. citizens deprived of their voting rights. One wonders how their votes might have changed their communities, and if those changes may have even reduced crime rates.

Another very serious obstacle faced by ex-offenders is in finding employment. While there is an alleged presumption that the ex-convict has paid his or her dues, and a general belief that people deserve a second chance, levels of discrimination against ex-offenders are enormous and often insurmountable. Alana Semuels writes in *The Atlantic*, "No matter how committed former convicts are to finding gainful employment, employers remain prejudiced, and a criminal record is still a very heavy weight to bear."[88] Unlike many other types of discrimination, this one is taken for granted and often believed to be legitimate. A checkbox beside the question "have you ever been convicted of a felony?" has long been a standard on job application forms. (Often applicants are even asked about a conviction for a misdemeanor.) Such prejudice leads to exclusion; and exclusion may lead to recidivism.

Only recently have people come to question the legitimacy of this form of prejudice as the "Ban the Box" campaign has emerged. This initiative urges employers—especially state and local governments—to exclude questions (checkboxes) about criminal history from first-round job applications. Proponents argue that employers should examine the applicants' qualifications first; and criminal history becomes relevant only afterward. In August 2017, the National Employment Law Project reported,

> Momentum for the policy has grown exponentially, particularly in recent years. Federally, President Obama endorsed ban-the-box by directing federal agencies to delay inquiries into job applicants' records until later in the hiring process. There are a total of 29 states representing nearly every region of the country that have adopted the policies. … Nine states … have removed the conviction history question on job applications for private employers, which advocates embrace as the next step in the evolution of these policies.[89]

Unfortunately, prejudice against ex-offenders overlaps with, and reinforces, racial prejudice to the extent that ban-the-box policies may be backfiring and elevating discrimination against minority job applicants. There is recent research indicating that in areas that have ban-the-box policies, minority applicants are less likely to be called back for second-round interviews than in areas that do not have these ban-the-box policies. Researchers suggest that this is explained by the fact that employers, when they cannot include the criminal history checkbox on the initial job application, often assume their minority applicants have such a history.[90] In other words, racial prejudice often includes an element of presumed criminality and ban-the-box policies may actually be advantaging whites with criminal histories to the detriment of minorities without criminal histories.

COMMUNITY-BASED CORRECTIONS

Unless all we want from our prisons is retribution, then we would hope that the costs of imprisonment—to both the offender and the taxpayer—are justified by the reduction of crime outside of the prison. Yet high recidivism rates suggest otherwise. In other words, it is the exception, and not the rule, that former inmates are successfully reintegrated into society once released. Proponents of *reintegration theory* argue that the key to reducing recidivism is enabling the offender to maintain contacts within the community. Former inmates without such contacts are set loose with no family support and little chance of obtaining decent employment. Reintegration theory is not new. It was one of the motivations for allowing letter writing privileges soon after the advent of prisons, and then prison visitations, and later conjugal visits—so that the prisoner could maintain family contacts. Later halfway houses and prison furloughs—both toward the latter part of prisoner's sentence—were made available so that the soon-to-be-released prisoner might establish employment contacts. In respect to reintegration strategies, though, the United States is behind the curve relative to many European correctional systems. One study contrasting the U.S. to Germany (and the Netherlands) reports,

> In Germany, recognizing that strong family and community connections are associated with successful reentry outcomes, corrections officials routinely award prisoners short term or extended home leave to visit with family or search for work or accommodation. Germany's Federal Constitutional Court has affirmed the importance of prison leave to the principles of resocialization and reintegration. Strikingly, the failure rate from home leave (i.e., the failure to return to prison from home leave) amounts to a mere one percent and many prisoners consider denial of leave as a more severe sanction than detention in solitary confinement.[91]

Of course, the best way of ensuring the maintenance of contacts between the offender and the community is to avoid severing them in the first place with incarceration. In fact, millions of offenders are placed on probation, and there are a variety of "intermediate sanctions" that can be applied.

Probation (and parole)

Probation in the United States is often traced to John Augustus, a successful shoemaker and philanthropist in mid-nineteenth century Boston. Inspired by his religious beliefs, he began sitting in court and volunteering to bail out and supervise offenders. He started out offering his services to male drunkards, but soon his work extended to other offenses as well as to women and juveniles offenders. Conducting "presentence investigations," he selected his clients based on which ones were most likely to succeed on "probation," a term he coined. He visited his clients in their homes, counseled them, and allowed them to come to his home. He became so busy with this work that he had to turn over the operations of his shoemaking business to his son. He kept records of his cases and, by his own account, he had worked with over 2,000 clients during his 18 years of volunteer service.[92] Upon his death in 1859, other philanthropists took on his work and, in 1878, Massachusetts established a state-funded probationary service. By the turn of the century, only six states had followed suit, but the concept of probation got a big boost with the establishment of the juvenile court in 1899; and later it was recognized as a viable alternative to incarceration for adults as well. While prisons in the United States hold over two million people, and the United States has the highest incarceration rate in the world, most people under correctional supervision are *not* in prison. Today, there are over twice as many people under community supervision than in jail or prison, with the majority (over 80 per cent) being on probation[93]

In lieu of a prison sentence, convicted offenders are often sentenced to probation. Parole, on the other hand, may be granted to prisoners once they have completed a certain portion of their sentence. Probation and parole are being discussed together here because they are both often defined by very similar conditions that the offender must meet, including, at a minimum, regular meetings with his or her probation/parole officer (PO) and staying out of trouble. Probation and parole have many vocal critics who argue that they mitigate the severity of punishment and compromise its deterrent effect. However, the criminal justice system very much depends upon them to keep costs down. As noted in the previous chapter, some 95 percent of criminal cases are resolved by a plea bargain. Thus, a small reduction in pleas would result in an enormous increase in cases going through the time-consuming and expensive trial process. Probation, besides being less costly to administer to convicted offenders than prison, is also used to great effect to entice defendants to plead guilty. And parole helps correctional systems by relieving prison overcrowding as well as by cutting the costs of imprisonment.

Over the years, the functions and expectations of POs have changed. In the 1940s and 1950s, POs acted primarily as counselors, trying to uncover and resolve the psychological and sociological conflicts that contributed to their clients' criminality. In the 1960s and 1970s, they served largely as resource managers, directing their clients to community resources that could help them with their problems, such as family counseling, drug treatment, and housing and employment services. From the 1980s to the present day, reflecting the crackdown on crime discussed earlier in this chapter, POs serve mainly as officers of the law, strictly enforcing probation conditions, often "revoking" their clients for probation violations and sending them to jail or prison to serve out their sentences.

In fact, the famously dismal recidivism rates in the United States are somewhat misleading because a large number of offenders returning to prison are returned, not for violating criminal codes, but for violating the terms of their probation or parole. These are called "technical violations" and can include violations such as drinking alcohol, failing or refusing to show up for a drug test, curfew violations, and traveling outside a designated area. As probation is meant to be an alternative to prison, and parole is meant to shorten the period of incarceration, both are thought to mitigate mass incarceration. However, the restrictions imposed by probation and parole may, in fact, be a driver of mass incarceration. The alarming recidivism rates reported earlier in this chapter are familiar to all practitioners in criminal justice. They do not, however, distinguish between rearrests for criminal activities and those for technical violations. For example, Dana Goldstein of the Marshall Project reports, "Most of the returns to prison in New York—78 percent—were triggered not by fresh offenses but by parole violations, such as failing drug tests or skipped meetings with parole officers."[94]

Quite often when there is a criminal case where there is not enough evidence to secure a conviction, or when there is a relatively minor offense that is not worthy of a prison or jail sentence, the defendant may be coaxed to plead guilty in return for probation. Then he or she may be placed on severe restrictions, and then sent to prison for a technical violation. This is more likely to happen to a poor defendant who cannot afford the advice of a good attorney.

Alternative sanctions

There is a huge variety of sanctions that are being employed in the criminal justice system, other than incarceration and probation. These are so varied that it is difficult to discuss them in a systematic way. Sometimes they are called "intermediate sanctions," suggesting that they fall on a continuum between probation and incarceration. However, while some alternative sanctions—such as house arrest, electronic monitoring, wilderness programs, and boot camps—do indeed seem to be "intermediate," others—such as fines and community service—often seem to be much milder than probation. Some alternative sanctions may be applied before conviction, but most are applied afterwards. Some are used in some jurisdictions and not in others. Some are used in conjunction with probation or other alternative sanctions; some are not. Some are formal programs; others are informal. Some have a well-established track record, while others are quite experimental. Below, we will discuss only a few alternative sanctions and the issues that arise with them.

Fines

Fines are an alternative sanction with which most of us are familiar, especially when it comes to traffic violations. Sometimes they are used in conjunction with a jail sentence; often they are used in lieu of jail time. Ideally, the advantage of fines as a sanction is that they can be adjusted to fit the financial means of the offender. Thus, a wealthy offender can be made to feel the same "pain" as a poor offender. However, this is rarely the case. Instead, it is more often the case that rich and poor offenders are given much the same fines; and these fines are often an onerous burden for poor offenders. Some jurisdictions impose monetary penalties on offenders who do not pay their fines on time. In other words, poor offenders are trapped in a cycle where they are paying fines on fines and find themselves in a relationship with the city government much like that of a victim and his loan shark. (Something like this also happens in cases where probationers are required to pay for their own probation services.)

When cities and municipalities face budgetary problems, sometimes they come to rely on the proceeds from fines to meet their operating expenses. In such cases, the authorities may become overly aggressive in issuing fines. According to a U.S. Justice Department investigation, this was the situation that contributed to racial unrest in Ferguson, Missouri in 2014 (see Chapter 5). CNN summarized the investigation's report,

> Just about every branch of Ferguson government—police, municipal court, city hall—participated in "unlawful" targeting of African-American residents … for tickets and fines, the Justice Department concluded this week. The millions of dollars in fines and fees paid by black residents served an ultimate goal of satisfying "revenue rather than public safety needs."[95]

Forfeiture

It has long been the belief that criminals should not benefit from their "ill-gotten gains." Forfeiture of money and valuable property can disrupt the ability of organizations involved in illegal activities—drug trafficking, gambling, terrorism—to carry out those activities; and since the acquisition of money and valuable property is so often the motivation behind criminal activity, forfeiture should remove that motivation. Unfortunately, forfeiture can also be the motivation for overly aggressive law enforcement, as the proceeds often go to the agencies that conducted the investigation and/or made the arrest. Much like the problem with fines discussed above, when law enforcement agencies come to rely on the proceeds from forfeitures, their priorities and tactics may become distorted.

This is especially the case for drug-related crimes. In one case, authorities seized a $2.5 million yacht after finding 10 marijuana seeds and two stems onboard.[96] Parents' houses have been seized when their kids have been apprehended for selling drugs. In Arkansas, a sheriff was "privately selling cars he had seized to himself and others at a price at or well below their appraised values."[97] In California, authorities raided a $5 million ranch they thought was involved in the drug trade. The owner was killed in the raid. It turned out the authorities had obtained an appraisal of the property weeks before the raid.[98] In some cases "policing for profit" can lead the authorities to prioritize less serious crimes. According to one senior Customs official, if the police "had a guy with a ton of marijuana and no assets versus a guy with two joints and a Lear jet, I guarantee you they will bust the guy with the Lear jet."[99]

Restitution

Depending on the crime, most or all jurisdictions have it in their authority to require the offender to "restore" the victim to his or her previous state through a financial payment(s). This sanction is different from the payment of a fine because the money goes to the victim. Restitution may be ordered in lieu of a jail or prison term, or it may be used in conjunction with a period of incarceration. In the case of the former, critics often charge that it is too lenient on the offender. Other than that, restitution has become quite popular as an alternative sanction because it saves the state money on incarceration, it spares the offender the criminogenic influences of incarceration, and it benefits the victims of crime, who often feel the court only cares about them for their testimony.

Restorative justice

Today's system of criminal justice is predicated on the notion that a crime is an offense against the state, and the only role to be played by the victim is that of giving testimony. Restorative justice is predicated on the idea that crimes are committed against individuals and the community, and gives each a greater role to play in the criminal justice process. The offender, the victim, and sometimes community representatives are brought together in mediated conversations to discuss how the victim can best be restored to his or her previous state. John Braithwaite, a leading proponent of restorative justice, writes,

> Restorative justice is a process where all stakeholders affected by an injustice have an opportunity to discuss how they have been affected by the injustice and to decide what should be done to repair the harm. With crime, restorative justice is about the idea that because crime hurts, justice should heal. It follows that conversations with those who have been hurt and with those who have inflicted the harm must be central to the process.[100]

Financial restitution is often involved, but the victim may ask for something other than money; for example, the victim of violence may ask that the offender attend anger management classes and that he or she perform community service. In addition to including and restoring the victim, restorative justice is believed to have rehabilitative benefits for the offender, giving him or her a chance to personalize the victim and recognize and take ownership of the harm that their acts have caused. As such, the process offers the offender an opportunity to redeem him- or herself (see "John Braithwaite" in Chapter 4). Restorative justice programs are seen to provide a more humane means of bringing about justice than traditional methods and they have gained a great deal of traction both inside and outside the United States over the last two decades.

Community service

Courts also have it in their authority to sentence an offender to a certain number of hours of work for a non-profit or government agency. An original intent for this alternative sanction was to level the playing field for poor misdemeanants who could not afford financial penalties, while their wealthier counterparts could. Besides the cost savings of community service vis-à-vis incarceration, it often appeals to the authorities and the public who feel community service builds character and, therefore, may contribute to the offender's rehabilitation. Today, it is still mostly used for misdemeanors.

Many alternative sanctions are considered as "diversion programs." As we saw in the previous chapter, diversion programs are meant to divert offenders out of the criminal justice system, or to minimize their penetration into the system. The intentions behind diversion programs are benevolent; and such programs are almost always less costly than probation and, certainly, than incarceration. However, alternative sanctions are often subject to criticism. Critics from the right charge that such programs are too lenient on offenders.

Criticism of alternative sanctions from the left falls into two camps. Since alternative sanctions are often at the discretion of the prosecutor, the judge, or even the police, critics charge that there is often discrimination in the way they are applied. That is, they argue that alternative sanctions are more likely be issued to affluent whites, while poor minorities get more severe traditional sanctions. The other criticism from the left refers to the *net-widening* effect of alternative sanctions, particularly diversion programs (see Chapter 6). Since these may be much milder than traditional sanctions, the authorities hand them out with much less restraint, sometimes in lieu of formally pressing charges—that is, without due process. If alternative sanctions were not available, then many of these cases would not have been pursued by the criminal justice authorities. As milder alternatives are available, though, rather than minimizing penetration into the system, many more people are being caught up in the "net" and find themselves under the state's supervision.

THE DEATH PENALTY

In the case of *Furman v. Georgia* in 1972, the United States Supreme Court placed a moratorium on all executions, holding that the death penalty was applied inconsistently and that most state statutes failed to adequately "assure that the death penalty would not be administered in a capricious or discriminatory manner."[101] States rewrote their statutes and capital punishment was reinstated in 1976 in the case of *Gregg v Georgia*. Since reinstatement, over 1,400 people have been executed in the United States. The federal judicial system allows capital punishment, as do the judicial systems of 31 states (although two of those states—Kansas and New Hampshire—have not executed anyone since reinstatement).

In the *Furman* case, Justice Brennan cited "evolving standards of decency," referring to the fact that what might not have been considered "cruel and unusual" punishment by the framers of the Constitution might be so considered in more recent times. Indeed, over the last few centuries, across much of the world—especially in democratic countries and in emerging democracies—public sentiments about the limits of punishment have evolved in the direction of leniency. The American sentiment toward the death penalty may be lagging behind in this evolution, but there is evidence that some evolution is taking place. According to opinion polls, American support for the death penalty has been dropping since the height of the crackdown on crime in the 1990s (from 84 percent in favor in 1994 down to 60 percent in 2016);[102] death by lethal injection has become the norm because it was thought to be more humane than the alternatives; and there have been a number of Supreme Court decisions in recent years limiting the use of the death penalty. In particular, the Court banned the use of the death penalty for "mentally retarded" defendants in 2002; and in 2005 the Court banned its use for offenders who committed their crimes while still a juvenile.

As this book goes to press, there are three very controversial issues surrounding the death penalty. The first and most persistent of these is whether the death penalty is applied in a racially discriminatory manner. In the 1986 U.S. Supreme Court case of *McCleskey v. Kemp*, much of the defendant's case revolved around the now-famous study by David Baldus and his colleagues which found that, in Georgia, "blacks who killed whites were sentenced to death 22 times more frequently than blacks who killed blacks, and seven times more frequently than whites who killed blacks."[103] (The Court upheld McCleskey's death sentence, however, holding that the data did not prove discrimination in his particular case.) A 2003 study by University of Maryland researchers (commissioned by the Governor of Maryland) found that defendants—white or black—were more likely to be sentenced to death if the victim were white than if he or she were black. Similar results have been found in New Jersey and North Carolina.[104] Today, whites and African Americans each make up about 42 percent of the death row inmate population,[105] even though the general population in the United States is 77 percent white and only 13 percent is African American.[106] (That is, a proportionate representation of death row inmates would have five times more whites than blacks, rather than roughly equal numbers.) Whether this disparity is due to discrimination in prosecutors' charging of defendants, or on the part of juries, or whether it is due to the relative frequency with which blacks and whites commit capital crimes—these matters are still up for debate.

Another controversial issue related to the death penalty has to do with the rise in the numbers of people who have been exonerated of the crimes for which they were convicted—of people who have been convicted of both capital and non-capital crimes. Proponents of the death penalty have long felt secure that, with all of the legal safeguards in place, no one who is innocent will ever be executed. Indeed, for generations, prisoners did not have the resources to challenge the evidence against them post-conviction; and criminalistics had not advanced to the point that it has today. In the past few decades, a number of non-profit organizations—most famously, the Innocence Project—have emerged to provide the resources to inmates who have a convincing case; and the collection and analysis of DNA evidence has become commonplace.

The National Registry of Exonerations reports that over 2,000 convicts have been exonerated since 1989;[107] and the Death Penalty Information

Center reports that 159 death row inmates have been exonerated since 1973.[108] Again, race plays a role. According to a report by the National Registry of Exonerations,

> African Americans are only 13% of the American population but a majority of innocent defendants wrongfully convicted of crimes and later exonerated. They constitute 47% of the 1,900 exonerations listed in the National Registry of Exonerations (as of October 2016), and the great majority of more than 1,800 additional innocent defendants who were framed and convicted of crimes in 15 large-scale police scandals and later cleared in "group exonerations."[109]

Lastly, another controversy that has been swirling around the use of capital punishment in recent years has to do with chemicals being used in executions by lethal injection. Since the first execution by lethal injection in 1982, the standard drug protocol involved the administration of three drugs in a timed sequence: an anesthetic to put the condemned inmate to sleep, a paralytic to stop the breathing, and potassium chloride to stop the heart. Such a combination is believed to be more humane than alternative forms of execution and it provides a counter to critics who charge the death penalty constitutes cruel and unusual punishment. However, many American drug companies have ceased manufacturing some of the drugs that were previously used in these protocols, and foreign manufacturers have either refused to export drugs to be used in executions, or they have been banned from doing so by their governments. Consequently, different states have been experimenting with different drugs in different combinations, sometimes with disastrous results. In Ohio in 2014, for example, Dennis McGuire "appeared to gasp and convulse for roughly 10 minutes before he died."[110] That same year in Arizona, Joseph Woods took two hours to die. He is said to have "gasped and struggled to breathe for about an hour and 40 minutes."[111] In 2017, concerned about the expiration date on one of the execution drugs it had in stock, Arkansas planned the execution of eight inmates in one month. (Courts intervened and issued stays for half of those inmates.) Proponents of the death penalty are well aware that incidents such as these cast death by lethal injection in a bad light and can alter both public and judicial opinions about the practice, and about the death penalty in general. In fact, in 2014 the Tennessee legislature moved to make the electric chair mandatory should drugs for lethal injection become unavailable.

CONCLUSIONS

Perhaps the most singular feature of the American correctional system is the fact that the United States stands apart from other advanced Western industrialized democracies in the relative ease with which it dispenses relatively harsh punishments for criminal wrongdoing.

Ironically, Americans hold up the value of freedom as the country's greatest attribute; yet its criminal justice system shows less restraint in depriving people—especially poor minorities—of their freedom than its counterparts among industrialized democracies.

As we have discussed, the U.S. has the highest incarceration rate in the world, largely because of the length of sentences that it metes out. The vast majority of those sentences are based on plea bargains, which means the defendants' right to due process has been compromised. Prison conditions are sometimes quite brutal, where prisoners are not adequately protected from one another, and extended periods of solitary confinement are allowed. (Other countries have refused to extradite people accused of crime in the United States because their courts have held that incarceration in the U.S. amounts to cruel and unusual punishment.)[112] And the United States is among the few advanced industrialized democracies that allows the death penalty; most of the others that do allow it never—or almost never—use it.

If all of these practices were proven to lower crime and recidivism rates, making Americans safer, that may well be an adequate explanation for the relatively harsh treatments for the accused and the convicted in the United States. Yet, they have not been proven to make Americans safer, leading many observers to believe that perhaps the major driver of American criminal justice has indeed been retribution.

Another explanation for why criminal justice policies are perpetuated even though they have not proven to be effective in reducing crime is that perhaps the true purpose of criminal justice policy is indeed to maintain the status quo, along with its existing inequalities. As we noted in our discussion of conflict theory (Chapter 3), by targeting and punishing crimes committed by the poor, the criminal justice system serves two important objectives that contribute to this goal: it legitimizes the activities of the rich that can do harm to far more people than crimes committed by the poor; and it promotes division among the working classes, causing them to fear one another, rather than unite to form a more just and equitable society.

Some of the inequities that are rife in the system are being addressed. For example, there are efforts to reform minimum sentencing guidelines, especially with regard to nonviolent drug crimes. Bail reform is being undertaken—and met with resistance—in a number of states. There is also an increasing number of reform-minded candidates running for and winning elections for district attorney's offices.[113]

The success of future reforms will depend upon our recognition of inequalities within the system. So many of the inequities built into the American criminal justice system deal with social class. There can be little doubt that some people can afford more justice than others. Similarly, the success of future reforms also depends very much on white Americans being woke to the racism that permeates the system.

The success of future reform also depends upon continued criminological research. As criminological research becomes better able to prove inequitable outcomes are due to inequitable policies, reform becomes all the more possible. It was, after all, the works of criminologists and sociologists that alerted policymakers to the racist implications of mass incarceration, starting over two decades ago.[114] Now, modest, but important, reforms are being undertaken.[115]

NOTES

1 Matthew Durose, Alexia Cooper and Howard N. Snyder, Recidivism of prisoners released in thirty states in 2005: Patterns from 2005 to 2010, Bureau of Justice Statistics, NCJ 244205. www.bjs.gov/index.cfm?ty=pbdetail&iid=4986. Retrieved August 8, 2017.

2 Ibid. See also Dana Goldstein, "The misleading math of 'recidivism': Even the Supreme Court gets it wrong." The Marshall Project, December 4, 2014. www.the marshallproject.org/2014/12/04/the-misleading-math-of-recidivism#.tjjiEdSGe. Retrieved August 8, 2017.

3 National Research Council. *The Growth of Incarceration in the United States: Exploring Causes and Consequences. Committee on Causes and Consequences of High Rates of Incarceration*, J. Travis, B. Western, and S. Redburn, Editors. Committee on Law and Justice, Division of Behavioral and Social Sciences and Education. Washington, DC: The National Academies Press, 2014.

4 Quoting Norval Morris and David Rothman, "All one can say about public sentiment on these issues is that whatever practices are followed in a society at any time, the majority of citizens perceive these practices as being too lenient toward the criminal." *The Oxford History of the Prison: The Practice of Punishment in Western Society*, New York; Oxford University Press, 1995, p. x.

5 Ibid.

6 "Criminal Transportation," The National Archives. www.nationalarchives.gov.uk/help-with-your-research/research-guides/criminal-transportation/. Retrieved July 16, 2017.

7 Michael Welch, *Punishment in America: Social Control and the Ironies of Imprisonment*, Thousand Oaks, CA: Sage, 1999.

8 Jessica Mitford, *Kind and Usual Punishment: The Prison Business*. New York: Alfred a Knopf, 1975, p. 31.

9 www.easternstate.org/research/history-eastern-state/timeline. Retrieved June 29, 2017.

10 Ibid.

11 Quoted in Daniel Van Ness, *Crime and its Victims: What we Can Do*, Downers Grove, IL: InterVarsity Press, 1986, p. 77.

12 Peter Wagner and Bernadette Rabuy, "Mass Incarceration: The Whole Pie 2016" Press Release, Graphic: How many people are locked up in the United States? The Prison Policy Initiative, March 14, 2016. www.prisonpolicy.org/reports/pie2016.html.

13 Bureau of Prisons, "About our Facilities." www.bop.gov/about/facilities/federal_prisons.jsp. Retrieved July 3, 2017.

14 Transcribed from podcast. *Only a Game*, National Public Radio. Originally broadcast June 30, 2017. www.npr.org/podcasts/510052/only-a-game. Retrieved July 3, 2017.

15 Bureau of Prisons, "About our Facilities."

16 Richard Serrano, "U.S. 'supermax' prison: Alcatraz of the Rockies is seen as 'inhuman and degrading,'" *Los Angeles Times*. August 9, 2015. www.latimes.com/nation/la-na-extradite-supermax-20150809-story.html. Retrieved July 3, 2017.

17 Tom Jackman, "Mass reduction of California prison population didn't cause a rise in crime, two studies find," *Washington Post*, May 18, 2016. www.washingtonpost.com/news/true-crime/wp/2016/05/18/mass-release-of-california-prisoners-didnt-cause-rise-in-crime-two-studies-find/?utm_term=.819f2cb27e15. Retrieved July 5, 2017.

18 Ibid.

19 "Over 700,000" from Bureau of Justice Statistics, "The Nation's jails held few inmates at midyear 2014 compared to their peak in 2008," Press release, June 11, 2015. www.bjs.gov/content/pub/press/jim14pr.cfm. Retrieved July 7, 2017. The 11 million figure counts jail admissions and does not identify when the same individual is admitted more than once in a given year. Peter Wagner, "Jails matter: But who's listening?" citing data from the Bureau of Justice Statistics, Prison Policy Initiative, August 14, 2015, www.prisonpolicy.org/blog/2015/08/14/jailsmatter/. Retrieved July 6, 2017.

20 Ram Subramanian, Ruth Delaney, Stephen Roberts, Nancy Fishman, Peggy McGarry, "Incarceration's front door: The misuse of jails in America," Vera Institute, Center on Sentencing and Corrections, February 2015, p. 4. https://storage.googleapis.com/vera-web-assets/downloads/Publications/incarcerations-front-door-the-misuse-of-jails-in-america/legacy_downloads/incarcerations-front-door-report_02.pdf. Retrieved July 7, 2017.

21 Todd, Clear, Michael Reisig, Carolyn Petrosino, and George Cole, *American Corrections: In Brief*, Boston: Cengage Learning, 2015, p. 60.

22 Subramanian et al. p. 4. Todd Minton and Zheng Zeng, "Jail inmates in 2015," Bureau of Justice Statistics, NCJ250394, December, 2016. www.bjs.gov/content/pub/pdf/ji15.pdf. Retrieved July 8, 2017.

23 The Vera Institute, "Incarceration's Front Door: The Misuse of Jails in America," Report Summary. February 2015. www.vera.org/downloads/publications/incarcerations-front-door-summary.pdf. Retrieved December 12, 2019.

24 Ibid., p. 14.

25 Miriam Aroni Krinsky and Christian Gossett, "With money bail, system continues to criminalize poverty," *USAToday*, opinion, July 27, 2017. www.usatoday.com/story/opinion/policing/2017/07/28/alternatives-bail-police-policing-the-usa-money/513032001/. Retrieved September 14, 2017.

26 Jamiles Larty, "New York Tried to Get Rid of Bail. Then the Backlash Came," *Politico*, April 23, 2020. www.politico.com/news/magazine/2020/04/23/bail-reform-coronavirus-new-york-backlash-148299. Retrieved April 27, 2020.

27 Ibid., pp. 11–12.

28 Clayton Mosher and Scott Akins, *Drugs and Drug Policy*, 2nd edition, Los Angeles: Sage, 2014, p. 454.

29 Kelly Herring, "Was a prison built every 10 days to house a fast growing population of non-violent inmates?, Politifact, July 31, 2015. www.politifact.com/truth-o-meter/statements/2015/jul/31/cory-booker/was-prison-built-every-10-days-house-fast-growing-/. Retrieved July 10, 2017.

30 The Drug Policy Alliance, "Cocaine and crack facts," www.drugpolicy.org/drug-facts/cocaine-and-crack-facts. Retrieved July 10, 2017.

31 Mosher and Akins, *Drugs and Drug Policy*. The Drug Policy Alliance. In 1995, the U.S. Sentencing Commission recommended that the ratio of crack sentencing to powder sentencing be reduced from 100 to 1 to 1 to 1. The Commission's recommendation was rejected by the President and the U.S. Congress. It was not until the Fair Sentencing Act passed in 2010 that the ratio was reduced to 18 to 1.

32 See Mosher and Akins, *Drugs and Drug Policy*, pp. 440–450.

33 Dan Baum, "Legalize it all: How to win the war on drugs," *Harper's Magazine*, April 2016. https://harpers.org/archive/2016/04/legalize-it-all/. Retrieved July 2017.

34 Riley Yates and Steve Esack, "Law treated black crack addicts more severely than today's heroin offenders," *The Morning Call*, December 3, 2016. www.mcall.com/news/local/allentown/mc-pennsylvania-war-on-drugs-heroin-versus-crack-epidemic-2-20161203-story.html. Retrieved July 11, 2017.

35 For a detailed discussion, see Nils Christie's *Crime Control as Industry: Towards Gulags, Western Style*. London: Routledge, 1993.

36 Eric Lotke, "The Prison-Industrial Complex," *Multinational Monitor*, vol. 17, no. 11, November 1996.

37 Richard Swift, "Crime and Civilization," an interview with Nils Christie, *New Internationalist*, no. 282, August 1996.

38 Ibid., 11.

39 Lotke, "The Prison-Industrial Complex."

40 Steven R. Donziger, *The Real War on Crime: The Report of the National Criminal Justice Commission*. New York: HarperCollins, 1996, p. 95.

41 CNBC Presents, "Billions Behind Bars: Inside America's Prison Industry." CNBC.com, October 11, 2011. http://m.cnbc.com/us_news/44706333. Retrieved August 13, 2014.

42 Quoted in Lotke, "The Prison-Industrial Complex."

43 Stephanie Clifford and Jessica Silver-Greenberg, "In Prisons, Sky-High Phone Rates and Money Transfer Fees," *New York Times*, June 26, 2014. www.nytimes.com/2014/06/27/business/in-prisons-sky-high-phone-rates-and-money-transfer-fees.html?_r=0. Retrieved July 12, 2014.

44 Matt Taibbi, *Divide: American Injustice in the Age of the Wealth Gap*. New York: Speigel and Grau, 2014, 214.

45 Laura Sullivan, "Prison Economics Help Drive Immigration Law," National Public Radio, October 28, 2010. www.npr.org/2010/10/28/130833741/prison-economics-help-drive-ariz-immigration-law. Retrieved July 12, 2014.

46 Livia Luan, "Profiting from Enforcement: The Role of Private Prisons in U.S. Immigration Detention," Migration Policy Institute, May 2, 2018. www.migrationpolicy.org/article/profiting-enforcement-role-private-prisons-us-immigration-detention. Retrieved March 18, 2020.

47 Quoted in Fox Butterfield, "Study Tracks Boom in Prisons," *New York Times*, April 30, 2004. www.nytimes.com/2004/04/30/us/study-tracks-boom-in-prisons-and-notes-impact-on-counties.html. Retrieved September 22, 2014.

48 Gresham Sykes, *The Society of Captives: A Study of a Maximum Security Prison*. Princeton, NJ: Princeton University Press, 1958. Reprinted 1972.

49 John Irwin and Donald Cressey, "Thieves, convicts and the inmate culture," *Social Problems*, vol. 19, Fall 1962, pp. 142–155.

50 Quoted in Graeme Wood, "How gangs took over prisons," *The Atlantic*, October, 2014. www.theatlantic.com/magazine/archive/2014/10/how-gangs-took-over-prisons/379330/. Retrieved July 17, 2017.

51 Gresham Sykes, *The Society of Captives*, p. 57.

52 Ibid., p. 58. Emphasis added.

53 "David Skarbek on Prison Gangs," an interview with Russ Roberts, Library of Economics and Liberty, March 30, 2015. www.econtalk.org/archives/2015/03/david_skarbek_o.html. Retrieved July 18, 2017. The interview concerned Skarbek's book *The Social Order of the Underworld: How Prison Gangs Govern the American Penal System*. New York: Oxford University Press, 2014.

54 Quoted in Graeme Wood, "How gangs took over prison."

55 Ann Carson and Elizabeth Anderson, *Prisoners in 2015*, Bureau of Justice Statistics, NCJ250229, December 2016, www.bjs.gov/content/pub/pdf/p15.pdf. Retrieved July 19, 2017.

56 Extrapolated from "Table 1: Sentenced prisoners in State and Federal institutions: Number and incarceration rates, 1925–1981," Prisoners 1925–1981, Bureau of Justice Statistics, December 1982 www.bjs.gov/content/pub/pdf/p2581.pdf and "Table 1: Prisoners under the jurisdiction of state or federal correctional authorities, December 31, 2000–2010" Prisoners in 2010, U.S. Department of Justice, NCJ 236096, December 2011. www.bjs.gov/content/pub/pdf/p10.pdf. Retrieved July 21, 2017.

57 "Incarcerated women and girls," The Sentencing Project, Fact Sheet. www.sentencingproject.org/wp-content/uploads/2016/02/Incarcerated-Women-and-Girls.pdf. Retrieved July 19, 2017.

58 Kimberly Greer, "The changing nature of interpersonal relationships in a women's prison," *The Prison Journal*, vol. 80, no. 4, December 2000, pp. 442–468.

59 Ibid., p. 445. "… affectional ties …" quoted from J.M. Pollack, *Counseling Women in Prison*. Thousand Oaks, CA: Sage, 1998.

60 "Children and families of the incarcerated fact sheet," National Resource Center on Children and Families of the Incarcerated," Camden, NJ: Rutgers University, 2014. http://dept.camden.rutgers.edu/nrccfi/files/nrccfi-fact-sheet-2014.pdf. Retrieved July 21, 2017.

61 Quoted in Ernest Drucker, *A Plague of Prisons*, New York: The New Press, 2011, p. 144.

62 Ibid., p. 146.

63 Eli Hager and Anna Flagg, "Parenthood Lost: How Incarcerated Parents Are Losing Their Children Forever," *Washington Post*, December 3, 2018. www.washingtonpost.com/national/parenthood-lost-how-incarcerated-parents-are-losing-their-children-forever/2018/12/02/e97ebcfe-dc83-11e8-b3f0-62607289efee_story.html. Retrieved March 18, 2020.

64 "Mothers, infants and imprisonment," Women Prison Association, May 2009, www.prisonlegalnews.org/media/publications/womens_prison_assoc_report_on_prison_nurseries_and_community_alternatives_2009.pdf. Retrieved July 21, 2017.

65 Ibid., p. 5.

66 Sarah Yager, "Prison born," *The Atlantic*, July/August 2015. www.theatlantic.com/magazine/archive/2015/07/prison-born/395297/. Retrieved July 21, 2017.

67 Ibid., and "Mothers, infants and imprisonment."

68 Yager, "Prison born."

69 Ibid., and Marie Douglas, "The Mutter-Kind-Heim at Frankfurt am Main: 'Come together—Go together," An observation," from *Criminology: A Cross-Cultural Perspective*, R. Heiner, ed., Minneapolis/St. Paul: West Publishing, 1995, pp. 254–260.

70 Center on Juvenile and Criminal justice, "Juvenile Justice History," www.cjcj.org/education1/juvenile-justice-history.html. Retrieved July 25, 2017.

71 Ibid.

72 Sarah Hockenberry, Andrew Wachter and Anthony Sladky, "Juvenile Residential Facility Census, 2014, Selected Findings," Office of Juvenile Justice and Delinquency Prevention, U.S. Department of Justice, September 2016, www.ojjdp.gov/pubs/250123.pdf. Retrieved July 27, 2017.

73 Patrick Griffin, Patricia Torbert, Linda Szymanski, "Trying Juveniles as Adults in Criminal Court," Department of Juvenile Justice and Delinquency Prevention, 1998. www.ojjdp.gov/pubs/tryingjuvasadult/transfer.html.

74 Jessica Lahey, "The steep costs of keeping juveniles in adult prisons," The Atlantic, January 8, 2016. www.theatlantic.com/education/archive/2016/01/the-cost-of-keeping-juveniles-in-adult-prisons/423201/. Retrieved July 28, 2017.

75 Ibid. See also Malcolm Young and Jenni Gainsborough, "Prosecuting juveniles in adult court," The Sentencing Project, 2000. www.prisonpolicy.org/scans/sp/juvenile.pdf. Retrieved July 27, 2017.

76 "Trends in juvenile justice state legislation, 2001–2011," National Conference of State Legislatures, August 7, 2012, www.ncsl.org/documents/cj/TrendsInJuvenileJustice.pdf. Retrieved July 27, 2017.

77 Doris James and Lauren Glaze, "Mental health problems of prison and jail inmates," Bureau of Justice Statistics, NCJ 213600, revised December 14, 2006. www.bjs.gov/content/pub/pdf/mhppji.pdf. Retrieved July 28, 2017.

78 Ibid.

79 Emanuella Grinberg, "Prison suicides are on the rise nationally and it's pretty bad in Massachusetts," CNN, April 19, 2017. www.cnn.com/2017/04/19/health/prison-suicides-massachusetts-trnd/index.html. Retrieved July 28, 2017.

80 "The impact of aging inmate population on the Federal Bureau of Prisons," Executive Summary, Office of the Inspector General, USDOJ, revised February 2016. https://oig.justice.gov/reports/2015/e1505.pdf. Retrieved July 28, 2017.

81 Michael Ollove, "Elderly inmates burden state prisons," Pew Charitable Trust, March 17, 2016. www.pewtrusts.org/en/research-and-analysis/blogs/stateline/2016/03/17/elderly-inmates-burden-state-prisons. Retrieved July 28, 2017.

82 Ibid.

83 "The Americans with Disabilities Act and prison conditions," Disabled-world.com newsletter. www.disabled-world.com/disability/ada/prisons.php. Retrieved July 28, 2017.

84 Ibid.

85 Jean Chung, "Felony disenfranchisement: A primer," The Sentencing Project, May 10, 2016. www.sentencingproject.org/publications/felony-disenfranchisement-a-primer/. Retrieved August 11, 2017.

86 Ibid.

87 Ibid.

88 Alana Semuels, "When banning one kind of discrimination results in another" *The Atlantic*, August 4, 2016. www.theatlantic.com/business/archive/2016/08/consequences-of-ban-the-box/494435/. Retrieved August 12, 2017.

89 Beth Avery and Phil Hernandez, "Ban the box: U.S. cities and counties and states adopt fair hiring policies," National Employment Law Project, Toolkit, August 1, 2017. www.nelp.org/publication/ban-the-box-fair-chance-hiring-state-and-local-guide/. Retrieved August 12, 2017.

90 Semuels, "When banning one kind of discrimination results in another."

91 Rob Subramanian and Alison Shames, "Sentencing and Prison Practices in Germany and the Netherlands: Implications for the United States," The Vera Institute, Center on Sentencing and Corrections, October 2013. https://storage.googleapis.com/vera-web-assets/downloads/Publications/sentencing-and-prison-practices-in-germany-and-the-netherlands-implications-for-the-united-states/legacy_downloads/european-american-prison-report-v3.pdf. Retrieved August 5, 2017.

92 Edward Wallach Sieh, *Community Corrections and Human Dignity*, Jones and Barlett Learning, 2006.

93 Danielle Kaeble and Thomas Bonczar, "Probation and parole in the United States, 2015," Bureau of Justice Statistics. NCJ 250230 February 22, 2017. www.bjs.gov/content/pub/pdf/ppus15.pdf. Retrieved August 8, 2017.

94 Dana Goldstein, "The misleading math of 'recidivism': Even the Supreme Court gets it wrong." The Marshall Project, December 4, 2014. www.themarshallproject.org/2014/12/04/the-misleading-math-of-recidivism#.tjjiEdSGe. Retrieved August 8, 2017.

95 Michael Martinez, Alexandra Meeks and Ed Lavandera, "Policing for profit: How Ferguson's fines violated rights of African Americans," CNN, March 6, 2015. www.cnn.com/2015/03/06/us/ferguson-missouri-racism-tickets-fines/index.html. Retrieved August 14, 2017.

96 Mosher and Akins, *Drugs and Drug Policy*.

97 Ibid., p. 464.

98 Ibid.

99 Ibid., p. 465.

100 John Braithwaite, "Restorative justice and de-professionalization," *Project Muse: The Good Society*, vol. 13, no. 1, pp. 28–31. Penn State University Press, 2004. https://muse.jhu.edu/article/175203/pdf. Retrieved August 31, 2017.

101 Wording of this passage is not directly from USSC decision, but from "Furman vs. Georgia," Oyez, www.oyez.org/cases/1971/69-5030. Retrieved September 1, 2017.

102 "U.S. death penalty support at 60%," Gallup, October 25, 2016. www.gallup.com/poll/196676/death-penalty-support.aspx. Retrieved September 1, 2017.

103 Quoted from Justice on Trial: Racial Disparities in the American Criminal Justice System. Leadership Conference on Civil Rights and Leadership Conference Education Fund, Diane Publishing Co., 2000. Summarizing David Baldus, Charles Pulaski and George Wentworth, "Comparative review of death sentences: An empirical study of the Georgia experience," *Journal of Criminal Law and Criminology*, vol. 74, fall 1983, pp. 661–753.

104 "Race and the death penalty," American Civil Liberties Union, www.aclu.org/other/race-and-death-penalty. Retrieved September 1, 2017.

105 "Death row USA, Spring 2017," A quarterly report of the Criminal Justice Project of the NAACP Legal Defense and Educational Fund. https://deathpenaltyinfo.org/documents/DRUSASpring2017.pdf. Retrieved September 1, 2017.

106 "Quick facts," United States Census Bureau, July 1, 2016. www.census.gov/quick-facts/fact/table/US/PST045216. Retrieved September 1, 2017.

107 The National Registry of Exonerations, A Project of the University of California Irvine Newkirk Center for Science & Society, University of Michigan Law School & Michigan State University College of Law. www.law.umich.edu/special/exoneration/Pages/Exoneration-by-Year.aspx. Retrieved September 3, 2017.

108 "The innocence list," The Death Penalty Information Center. https://deathpenalty info.org/innocence-list-those-freed-death-row. Retrieved September 3, 2017.

109 Samuel Gross, Maurice Possley and Klara Stephens, "Race and wrongful convictions in the United States," The National Registry of Exonerations, March 7, 2017. www.law. umich.edu/special/exoneration/Documents/Race_and_Wrongful_Convictions.pdf. Retrieved September, 3, 2017.

110 "Controversial execution in Ohio uses new drug combination," CNN, January 17, 2014. www.cnn.com/2014/01/16/justice/ohio-dennis-mcguire-execution/. Retrieved September 2, 2017.

111 "Another botched execution? Inmate gasps during two-hour execution," CNN, September 8, 2014. www.cnn.com/2014/07/23/justice/arizona-execution-controversy/. Retrieved September 2, 2017.

112 For example, in the case of alleged terrorist Ali Charaf Damache, the Irish court refused extradition, concerned he would be put in "supermax" prison and "prolonged exposure to involuntary solitary confinement ... is damaging to the integrity of the mind and personality, and is damaging to the bodily integrity of the person." Richard Serrano, "U.S. 'supermax' prison: Alcatraz of the Rockies is seen as 'inhuman and degrading,'" Los Angeles Times. August 9, 2015. www.latimes.com/nation/la-na-extradite-supermax-20150809-story.html. Retrieved July 3, 2017. Another example is the case of Henry Hendrickson who is alleged to have smuggled 50 tons of hashish. In 1999, the Norwegian Supreme Court unanimously refused to extradite him, holding that U.S. prisons were inhumane. "Norway won't turn over American," AP News Archive, August 24, 1999. www.apnewsarchive.com/1999/Norway-Won-t-Turn-Over-American/id-104d96e389b4223eb7db6061a 0b8863e. Retrieved September 3, 2017.

113 Bazelon, Charged: The New Movement to Transform American Prosecution and End Mass Incarceration.

114 See, for examples, Mass Imprisonment: Social Causes and Consequences, David Garland, editor, London: Sage, 2001; Bruce Western, Punishment and Inequality in America, New York: Russell Sage Foundation, 2006; Michael Tonry, Punishing Race: A Continuing American Dilemma, New York: Oxford, 2011.

115 Unfortunately, it was not only the research that led to sentencing reform. As noted elsewhere in this volume, reform was also motivated by cost containment and by the fact that the face of addiction in the public imagination became a white heroin addict, rather than the black crack addict.

Index

Page numbers in **bold** denote tables, those in *italics* denote figures.

For Product Safety Concerns and Information please contact our EU
representative GPSR@taylorandfrancis.com
Taylor & Francis Verlag GmbH, Kaufingerstraße 24, 80331 München, Germany

www.ingramcontent.com/pod-product-compliance
Lightning Source LLC
Chambersburg PA
CBHW050642280326
41932CB00015B/2746

9 780367 321635